Butterflies of Georgia

Watercolor drawing of the Monarch life history by John Abbot published in 1797 in Volume I of *The Rarer Lepidopterous Insects of Georgia*, by Dr. James Edward Smith.

John Abbot wrote, "This caterpillar eats the butterfly weed, *Asclepias curassavica*. On the 24th of April it suspended itself by the tail; changed to a chrysalis next day, and on the 11th of May the butterfly came out. It is not a very common species."

Dr. Smith wrote, with reference to Abbot's drawing, "All authors have been puzzled about the varieties, as they call them, of *P. Plexippus, Chrysippus*, etc. and surely the world are obliged to Professor Fabricius for distinguishing this and many others which resemble it. If their metamorphoses were known, as in that before us, we should probably be still more satisfied of their being distinct."

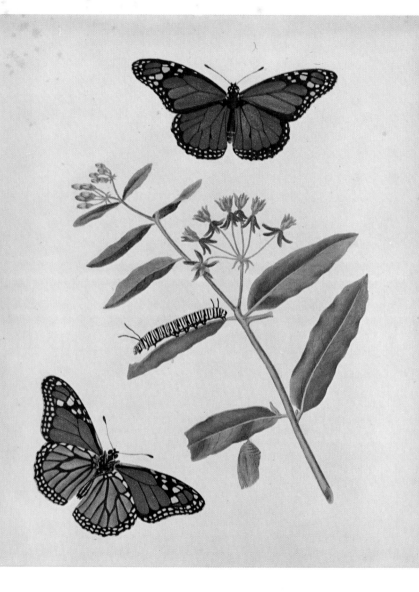

Butterflies of Georgia

by Lucien Harris, Jr.

Foreword by Alexander B. Klots

Norman
University of Oklahoma Press

Library of Congress Cataloging in Publication Data
Harris, Lucien, 1899–
    Butterflies of Georgia.
    Bibliography: p. 305
    1. Butterflies—Georgia. I. Title.
QL551.G4H28   595.7'89'09758   73–160493
ISBN 0–8061–0965–3
Copyright 1972 by the University of Oklahoma Press, Publishing
Division of the University. Manufactured in the U.S.A. First
edition.

To Louise,
to our two sons Robin and Lucien,
and to our good friend
the late Herbert L. Stoddard, Sr.

The publication of *Butterflies of Georgia* has been made possible by contributions from:

J. F. Bell Foundation	Mr. & Mrs. Leon Neel
Bolton Foundation	Olin Foundation
Ireland Foundation	Mrs. Phillip G. Rust
M. H. Ireland	Betsy Schafer
Claire Jonklaas	Walter Sedgwick
Clarence Jung	J. H. Thompson Fund

The color plates in this book were made possible by a special contribution from Mrs. Parker Poe.

FOREWORD

THIS BOOK, the third (and greatly expanded) list of the butterflies of Georgia by Lucien Harris, Jr., will be welcomed by all
who are interested in North American Lepidoptera, as well as
by students of zoogeography and ecology. The book is especially timely because it incorporates the results of the great
amount of intelligently planned collecting that has been done
in this state in recent years, and enables these results to be
coordinated with those of similar work carried out in Florida
and Mississippi.

To the lepidopterist, Georgia is especially interesting for a
number of reasons. It is interesting historically because it is
where John Abbot, one of the first and certainly the greatest
of our pioneer lepidopterists, lived and worked during colonial
times. The life histories that he worked out and painted are
still our prime source of information about many species of
American butterflies. Although recent legalistic interpretation
of the *International Code of Zoological Nomenclature* has
deprived Abbot of even partial formal "authorship" of the
many species that he was the first to collect, rear, describe, and
delineate, his work, published by others, towers secure.

Georgia is also particularly interesting to lepidopterists because of the special diversity of its terrain and fauna. Along
the low-lying coastal plain, with its distinctive "sea islands,"

are found many species of the deep South that extend more or less northward, some of them as distinct clines or subspecies. Inland are to be found many of the essentially northern species that extend far southward along the Appalachians and gradually disappear as the mountains decrease in altitude. Between the coastal plain and the mountains is the large complex piedmont area in which the lowland and montane populations come together, and the study of this area may provide especially valuable information about the approximation, contact, or overlapping of their ranges. Finally, some species characteristic of the Midwest and West reach their eastern limits in Georgia.

It is curious that Georgia is one of those states that have long been less well known to lepidopterists than many more glamorous collecting areas. For example, its proximity to Florida has made many collectors hasten through it following the lure of a more exotic, tropical fauna. In recent years, however, collecting in Georgia has come into its own again. One species new to science has been discovered and named, "lost" species have been rediscovered, new life-history work has been done, and a great many new locality and environment records have been established. Much important work still remains to be done; but this book provides a broad and reliable foundation on which future workers can build.

ALEXANDER B. KLOTS

CONTENTS

ILLUSTRATIONS

xiii

Euphyes arpa
Euphyes palatka
Eparygyreus clarus

Calpodes ethlius
Megathymus harrisi
Megathymus cofaqui

BLACK AND WHITE PLATES

Panoquina panoquin
Panoquina ocola
Oligoria maculata
Lerodea eufala

Amblyscirtes samoset
Amblyscirtes aesculapius
Amblyscirtes carolina
Amblyscirtes vialis

Amblyscirtes c. belli
Amblyscirtes alternata
Atrytonopsis hianna

Atrytonopsis loammi
Euphyes bimacula
Euphyes v. metacomet

Euphyes berryi
Euphyes dion

Poanes zabulon
Poanes hobomok

Poanes viator
Problema byssus
Problema bulenta

Atrytone arogos
Atrytone delaware
Atalopedes campestris

Polites themistocles
Polites origines
Polites vibex
Hesperia metea

Hesperia sassacus
Hesperia meskei
Hesperia attalus
Hylephila phyleus

Copaeodes minima
Ancyloxypha numitor
Pholisora catullus
Staphylus hayhurstii
Pompeius verna

Wallengrenia otho
Wallangrenia egeremet
Polites coras
Polites baracoa

DISTRIBUTION CHART

Distribution of species found in Georgia based on collected specimens and records of occurrence. The sequence follows the C.F. dosPassos list published by the Lepidopterists Society (1964) except for some recent nomenclatural revisions.

Mtn	Pmt	Ctl	BUTTERFLY	Jan	Feb	Mar	Apr	May	Jun	Jul	Aug	Sep	Oct	Nov	Dec	COMMENTS
X	X	X	M. y. yuccae	X	X	X	X	X								
	X	X	M. cofaqui													Known from type--no date
X	X	X	M. harrisi						X	X	X				X	Nov. spec. is a sight record
	X	X	P. panoquin				X	X	X	X	X					
X	X	X	P. ocola					X	X	X	X	X	X			
X	X	X	C. ethlius						X	X	X	X	X			
	X	X	O. maculata				X	X	X	X	X	X				
	X	X	L. eufala	X		X	X	X	X	X	X	X				
X	X		A. samoset				X	X								
X	X	X	A. aesculapius				X	X	X	X	X	X				
X	X	X	A. carolina					X	X	X	X	X				
X	X	X	A. vialis				X	X	X	X	X	X				
	X		A. c. belli					X	X	X	X	X				
X	X	X	A. alternata					X	X	X	X					
X	X	X	A. h. hianna				X	X	X	X						
	X		A. loammi													No confirmed records
	X	X	E. arpa													No date-Abbot fig. in BDV & LeC
	X	X	E. palatka					X	X							
X		X	E. d. alabamae					X	X			X				
	X	X	E. berryi					X	X	X	X					
	X	X	E. bimacula				X									
X	X	X	E. v. metacomet			X	X	X	X	X	X	X				
X	X	X	P. hobomok			X	X	X								
X	X	X	P. zabulon				X	X	X	X	X	X				
X	X	X	P. a. howardi									X				
X	X	X	P. yehl				X	X			X	X				
X	X	X	P. viator				X	X	X	X	X	X		X		
X	X	X	P. byssus				X	X	X	X	X	X				
		X	P. bulenta							X						

							Mtn			Pmt		Ctl	
		X	A. arogos				X	X		X			
X	X	X	A. d. delaware				X	X	X	X	X		
X	X	X	A. campestris			X	X	X	X	X	X	X	
X	X	X	P. v. sequoyah				X	X	X	X	X		
	X	X	W. otho		X	X	X	X	X	X	X		
X	X		W. egermet			X	X	X	X	X			
X			P. coras				X			X			
		X	P. baracoa				X	X	X	X			
	X	X	P. themistocles				X		X	X			
X	X	X	P. origines				X	X	X	X			
X	X	X	P. v. vibex				X	X	X	X	X	X	
X	X		H. metea			X	X						
	X	X	H. s. sassacus				X						
	X	X	H. meskei				X	X	X	X			
		X	H. a. seminole						X				
X	X	X	H. phyleus		X		X	X	X	X	X	X	
	X	X	C. minima				X	X	X	X			
X	X	X	A. numitor			X	X	X	X	X			
X	X	X	L. accius	X		X	X	X	X	X	X		
	X	X	N. lherminier			X	X	X	X	X			
X	X	X	P. catullus			X	X		X	X	X		
X	X	X	P. c. communis		X	X	X		X	X	X	X	
X			E. icelus			X	X	X	X				
X	X	X	E. b. brizo		X	X	X			.			
X	X	X	E. baptisiae			X	X	X					
X	X	X	E. zarucco	X	X	X	X	X	X	X	X		
X	X	X	E. martialis		X	X	X	X	X	X			
X	X	X	E. horatius		X	X							
X	X	X	E. juvenalis		X	X	X	X					
X	X	X	S. m. hayhurstii			X	X	X	X				
X	X	X	T. bathyllus		X	X	X		X	X	X		
X	X	X	T. pylades		X	X	X	X	X	X	X		
X	X	X	T. confusis		X	X	X			X			
X	X	X	A. lyciades		X	X		X	X	X			
X	X	X	A. cellus			X	X		X	X			
X	X	U. proteus	X	X		X		X	X	X	X		

* Mtn = Mountain; Pmt = Piedmont; Ctl = Coastal

REGIONS*			BUTTERFLY	MONTHS OF OCCURRENCE												COMMENTS
Mtn	Pmt	CtI		Jan	Feb	Mar	Apr	May	Jun	Jul	Aug	Sep	Oct	Nov	Dec	
X	X	X	E. c. clarus			X	X	X	X	X	X	X	X			
X	X	X	B. philenor		X	X	X	X	X	X	X	X	X	X		
		X	B. p. lucayus						X							
X	X	X	B. p. asterius		X	X	X		X	X	X	X				
	X	X	P. c. cresphontes			X		X		X	X	X	X			
X	X	X	P. glaucus	X		X	X	X	X	X	X	X	X			
X	X	X	P. t. troilus	X	X	X	X	X	X	X	X	X	X	X		
		X	P. t. ilioneus									X				Lower Coastal Plain
	X	X	P. palamedes			X	X	X	X	X	X	X	X			
	X	X	G. marcellus		X	X	X	X	X	X	X	X	X			
X	X	X	P. p. protodice			X	X	X	X	X	X	X	X			
X			P. virginiensis			X	X									
X	X	X	P. rapae	X		X	X	X	X	X	X	X	X	X		
		X	A. m. phileta				X	X			X					
X	X	X	C. eurytheme	X		X	X	X	X	X	X	X	X	X		
X	X	X	C. philodice			X	X	X	X	X	X	X	X	X		
X	X	X	C. cesonia	X	X	X	X		X	X	X	X	X	X		
X	X	X	P. s. eubule	X	X	X	X	X	X	X	X	X	X	X		
X	X	X	P. philea									X	X	X		
		X	P. s. floridensis								X					
X	X	X	E. d. daira	X	X	X	X	X	X	X	X	X	X			
X	X	X	E. lisa	X	X	X	X	X	X	X	X	X	X		X	
X	X	X	E. nicippe	X		X	X	X	X	X	X	X	X	X		
	X	X	N. iole			X		X	X	X	X	X	X	X	X	
X	X		A. m. annickae			X	X						X	X	X	
		X	A. m. midea			X	X									
X	X	X	L. v. pumila						X	X		X	X	X		
X	X	X	C. t. mopsus						X	X						
		X	S. l. tiparops				X	X								Lower Coastal Plain
X	X		S. l. strigosa				X		X	X						Mts., Piedmont, Upper Coastal
X	X		S. kingi				X		X	X						
X	X		S. c. calanus				X									
X	X	X	S. c. falacer				X	X	X							

Species	Notes
S. caryaevorus	
S. edwardsii	
C. cecrops	
C. irus	
C. h. henrici	
C. h. margaretae	
C. a. croesioides	
C. n. niphon	
C. g. gryneus	
A. halesus	June specimen was very worn
E. favonius	
E. o. ontario	
P. m-album	
S. m. melinus	
F. t. tarquinius	
L. p. americana	
B. i. pseudofea	
H. c. antibubastus	
E. c. comyntas	
G. l. lygdamus	No dates--type locality Screven Co.
G. l. nittanyensis	
C. a. pseudargiolus	
L. b. bachmanii	
A. a. andria	
A. c. celtis	Piedmont and Upper Coastal
A. c. alicia	Lower Coastal Plain only
A. c. clyton	
A. c. flora	Lower Coastal Plain
L. a. astyanax	
L. a. archippus	
A. j. guantanamo	Chatham Co. sight records
V. atalanta	
V. virginiensis	
V. cardui	
J. c. coenia	
N. a. antiopa	
P. interrogationis	

Species											Notes
P. comma	X	X	X						X		
P. f. smythi	X						X				
C. nycteis	X	X			X	X	X				
C. g. gorgone	X			X	X	X	X				
P. t. seminole	X			X	X	X	X	X			
P. t. tharos	X	X	X	X	X	X	X				
P. batesii	X					X					
P. phaon	X	X		X	X		X	X	X		Strays taken in Piedmont
E. p. phaeton	X			X			X				
S. idalia	X										No data; reported by S.H. Scudder
S. diana	X	X			X	X	X				
S. c. cybele	X			X	X	X	X				
S. a. aphrodite				X	X						
E. claudia	X	X	X	X	X	X	X	X			
H. c. tuckeri					X	X	X	X	X		Strays taken in Piedmont
A. v. nigrior	X	X			X	X	X	X			
D. p. plexippus	X	X		X	X	X	X	X			
D. g. berenice	X			X	X	X	X				
L. portlandia	X	X		X	X	X					
L. creola	X	X		X	X	X					
L. e. appalachia	X	X	X	X	X	X					
E. gemma	X	X	X	X	X	X	X				
E. a. areolata	X	X	X	X	X						
E. h. sosybia	X	X	X	X	X	X		X			
E. c. cymela	X	X	X	X	X						
C. p. abbotti	X		X	X							
C. p. alope	X	X	X	X	X	X					

Lower Coastal Plain

Mts., Piedmont, Upper Coastal

Butterflies of Georgia

INTRODUCTION

THE PURPOSE of this introduction is to "set the stage" for what follows. I believe that the stage can best be set by sketching the lives of two of the towering figures in the field of wildlife study in the South, by telling something about the natural features that make Georgia such a rich reserve for wildlife, by explaining the background and organization of this book, and by acknowledging the help that has made it possible.

It would be very difficult to write a book on Georgia wildlife, and especially on the butterflies or bird life of Georgia, without referring in many ways to John Abbot and Herbert Lee Stoddard, Sr. The following brief biographical sketches of these two men will provide some historical perspective, mention the unique contributions that these two pioneering naturalists made to the study of wildlife in the South, and help to bring into sharper focus my own study of the butterflies of the Georgia region.

JOHN ABBOT

John Abbot (?–1841?) was Georgia's pioneer naturalist-artist. Little was known of Abbot's early life until his manuscript, "Notes on My Life," was found stored in a locked file in the Department of Zoology at Yale University. In it, Abbot wrote:

3

My father was an Attorney-at-Law, I was his second son, my brother dying before I was born. At the time of my leaving England, I had two sisters, Elizabeth and Charlotte, and a brother Thomas then seven years old.

My peculiar liking for insects was long before I was acquainted with any method of catching or keeping them. I remember knocking down a Libelula (dragonfly) and pinning it, when I was told it would sting as bad as a rattlesnake bite.[1]

Abbot developed an early love for books and an early talent for drawing. His father, who had a large and valuable collection of prints of some of the best masters as well as many good paintings, arranged for Abbot to have drawing lessons. Fortunately for Abbot, his teacher, a Mr. Boneau, likewise had an interest in insects, and had been a collector. It was through him that Abbot was introduced to a Mr. Rice, who in turn introduced him to Mr. Dru Drury, who had been president of the Linnean Society, and who had a fine collection of British and foreign insects.

In his "Notes" Abbot continued, "I leave you to judge my pleasure and astonishment at the sight of his cabinets, the first I had ever seen of the kind. He very politely offered to lend me insects to draw and we immediately became well acquainted. That hour may be said to have given a new turn to my future life. I had immediately a mahogany cabinet made of 26 drawers, covered with sliding tops of glass, it cost me 6 guineas, and begun to collect with unceasing industry."

By the time he was twenty, Abbot had become recognized as an artist and naturalist of great ability and promise by many of the entomologists and ornithologists of England. It was not long before he began to entertain thoughts of going abroad to collect insects. In 1773, he determined to come to America, and finally decided on Virginia after reading a history that gave a glowing account of that area.[2] In the summer of that

[1] Remington, C. L., *Lepidopterists' News* 2 (3):28, 1948.
[2] Abbot sold his large cabinet of insects and had three smaller ones made to bring with him. Before coming to America, he had completed at least two

year, he sailed for Virginia, and after a voyage of six weeks, the ship anchored near the mouth of the James River.

A fellow passenger who became Abbot's friend was a Mr. Goodall, who had relatives in Georgia. Goodall was returning with his English bride to set up a store in Hanover County, Virginia. He had been furnished with a cargo of goods by his uncle, a rich merchant in London. Goodall lived one hundred miles from the mouth of the James River, and he agreed to let Abbot board with him.

Abbot lived two years in Virginia, and during that time he became acquainted with Goodall's cousin, William Goodall. William Goodall lived in Georgia, had married in Virginia, and now wanted to go back to Georgia, but "had not the means to bear his expenses," as Abbot expressed it. In Virginia, Abbot did not find the variety of insects he had hoped to collect. He became further discouraged when a cabinet of specimens he was sending to London went down with the ship in a storm off the English coast. Abbot wrote:

The colonies having appointed a day after which all intercourse with England was to be stopped, I fixed up another cabinet of insects to send to England. It was on board the boat in the river being taken to the ship when a terrible September storm arose in the night and the boat was lost together with my insects again, but to make amends I have not lost any I have sent from Georgia.

The times now becoming very troublesome and hearing that Georgia had not then joined the other colonies, I joined Mr. William Goodall to come to Georgia together. I furnished two horses and was to bear all our expenses, he one horse and a cart to carry his wife and child and a little negro boy and our baggage.

The journey began in December, 1775, and ended in early February, 1776, about thirty miles below Augusta. The party settled on some land that adjoined that of William Moore, who

albums of drawings of insects, one now at Harvard University containing 42 drawings with 235 figures. The other album, containing 98 drawings, is in the Library of the Carnegie Museum in Pittsburgh, the gift of Andrei Avinoff, the late director of that museum.

was William Goodall's brother-in-law. While waiting for a log house to be built for William Goodall, the party stayed in the home of Pleasant Goodall, William's half-brother. After William Goodall's home was completed, Abbot resided with the family until he established his own home.

Abbot married Penelope Warren and settled near the Goodalls in Burke County. Their son, John Abbot, Jr., was born in 1779 and died in Savannah on August 18, 1826, at the age of 47 years. John Abbot, Sr., spent most of his life in Burke, Screven, and Bulloch counties, although records indicate that he may have lived for various periods in Savannah.[3]

After 1820, Abbot's name is described in legal papers as a resident of Bulloch County, which adjoins Screven County. He died in Bulloch County on the plantation of William E. McElveen, his beloved friend, who had given him a small home on his place to live out the advanced years of his life. A deed recorded in Bulloch County (Record Book No. 5, page 292) shows that Abbot bequeathed his personal property and other possessions to McElveen on June 4, 1839. He died in December, 1840, or in early January, 1841, and is buried in the McElveen family cemetery. For many years, his grave was unmarked, but on May 25, 1957, a Georgia Historical Marker was placed in the cemetery with appropriate ceremonies. There is also a monument bearing a bronze plaque of Abbot.

Throughout his long life, Abbot continued to collect, rear, and depict in fine watercolor drawings the many kinds of insects and spiders that he found. He made drawings of birds

[3] Perhaps a word of explanation should be given about Screven County (also spelled Scriven in the early days) and its relation to Burke County. When Abbot came to Georgia in 1776, Screven County had not yet been formed. It was created by the State Legislature from parts of Burke and Effingham counties in 1793. The legislature also authorized the building of a new town, Jacksonborough, to be the county seat of Screven County. Except for one house, known as the Goodall house, this once-thriving town no longer exists. On December 14, 1847, the county government was moved to Sylvania.

and collected specimens which he sold to museums and ornithologists. Some of his drawings and specimens were of species that had not yet received scientific names.

A great many of his drawings of birds have been carefully preserved by libraries and other institutions in America, England, and Europe. The great interest in Abbot's bird drawings has led to additional research into his life, and much biographical information has appeared in ornithological publications. Abbot, before leaving England, had made a business arrangement with John Francillon, as his agent, to handle the sale of Abbot's drawings and collections of such natural history specimens as he might assemble in America. The arrangement appears to have been a good one for both Abbot and Francillon, for it lasted many years.

Because his work was sold through his agent, Abbot apparently did not know the names of many of the collectors or institutions purchasing his materials, or the use to which the materials were put. For example, two volumes of *The Rarer Lepidopterous Insects of Georgia*, by Dr. James Edward Smith, was published in London in 1797. Through Francillon, Dr. Smith had acquired some of Abbot's drawings, which depicted, in natural size and color, many species of butterflies and moths with their caterpillars, pupae, and food plants, plus such data and notes as Abbot had recorded for each one. Dr. Smith gave due credit to Abbot in the foreword to his book and in the notes on each species; but, as Abbot's friend in Savannah, Dr. Augustus G. Oemler, wrote to a friend, Abbot did not learn of the work until several years after its publication.

In *Histoire Generale et Iconographie des Lepidopteres et des Chenilles de L'Amerique Septentrionale*, published in Paris between 1829 and 1833 under the authorship of Dr. J. A. Boisduval of Paris and Major John E. LeConte of New York and Philadelphia, many life-size, full-color illustrations, but by no means all, were from Abbot's drawings. One of Abbot's drawings in this volume depicted *Melitaea ismeria,* which later collectors could not find. Another drawing figured a skipper, *Problema bulenta,* which was known only from Abbot's picture until it was rediscovered in July, 1925, by the late Frank Morton Jones.

It is a real tribute to Abbot's skill as an artist and to his keen observations as a naturalist that only a few of his hundreds of drawings have been unidentifiable. In the book by Boisduval and LeConte, some difficulty in identification can be attributed to the process used in reproducing the pictures. In the introduction to later printings of that book, Dr. Boisduval stated that criticisms had been received of the way some of Abbot's pictures were reproduced and, therefore, in later editions some restoration had been made.

An example of the volume of materials that Abbot shipped to Francillon is cited in an article by Elsa G. Allen.[4] She quotes a letter from Francillon, dated London, August 10, 1793, which reads: "I have received from my friend at Savannah, Georgia (the person who drew the hundred birds) a wonderful fine collection of the Drawings of the Insects of that Country . . . the contents are 1021 sheets of Drawings, containing 1664 different species or 1833 figures . . . with a manuscript description of the natural history of each insect."

In the same article, Mrs. Allen quotes from another Francillon letter, dated London, December 26, 1809: "I have the pleasure of enclosing to you forty-four more drawings of Birds for the Manchester Library which I have just received from Mr. Abbot of Savannah, Georgia which I hope will be approved of and I have enclosed a Bill with them, and if not inconvenient to the proprietors of the Library I shall be obliged to them to favor me with the amount as soon as it may suit them, as I shall very soon have an opportunity of remitting it with some other money and articles in a Box to Mr. Abbot."

Information about this remarkable artist, naturalist, and

4 *Auk* 59:570, 1942.

collector has gradually been assembled through the years by patient research, much of it by ornithologists. The late Mrs. Elsa G. Allen of Ithaca, New York, generously permitted me to read the unpublished manuscript of her latest biography of Abbot. During an extensive period of research, she visited many places, including London, Paris, and Georgia, where Abbot drawings, letters, specimens, and other materials have been preserved. Some of the principal sources on Abbot are given in the Bibliography on John Abbot at the end of this book.

HERBERT LEE STODDARD, SR.

Herbert Lee Stoddard (1889–1970) may, in many ways, be compared with John Abbot, for both had a deep understanding and knowledge of their environment and its wildlife.

Herbert Stoddard's interest in nature began at an early age, when the family moved in 1893 from Rockford, Illinois, to Chuluota, Florida, approximately twenty miles east of Orlando. He has left a vivid account of his early years there in his *Memoirs of a Naturalist* (University of Oklahoma Press, 1969). He was fortunate in meeting "Mister Barber," a retired government surveyor who knew the names of birds, animals, and other wildlife that inhabited the virgin forests, lakes, streams, and prairies of Florida.

He quickly became attuned to his surroundings, and many things he observed became lasting memories. He enjoyed recalling his youthful adventures and observations and sharing them with friends. Later, he put to excellent use many of the things he learned through keen and perceptive observation. He watched the cattlemen of those early days burn certain areas of the prairie at the right time of year and under the most favorable weather conditions, a burn that resulted in a new growth of fresh grass on the cattle range. Later, when he settled in south Georgia on Sherwood Plantation, with its thousand acres of woods and fields, he put his knowledge of controlled burning into practice. He became an expert in the proper use of fire and its relation to the total environment long before ecology became a household word.

When I first visited Sherwood Plantation, I noted that there were more butterflies and moths to be seen than in most other areas of the state. I also observed the presence of more quail and other species of birds, as well as other forms of wildlife.[5] All had found favorable habitats in which they could live and multiply. This was brought about by the wise methods employed to manage the land for its maximum use in producing timber as well as wildlife.

At an early age, Stoddard became interested in taxidermy, which led to positions with the Milwaukee Public Museum and the Field Museum of Chicago. His skill as a taxidermist was put to good use throughout his life. This skill made it possible for him to preserve thousands of skins from the many species of birds that were killed annually during periods of migration when they struck a 1,010-foot television tower on Tall Timbers Research Station in Leon County, Florida, only a few miles from Stoddard's home.[6]

In August, 1929, I invited a group of men to an informal meeting at Emory University. Although they were specialists in various branches of science, they shared a general interest in natural history and conservation. Present at the meeting were: W. B. Baker, botanist; P. W. Fattig, entomologist; Earle R. Greene, ornithologist; H. Reid Hunter, dendrologist; Wallace

[5] Herbert Stoddard's scientific studies of the Bob White Quail were reported in detail in his monumental book *The Bob White Quail* (Scribner, 1931). Although now out of print, the book is available in many public libraries.

[6] Daily visits were made at dawn for eleven consecutive years to pick up birds killed at the tower. The largest kill occurred at the time he began his visits: more than 1,000 dead birds were picked up on the morning of October 9, 1955, during the peak of a migration, when the tower was obscured by fog. During the eleven-year period, Stoddard and the Tall Timbers Research Station shared the specimens with a number of institutions. The study was published in *Bull. Tall Timbers* Res. Sta. (8), 1967.

Rogers, ornithologist and nature photographer; R. C. Rhodes, protozoologist; Ralph E. Wager, general biologist and ornithologist; and myself, a lepidopterist.

It was suggested that we meet monthly and that we call our group the Naturalist Club. We soon began taking field trips to explore such diverse areas as Stone Mountain and the Okefenokee Swamp. We began to publish bulletins and renamed our organization The Georgia Society of Naturalists. Herbert Stoddard became a member in 1933.[7] Many humorous incidents occurred during our expeditions into the Okefenokee Swamp, and Stoddard, with his keen sense of humor, would join in the general laughter at the mishaps of the intrepid members of our Society.

The members of the Society agreed that the Okefenokee was a unique area that deserved to be designated as a National Wildlife Refuge. We worked hard toward this objective; and it was a never-to-be-forgotten day when we received word from Washington that our efforts had been successful. The first manager of the Okefenokee National Wildlife Refuge was Earle R. Greene, a charter member of the Georgia Society of Naturalists. He is a dedicated conservationist and a man who served well in this position and in the many others to which he was named. Now retired, his legacy is told in *A Lifetime with the Birds* (Edward Brothers, Ann Arbor, Michigan, 1966).

In May, 1934, the Georgia Society of Naturalists received an invitation from Mr. and Mrs. Henry L. Beadel, owners of Tall Timbers Plantation, to explore the plantation and have dinner with them. It was through the friendship of Stoddard and Mr. Beadel that the invitation was extended. Following our visit to Tall Timbers, our group also explored Wakulla

---

[7] Herbert L. Stoddard was active in various ornithological organizations. He was a fellow of the American Ornithologists' Union, a charter member and president of the Georgia Ornithological Society, and a charter member of both the Wildlife Society and the Inland Bird Banding Society.

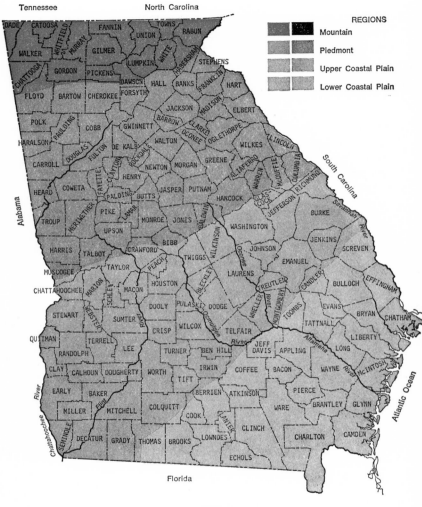

GEORGIA

Georgia is the largest state east of the Mississippi and has a diversified topography. The highest point is the summit of Brasstown Bald, elevation 4,768 feet, in Towns County in the Mountain Region. From the Mountain Region, the elevation descends through the Piedmont and Coastal regions to sea level, where the Atlantic Ocean forms the eastern boundary.

Springs and Alligator Point, Florida, when these areas were still undeveloped and wildlife was abundant. Some years later, Stoddard made an important discovery on Alligator Point, when he found hundreds of Monarch butterflies clustered on young pine trees during their fall migration (see p. 287).

In later years, Mr. Beadel discussed privately with Stoddard, for whom he had great respect, the question of how Tall Timbers Plantation could be used best for scientific purposes, including among other important projects, studies of controlled burning and the selective cutting of timber. Mr. Beadel's will reflected those important discussions and, as a result, led to the founding of the Tall Timbers Research Station. Under the guidance of Stoddard as president—until his death in 1970 —and now under E. V. Komarek, Sr., as executive secretary, and an excellent board of directors, the aims of the founder are being achieved. The results of those admirable goals are made known in many ways, through research and publications, through annual fire conferences, and through special Fire Ecology Conference *Proceedings*.

The Herbert L. Stoddard, Sr., Research Building was erected to house the Herbert L. Stoddard, Sr., bird collection.[8] It also contains the Lucien Harris, Jr., butterfly and moth collections. Many of the specimens of Georgia butterflies in that collection figure in the *Butterflies of Georgia*.

ABOUT GEORGIA

It has been the pioneering efforts of such naturalists as John Abbot and Herbert Stoddard that set the course for us to follow in the study of wildlife in Georgia. Georgia is the largest state east of the Mississippi and has a diversified topography.

---

[8] When Thomas D. Burleigh's book *Georgia Birds* (University of Oklahoma Press, 1958) was published, The Herbert L. Stoddard, Sr., Scholarship Fund was established at the University of Georgia with income from the sale of the book. Some of the book's beautiful illustrations were made from life at Sherwood Plantation by the ornithologist-artist George M. Sutton.

The highest point is the summit of Brasstown Bald, elevation 4,768 feet, in Towns County in the Mountain Region. From the Mountain Region, the elevation descends through the Piedmont and Coastal regions to sea level, where the Atlantic Ocean forms the eastern boundary.

There are several mountains in the Piedmont Region that are generally isolated and of relatively low elevation. Examples are Blackjack and Kennesaw mountains in Cobb County, Stone Mountain in DeKalb County, and Pine Mountain in Harris County.

In the Coastal Region, the highest portion lies generally along the fall line, where the Piedmont and Coastal regions merge. There are two large swamps in the Coastal Region, the Altamaha River Swamp and the well-known Okefenokee Swamp.

Georgia has 159 counties. Although the amount of collecting in some counties has been negligible, enough collecting has been done in various sections of the state to give a representative cross section of the butterflies occurring in each region. Further collecting may add a number of species to the state list. There are several species of possible occurrence that have not been included for lack of confirmed state records, including *Erora laeta, Erynnis lucilius, Erynnis persius, Euphyes dukesi, Hesperia leonardus, Mitoura hesseli,* and *Nastra neamathla.*

One cannot predict with any degree of certainty the butterflies likely to be added to the state list. The following have been added in recent years: *Amblyscirtes carolina* f. *reversa, Amblyscirtes celia belli, Atrytonopsis hianna, Euphydryas phaeton, Euphyes berryi, Euphyes bimacula, Euristrymon ontario autolycus, Glaucopsyche lygdamus nittanyensis, Hesperia meskei, Callophrys, (Incisalia) augustinus croesioides, Megathymus harrisi, Phoebis statira floridensis, Phyciodes batesii, Pieris virginiensis, Polites coras, Polygonia comma, Satyrium caryaevorus,* and *Satyrium kingi.*

14

ABOUT THE BOOK

This is the first illustrated book on the butterflies of Georgia since John Abbot's two-volume study published in 1797.

Because Georgia is the type locality of many species of butterflies found throughout the South, it was seriously proposed, and considered, that the book be called *The Butterflies of Dixie, with Special Reference to Georgia.* Although this title was finally abandoned in favor of the present one, the fact remains that the book will have meaning and validity far beyond the boundaries of the state.

My first book on this subject, *A List of The Butterflies of Georgia*, was published in 1931. Although it was essentially an annotated checklist, it contained the original description and photograph of *Eurema daira* ab. *fusca.* A revised edition, edited by the late Austin H. Clark of the Smithsonian Institution, was published in 1950 under the title *The Butterflies of Georgia, Revised.* It contained much new material, with a comprehensive bibliography prepared by Mr. Clark. That bibliography, revised and with added recent materials, is included in this book.

The purpose of this book is to cover and illustrate every species of butterfly now known to occur in the state of Georgia. This coverage includes information on distribution, life history, foodplants, and habitat. Not only are records of locality and date of capture given, but the dates of capture are listed in sequence by days and months instead of by years. Included also is a Distribution Chart (page xvii), which lists the month or months of occurrence for each species and the regions in which they have been found, thus making this information readily available in brief form.

The source and sequence of the scientific names are based on "A Synonymic List of the Nearctic Rhopalocera," by Cyril F. dos Passos (*Mem. Lepidopterists' Soc.* (1), 1964), except for those of the subfamily Melitaeinae, which follow "A Revised Synonymic List of the Nearctic Melitaeinae with Taxonomic Notes (Nymphalidae)," by Cyril F. dos Passos (*J. Lepidopterists' Soc.* 23 (2): 115–125, 1969), and those of the subfamily Theclinae, which follow the proposals of Harry K. Clench in *How to Know the Butterflies*, by P. R. and A. H. Ehrlich (W. C. Brown Company, Dubuque, Iowa, 1961).

ACKNOWLEDGMENTS

I wish to express my sincere thanks to all who have helped in the preparation of this book. Many have supplied records of their Georgia specimens, others have identified or loaned specimens, and many have given valuable suggestions that have been incorporated here. I am greatly indebted to the following:

Alexander B. Klots, of the American Museum of Natural History, for his Foreword and for his continued interest and helpful suggestions;

Bryant Mather, co-author with Mrs. Katherine Mather of *The Butterflies of Mississippi*, for his editorial assistance and very helpful advice, which greatly improved the manuscript;

Wilson Baker, who collected in Screven County with Bryant Mather and who, because he was familiar with the county, took us to many places we would have otherwise missed;

J. C. Brooks, for the summary of his observations on the butterflies of Bibb County and the surrounding area, which he sent when he learned that this book was in preparation;

F. Martin Brown, for reading portions of the manuscript, especially the sections dealing with *Chlosyne g. gorgone*, *Phyciodes phaon*, and *Cercyonis p. pegala*;

The late Otto Buchholz, for supplying a record of the species he collected in Screven County from March to September, 1946, including *Euphyes berryi*, which was a new state record for Georgia;

John M. Burns, for reading the section dealing with the genus *Erynnis*;

Joe Carter, for supplying a female *Pholisora catullus* for the illustrations;

Cyril F. dos Passos, of the American Museum of Natural History, for providing an advance copy of his revision of the subfamily Melitaeinae;

William D. Field, of the Smithsonian Institution, for his interest and help with the genus *Melitaea*;

Herman Flaschka, for his Georgia records and the account of his experience with *Nymphalis antiopa*;

William T. M. Forbes, for the list of specimens taken in Savannah by M. H. Mead in the Mead Collection at Cornell University, and also for his letters dealing with the complex problems related to *Chlosyne gorgone* and *Melitaea ismeria* shortly after the publication of *The Butterflies of Georgia, Revised*;

H. Avery Freeman, who has given me guidance and encouragement, particularly with my treatment of the genera *Megathymus* and *Euristrymon*, especially the species *E. favonius* and *E. ontario*;

Louise, my wife, who has aided greatly both by collecting many rare specimens and by calling my attention to important specimens that turned out to be state records;

Lucien Harris III, who has a broad interest in the skippers (Hesperioidea) and collected several rare specimens, including a *Megathymus* new to our collection, which, when compared with a specimen collected by J. P. Knudsen, eventually led to the discovery of *M. harrisi*;

James Robin Harris, whose general interest in butterflies resulted in his collecting specimens of various groups, including specimens of hairstreaks from the Mountain Region near Helen, Georgia, which, when sent to A. B. Klots, were found to belong to a new species, later named *Satyrium kingi*, being studied by Klots and H. K. Clench;

J. Richard Heitzman, who generously supplied the life-history information that he had worked out for a number of species of skippers;

Sidney A. Hessel, who made a great deal of information available to me about *Mitoura hesseli*, a species that may possibly occur in Georgia but, so far, has not been found (it should be looked for in areas where the larval foodplant, White Cedar, occurs);

Charles P. Kimball, for his helpful interest (frequent reference is made in this book to Kimball's *The Lepidoptera of Florida*, which contains much information about species also found in Georgia);

H. L. King, who discovered a new species of hairstreak, *Satyrium kingi*, named for him by Klots and Clench in 1952;

John P. Knudsen, for his interest and helpful data, including his observations of the lepidoptera on the Oglethorpe College campus;

Mrs. Harriett Knowles, for typing the final manuscript;

E. V. Komarek, for his encouragement and his contagious enthusiasm—his guidance and planning have added much to this publication;

Roy Komarek, for his helpful assistance;

Desmond Lanktree, of the University of Western Ontario, for his suggestions and for supplying a list of Georgia specimens, collected by Hal and Ann Vogel, located in the Museum collection of the Department of Zoology at the University;

Thomas R. Manley, of Bloomsburg State College, Pennsylvania, for manuscript material for *Limenitis archippus*;

Fred T. Naumann, experienced collector and friend for many years, who made all of his records available as well as the notes in his journal;

Leon Neel, for reading and commenting on the manuscript, and for sharing some of his choice specimens from the Coastal Region, which include *Autochton cellus* and *Megathymus harrisi*;

Stanley S. Nicolay, for rare specimens of hairstreaks and

skippers, including *Satyrium kingi, S. favonius,* and *Problema bulenta;*

Walfried J. Reinthal, for assistance with the Hackberry butterflies (*Asterocampa*);

Ellery Sedgwick, Jr., for making his Georgia material available at the Tall Timbers Research Station;

Arthur M. Shapiro, of Cornell University, for information about *Poanes viator* in the M. H. Mead Collection at Cornell;

Harry Sicher, whose many Georgia specimens include a *Speyeria diana* collected on June 6, 1952—our earliest recorded date in the year for this species;

Gordon B. Small, Jr.—who discovered *Phyciodes (Tritanassa) texana seminole* at Savannah, and was the first to recognize and identify specimens of *S. caryaevorus* from Georgia—for much valuable information;

John C. Symmes, a fine collector with several state records to his credit (including *Pieris virginiensis, Phyciodes batesii, Euphyes bimacula,* and *Polites coras*), for his many helpful suggestions and his generosity in sharing rare specimens;

L. R. Tanner, for supplying a list of the specimens he collected on the University of Georgia campus at Athens and in the surrounding area of Clarke County;

Fred A. Urquhart, of Scarborough College, West Hill, Ontario, who gave me an opportunity to see some of the work involved in research then being carried out at the University of Toronto; and

C. B. Williams, the foremost authority on mass movements and migrations of butterflies, to whom I am indebted for his letters and copies of many of his publications.

My special thanks and appreciation go to the members of the Board of Tall Timbers Research Station for making this publication possible by providing illustrations of every species of butterfly found in Georgia. To all others who have collected in Georgia and have contributed to the information set forth herein, I offer my sincere thanks.

RECORDS:
COLLECTORS, MUSEUMS, AND INSTITUTIONS

THE LISTS of records that accompany the species accounts are arranged in chronological order, ignoring the year. Thus, a record for 5 May 1942 will precede one for 10 May 1930. An authority is cited for every record. The records come from three sources: (1) specimens in private or institutional collections, (2) statements in the literature, and occasionally (3) the statements of reliable collectors. An abbreviation of the collector's name is given after each record; if the specimen is located in a museum or an institution, a second abbreviation follows in parentheses. Thus, for example, a record marked "PWF (USNM)" indicates a specimen collected by Prof. P. W. Fattig in the collection of the United States National Museum. The following is an alphabetical list of the abbreviations used in this book:

AGR	Dr. A. Glenn Richards, Jr., St. Paul, Minnesota
AMNH	American Museum of Natural History
ANSP	Academy of Natural Sciences, Philadelphia
AT	Abner Towers, Atlanta, Georgia
BM	British Museum (Natural History)
BMR	Bryant Mather, Clinton, Mississippi
CFDP	Cyril F. dos Passos, Mendham, New Jersey
CM	Carnegie Museum, Pittsburgh
CU	Cornell University
DE	Donald Eff, Boulder, Colorado

ELT	E. L. Todd, address unknown
ESS	Ellery S. Sedgwick, Jr., Thomasville, Georgia
EUM	Emory University Museum, Atlanta
EVK	E. V. Komarek, Thomasville, Georgia
FMB	F. Martin Brown, Colorado Springs, Colorado
FMJ	Dr. Frank Morton Jones (deceased), Wilmington, Delaware
FMNH	Field Museum of Natural History, Chicago
FTN	Fred T. Naumann, Forsyth, Georgia
FWW	Fred W. Walker, address unknown
GBS	George B. Small, Jr., Panama Canal Zone
GH	Graham Heid, Atlanta (Sandy Springs), Georgia
HAF	Dr. H. A. Flaschka, Georgia Institute of Technology, Atlanta
HFS	Dr. H. F. Strohecker, Coral Gables, Florida
HLK	H. L. King, Sarasota, Florida
HOL	Dr. Horace O. Lund, University of Georgia, Athens
HS	Dr. Harry Sicher, Chicago, Illinois
HVAV	Hal and Ann Vogel (Georgia specimens at University of Western Ontario [UWO])
HWE	Henry W. Eustis (deceased), Augusta, Georgia
JC	Joe Carter, Atlanta, Georgia
JCBS	Dr. J. C. Brooks, Macon, Georgia
JCBY	Dr. J. C. Bradley, Ithaca, New York
JCS	John C. Symmes, Atlanta, Georgia
JMB	Dr. John M. Burns, Middletown, Connecticut
JN	Julie Neel, Thomasville, Georgia
JPK	John P. Knudsen, Raleigh, North Carolina
JRH	J. Robin Harris, Decatur, Georgia
KR	Kilian Roever, Phoenix, Arizona
LACM	Los Angeles County Museum
LHJ	Lucien Harris, Jr., Avondale Estates, Georgia
LHT	Lucien Harris III, Orlando, Florida
LN	Leon Neel, Thomasville, Georgia
LNH	Mrs. Louise N. Harris, Avondale Estates, Georgia
LRT	Leslie R. Tanner, Jamestown, North Dakota
MES	M. Eugene Smith, Madras (Coweta County), Georgia
MEVK	Mrs. E. V. Komarek, Thomasville, Georgia
MHM	M. H. Mead (deceased), Savannah, Georgia
MJCS	Mrs. John C. Symmes, Atlanta, Georgia
MLN	Mrs. Leon Neel, Thomasville, Georgia
OB	Otto Buchholz (deceased), Roselle Park, New Jersey

(specimens at the American Museum of Natural History [AMNH])

PK Paul Kight (deceased), Stone Mountain, Georgia

PMNH Peabody Museum of Natural History, Yale University

PWF Prof. P. W. Fattig (deceased), former Curator, Emory University Museum (EUM), Atlanta, Georgia

RAL R. A. Leussler (deceased), Omaha, Nebraska

RLC Dr. Ralph L. Chermock, Fairfield, Iowa

RWM Robert W. Montgomery, Poseyville, Indiana

RWP Dr. R. W. Pease, Jr., New Britain, Connecticut

SI Smithsonian Institution

SSN Col. S. S. Nicolay, Virginia Beach, Virginia

TRM Prof. and Mrs. Thomas R. Manley, Selinsgrove, Pa.

TTRS Tall Timbers Research Station, Tallahassee, Florida

UGM University of Georgia Museum, Athens

USNM United States National Museum

UWO University of Western Ontario, London, Ontario

WB Wilson Baker, Tall Timbers Research Station, Tallahassee, Florida

WFF W. F. Fiske (deceased), Assistant State Entomologist for Georgia, circa 1910

WJC W. J. Coxey, Philadelphia, Pennsylvania

SUPERFAMILY HESPERIOIDEA

Family MEGATHYMIDAE—Giant Skippers

Genus *Megathymus*

Yucca Skipper. *Megathymus yuccae yuccae*
Boisduval and LeConte (Page 129)

Distribution and Records: *M. y. yuccae*, the type locality of which is Aiken County, S. C. (H. A. Freeman, 1963), is found in close association with its larval food plants, *Yucca filamentosa* (Bear Grass), and *Y. aloifolia* (Spanish Bayonet). Two closely related species, *Y. gloriosa* (Spanish Dagger) and *Y. smalliana* (Small's Yucca), may also be food plants of *M. y. yuccae*. Bear Grass occurs widely throughout the state. We have only one record for the Yucca Skipper in the mountains, and further search is needed in that area where good stands of Bear Grass occur.

Mountain Region—*Dawson Co.*: Lake Lanier, 1 Mar 1961 JCS. Piedmont Region—*Meriweather Co.*: Stovall, Harmon Plantation, 7 Mar 1961 JCS. *Paulding Co.*: near Dallas, 28 Mar 1952 PWF. *Bartow Co.*: Etowah River, 30 Mar 1962 JCS. *DeKalb Co.*: Stone Mountain, 1 Apr 1951 LHJ (TTRS). *Fulton Co.*: Atlanta, Harris Trail, 1 Apr 1960 JCS (TTRS). *Greene Co.*: near Greensboro, 10 Apr 1952 PWF (TTRS). *Fulton Co.*: Atlanta, Harris Trail, 16 Apr 1960 JCS (TTRS); Atlanta, Harris Trail, 18 Apr 1958 JCS (TTRS); Atlanta, Harris Trail, 29 Apr 1958 LHJ (TTRS). *Greene Co.*: near Greensboro, 30 Apr 1953 LHJ (TTRS). *DeKalb Co.*: Stone Mountain, 5 May 1952 LHJ (TTRS).

Coastal Region—*Grady Co.*: Beachton, Springwood Plantation, ex pupa 14 Feb 1964 LHJ (TTRS); Beachton, Susina Plantation, 25 Mar 1965 LHJ (TTRS). *Charlton Co.*: Folkston, ex pupa 29 Apr 1953 LHJ (TTRS).

One of the best ways to locate a colony of the Yucca Skipper is to look for signs that may show the presence of the caterpillar in a Yucca plant. The place to look is in the center of the plant, where the flower stalk emerges. If a caterpillar is present, it will have begun the construction of a cocoonlike tent, which protects the opening to the tunnel occupied by the caterpillar. If a tent is found, the plant can be carefully dug up with a shovel so that the stout root is still attached to the plant (the tunnel occupied by the caterpillar is in the root). The entire plant can be transferred to a large pot or a box to be grown on, or to be transplanted in the ground at home. The caterpillar remains in the plant until the following spring, at which time it changes to a pupa while still in the plant. Then, usually in March or April, the butterfly emerges. It crawls outside the tent and clings to it while the wings gradually expand and become firm. This usually occurs in the morning, and the butterfly is ready to fly by midday.

A word of caution about handling Yucca plants: On some people with tender, sensitive skin, the juicy sap in the root may produce itching and blisters similar to the rash of poison ivy. It is best to use heavy gloves when handling these plants. Further, the sharp point on the tip of each leaf can be dangerous to the eyes when one is bending down to examine a plant.

The late Henry W. Eustis of Augusta taught me how to find the tent that the caterpillar makes in the crown of Bear Grass and on the end of the stem of Spanish Bayonet. Eustis had located a few colonies around Augusta and one in North

Augusta, which lies just across the Savannah River in Aiken County, South Carolina. The colony in North Augusta was in a yard that had been landscaped with Spanish Bayonet. Some months later, I found tents on Bear Grass in extreme southeast Georgia in Camden County. The adults that emerged were *M. y. yuccae.*

In 1964, Leon Neel, whose active work in forestry takes him into the woods over a wide area in southwest Georgia, found a number of *M. y. yuccae* tents on plants that were scattered about in the woods and along the edge of forest roads in Thomas and Grady counties. He helped me gather a number of infested plants from which Yucca Skippers emerged in the spring of 1965.

In the Piedmont Region of Georgia, good stands of Bear Grass may be found around the large outcroppings of granite that are located in a number of counties, including DeKalb, Elbert, Greene, Hancock, and Rockdale. Local colonies of the Yucca Skipper can usually be found in such areas.

Another type of habitat may be found in old fields and bottom land near rivers and creeks, where Yucca plants may grow rather profusely. John Symmes, an excellent collector and companion on many field trips, has located well-established colonies in such areas. He has found both *M. y. yuccae* and *M. harrisi* in this type of habitat.

The Yucca Skipper eggs are laid on Yucca leaves, usually on the underside. The larva emerges about ten days later. In a few days, the larva has worked its way into the large, fleshy root of the plant by literally eating its way into it. As the larva grows, it increases both the size of the tunnel and the size of the silken tent at the top of the tunnel to accommodate its growth. In a few months, the larva has reached full size. The tent and the upper end of the tunnel are lined with silk. The larva usually pupates in February, but may wait until March. The pupa is active, and can move up and down quickly and easily in the tunnel and tent.

The adult Yucca Skipper is seldom seen, even in its natural habitat, for it remains hidden during the day and flies in the late afternoon and early evening. The body of this and other skippers in the family contain much fat, and many cabinet specimens therefore become greasy.

A watercolor drawing of *M. y. yuccae* by John Abbot was reproduced by Boisduval and LeConte (1833) when they named this species. Freeman (1963), noting that Boisduval and LeConte had failed to specify a type locality for *M. y. yuccae* in their original description, wrote as follows: "Aiken County, South Carolina is here designated type locality as it is the nearest place to Abbot's home in Scrivin (sic) County, Georgia where he is known to have collected and where Yucca grows." Thus, although South Carolina has been so designated, it is clear that the circumstance of its designation is such as to in no way deny the possibility that the locality at which Abbot collected the specimen figured by Boisduval and LeConte may actually have been in Georgia.

Cofaqui Skipper. *Megathymus cofaqui* Strecker
(Page 129)

Distribution and Records: Herman Strecker, in his original description of *M. cofaqui*, designated a female as the holotype and gave the type locality as "Georgia." This specimen, which is still the only one known from Georgia, was collected by H. S. Morrison and is in the Field Museum of Natural History in Chicago. The label on it bears the inscription "AEG. cofaqui Streck., Georgia, Orig. type, H. S. Morrison."

We now know, through information received from F. Martin Brown, that Morrison was at Parramore Hill in Screven County between March and September, 1876. Brown learned of this when he read some of Morrison's letters to Strecker. I examined old Georgia maps and found "Parramore" shown on a railroad line in the northwest corner of Screven County, not far from Burke County. It was in these counties that John Abbot had lived and collected for many years prior to 1876, and it is understandable that Morrison would spend several months collecting in the same area. It seems reasonable to assume that Morrison collected the type specimen of *M. cofaqui* in this area. It is unfortunate that he did not list the date and locality of this important specimen.

Barnes and McDunnough (1912, pp. 34–35) figured Strecker's female holotype, the only specimen of which they had knowledge, stating that "the male sex is apparently unknown" and giving the habitat as "Georgia; Florida (fide Skinner)." Five years later, Grossbeck (1917, pp. 35–36) wrote: "The male of this species has, until now, remained undiscovered and, as it differs sufficiently from the female to be taken for another species I append the following description of it. . . . the allotype is from Boca Grande and is in the collection of Mr. Davis." W. H. Evans (1955, p. 467) wrote: "Cofaqui Strecker 1876: female Georgia. Fig. Strecker 1878 female."

H. A. Freeman (1955, p. 4) stated that "apparently Morrison caught the type of *cofaqui* somewhere along the eastern, coastal part of Georgia." But later (1963), he wrote: "The allotype was collected at Boca Grande, Florida, which is here designated as the type locality. The exact locality of origin of the holotype is believed to be somewhere in northern Florida near Georgia, collected by Morrison."

I am not an expert on the rules of zoological nomenclature, and therefore fail to understand the need for designating Boca Grande, Florida, as the type locality of a species validly described from Georgia more than 85 years earlier. Although doubt is cast on the accuracy of Strecker's designation of Georgia as the type locality for the holotype female, the basis for this doubt is not apparent: as I mentioned earlier, the records show that Morrison was collecting in Georgia at the relevant time in an appropriate area.

At the present time, *M. cofaqui* does appear to be more numerous on the west coast of Florida in the Sarasota–Fort Myers area than elsewhere. Boca Grande is located on Gasparilla Island, between Sarasota and Fort Myers.

The larva of *M. cofaqui* is about two inches long, with a small, brownish head and a whitish body. The larva bores into the stem and root of the Yucca or Spanish Bayonet.

Auburn E. Brower called my attention to an article written by J. G. Boniwell (1917) dealing primarily with *M. y. yuccae*, but referring to *M. cofaqui* briefly in three lines:

Some experiments with the larvae of *Megathymus cofaqui* the year before had convinced us that it had habits quite a lot different from its near kin *yuccae*. This year we succeeded in determining without any doubt the fact that the *cofaqui* does not make a silken pouch in the summer or fall like the *yuccae*, but remains entirely concealed until about two weeks prior to pupation, at which time it penetrates the surface and creates a short light-colored pouch, usually near the ground on rotten prostrate stems. We have yet to find a *cofaqui* in a strong healthy plant.

These observations were confirmed by H. L. King, J. P. Knudsen, and me when, at the invitation of King, we visited a colony he had located. We searched for the silken pouches or tents, and Knudsen found the first two. They were situated on the ground near the base of two Spanish Bayonets, and each tent had a silk-lined tunnel connecting with the root of a separate plant that had been the food plant.

King soon found a tent on the stalk of another Spanish Bayonet that was almost prostrate. After a diligent search, we each found several tents on the ground at the base of Spanish Bayonet plants. They were well hidden by dead leaves hanging from the lowest part of the stalk of each plant.

In February, 1954, I visited the Florida area again, and several tents were found. They, too, were usually on the ground, but a few were found on the plant just above the ground.

30

Charles P. Kimball discovered that *M. cofaqui* is double-brooded. He captured a female on November 22, 1952, at his winter home on Siesta Key at Sarasota. A year or two later, he collected another specimen in October. Further collecting of fall specimens by others indicate that a few individuals of the fall brood begin to emerge in August, with the number increasing in September and October and decreasing in November.

Harris' Skipper. *Megathymus harrisi* H. A. Freeman
(Page 129)

Distribution and Records: *M. harrisi*, the type locality of which is Georgia, occurs widely but locally throughout the state in close association with its larval food plant, *Yucca filamentosa* (Bear Grass). The best chance a collector has of finding *M. harrisi* is to locate good stands of the food plant.

Mountain Region—*White Co.*: US 129, ten miles north of Cleveland, 21 July 1952 LHJ (TTRS); US 129, ten miles north of Cleveland, 10 Aug 1952 LHJ (TTRS); US 129, ten miles north of Cleveland, 16 Aug 1942 JPK. *Rabun Co.*: Dick's Creek, near Lake Burton, sight record 5 Nov 1955, JCS.
Piedmont Region—*DeKalb Co.*: Stone Mountain, 3 July 1953 LHJ (TTRS); Stone Mountain, 9 July 1950 LHT (TTRS); Mt. Arabia, 25 July 1961 LHJ (TTRS). *Fulton Co.*: Atlanta, Harris Trail, 27 July 1958 LHJ (TTRS); Roswell, Wayt's Farm, 27 July 1965 JCS (TTRS). *Bibb Co.*: Macon, July 1930 HFS (TTRS). *Fulton Co.*: Roswell, Wayt's Farm, 11 Aug 1964 LHJ (TTRS). *Bibb Co.*: Macon, collected but escaped from net 11 Sept 1952 JPK and LHJ.
Coastal Region—*Thomas Co.*: Melrose Plantation, ex pupa 10 Aug 1964 LN.

On July 5, 1950, as my son Lucien and I were collecting along a path at the base of Stone Mountain in a wooded area, a large skipper darted out of the underbrush and lit on the trunk of a nearby tree. Lucien collected it, and we found that it was a species of *Megathymus*. We began to wonder at its presence in July, because all of the known Georgia species of

Megathymus fly in early spring. The specimen resembled *M. cofaqui*, so we surmised that this individual specimen had emerged out of season. A further search failed to turn up any more at that time. The specimen was tentatively labeled *M. cofaqui*, and placed in our collection.

In 1952, when I was looking at the collection of J. P. Knudsen at Oglethorpe College, I noticed a similar *Megathymus* specimen that Knudsen had collected. He had found the specimen on August 16, 1942, in White County, Georgia, as it flew across US 129 about ten miles north of the town of Cleveland. He, too, had labeled it *M. cofaqui*, and perhaps had also wondered about its late occurrence. Knudsen remembered the place where he had captured it, so we arranged a collecting trip that included Prof. P. W. Fattig, curator of the Emory University Museum. When we arrived at the place where Knudsen had collected his specimen, we each began to look for tents in the centers of Yucca plants that were growing along the edge of the highway. Not finding any, we began to search at the bases of the plants, where to our surprise, we found a number of tents. These tents were not *on* the plants, but were sticking up out of the ground beneath the plants, or very near them. Each tent was camouflaged on the exterior with particles of reddish soil that matched the surrounding ground. It was easy to overlook them, but with careful searching we found a number of tents. They were about the size and shape of the thumb of a lady's glove.

We went next to Stone Mountain, and looked for similar tents on the ground under Yucca plants. The trip was successful: after a diligent search, we found several. These tents were camouflaged with bits of granite, which blended perfectly with the ground. They were as easily overlooked as were the ones near Cleveland.

Knudsen was the first to discover an egg of the species. It was attached to the leaf of a Yucca plant, and a further search yielded three additional eggs. Knudsen took them home for further study. At the time the egg was first collected, its color was pale pink. One week before hatching, the egg was a pale rose-purple, lighter at the base and shading to a deep tone at the apex. As hatching time approached, the egg lost the purple cast and became white with a dark micropile. The larval head could be seen through the shell as a gray area within the egg.

At hatching time, the larva leaves the egg through a roughly circular hole 1 mm in diameter chewed at the apex of the egg. On emergence, the larva is about 6 mm long. The remainder of the shell is not eaten, and the young caterpillar crawls immediately to the base of a leaf of Yucca, and conceals itself in the crown of the plant. A little later, it gradually begins to eat its way into the main root of the plant.

The larva is creamy white, with a small black head that can be withdrawn into the first segment. As it grows, it extends and enlarges its living area in the root of the plant. It remains there until after it has reached its final instar. Almost a year later, through one of nature's amazing timing processes, the caterpillar, now about 2 inches long, begins to construct a silken tunnel out of the root and through the soil for a distance of a foot or more. It then turns upward until it has reached the surface of the ground, where it constructs a pouchlike tent of silk. The caterpillar remains in the tent for a week or two until it changes into a pupa. The pupal stage lasts from one to three weeks, after which the butterfly breaks through the pupal shell and crawls out of the tent. It clings to the tent for a few hours, until the wings have become fully expanded and dry. Then it is ready to fly, perhaps to find a mate and to complete the life cycle. (For additional details of the life histories of *M. cofaqui* and *M. harrisi*, see Harris, 1955.)

After a number of specimens had been collected, they were sent to H. A. Freeman for identification. He made detailed studies, and found that these specimens, although closely related to *M. cofaqui*, actually represented a new species. After further study, Freeman (1955) described and named the new species *M. harrisi*.

Information is needed on the general distribution of *M. harrisi*, particularly in the Mountain and Coastal regions. In the Mountain Region, the only record other than those for the Cleveland area is a sight record of a *Megathymus* made by John Symmes on November 5, 1955. He was on a deer hunt, and his stand was in a beech and oak hardwood hammock in a valley in the Dick's Creek area of Rabun County, not far from Lake Burton. It was a bright day, and the temperature was about 50° F. Symmes saw a large skipper flying slowly. It lit for a brief moment among the brown leaves on the ground, and then flew away. Symmes observed that the flight was typical of the *Megathymus* skippers. He noticed that it was light in color, and he thought that it might have been a faded and flown *M. harrisi*. The food plant, *Yucca filamentosa*, was present in the area.

J. P. Knudsen's specimen, which he collected in White County, was a slightly worn female taken on the wing near Yucca plants at about 4 P.M. on August 16, 1942.

At present, we have only one record for the Coastal Region. Leon Neel and I found a *Megathymus* tent near a fallen limb by a Yucca plant on the Melrose Plantation in Thomas County. We dug it up carefully. The tent contained a pupa, from which an *M. harrisi* emerged on August 10, 1964. It was our first south Georgia record, and is the only one at present. We also found an empty tent near the tent that contained the pupa.

An interesting account is given by Karl E. Karalus, Jr., (1957) of collecting a good series of adult skippers at Stone Mountain after first walking among Yucca plants expecting the butterflies to be flushed out, and then finding that they were not hiding among the plants, but were sitting on the trunks of nearby trees. Karalus stated:

We noticed that almost all were on the shady side of the tree, and all were on very bare areas of the trees from two to six feet above the ground. Some we managed to spot before they flew. They were resting with their heads pointing upwards, wings closed tightly, and hardly noticeable against the bark of the trees.

The day was hot and sunny, and it was after two o'clock when we discovered where the Giant Skippers were resting. They seemed very nervous and usually flew a long distance before settling again. Because of this, it was almost impossible to find them again if one missed capturing them on the first try—which we did in most cases.

Family HESPERIIDAE—True Skippers

Genus *Panoquina*

Salt-Marsh Skipper. *Panoquina panoquin* Scudder
(Page 136)

Distribution and Records: *P. panoquin* is a species of the Coastal Region that occurs in and near salt marshes, both along the mainland and on the coastal islands. It is a species of local distribution. It may be very abundant, in some places, and may occasionally be found at some distance from the marshes.

Mountain Region—None.
Piedmont Region—None.
Coastal Region—*Glynn Co.*: St. Simons Island, 22 Apr 1911 JCBS (CU); St. Simons Island, 23 Apr 1959 LNH (TTRS); Jekyll Island, 11 and 12 May 1958 JCS; St. Simons Island, 12 May 1911 JCBS (CU). *Chatham Co.*: Savannah, 20 May 1960 JCS; Tybee Island, 20 July 1913 JCBS (CU); Thunderbolt, Oglethorpe Cemetery, 30 July 1958 GBS; Thunderbolt, Oglethorpe Cemetery, 15 Aug 1958 GBS. *Glynn Co.*: St. Simons Island, 20 Aug 1951 LHJ (TTRS). *Chatham Co.*: Savannah, no dates MHM (CU).

On August 20, 1951, I found numerous *P. panoquin* in a grassy area along a road near the golf course on St. Simons Island. On April 23, 1959, Louise Harris found it abundant on flowers along a road near Christ Church on St. Simons Island, not far from Fort Frederica. It had previously been recorded from St. Simons Island by Dr. J. C. Bradley, who collected specimens on April 22 and May 12, 1911.

John Symmes collected a number of specimens on Jekyll Island on May 11 and 12, 1958. The skippers were feeding on the flowers of *Liqustrum* shrubs that had been planted around the grounds of the hotel. On July 30 and August 15, 1958, Gordon B. Small, Jr. found *P. panoquin* to be very common around the salt marsh at Oglethorpe Cemetery, which is located on the edge of Savannah near Thunderbolt.

There are two broods: the first appears in April and May, the second in July and August.

Ocola Skipper. *Panoquina ocola* Edwards (Page 136)

Distribution and Records: *P. ocola* occurs widely throughout the state, and may be common in some places.

Mountain Region—*Rabun Co.*: Lakemont, 3 Oct 1954 LHJ (TTRS).

Piedmont Region—*Bibb Co.*: Macon, 3 June 1931 HFS; Macon, 6 June 1931 HFS (TTRS). *Fulton Co.*: Oglethorpe College, frequent June–Oct 1954 JPK. *DeKalb Co.*: Stone Mountain, 27 July 1953 LHJ (TTRS). *Walton Co.*: Monroe, 14 Aug 1960 JCS. *Clarke Co.*: Athens, uncommon Aug and Sept 1931 JCS and AGR; Athens, uncommon Aug 1966 LRT. *Fulton Co.*: Atlanta, Riverside Drive, 24 Sept 1960 LHJ (TTRS). *Cobb Co.*: Marietta, 2 Oct 1960 JCS. *Bibb Co.*: Macon, 6 Oct 1928 HFS.

Coastal Region—*Chatham Co.*: Savannah, 27 May 1960 JCS. *Screven Co.*: Sylvania, several taken May–Sept 1946 OB (AMNH). *Lowndes Co.*: Valdosta, 11 July 1930 HFS.

J. P. Knudsen (1954) found it to be frequent on the Oglethorpe College campus and stated, "Not rare on pickerel weed and buttonbush in low areas during midsummer." At Athens, in Clarke County, L. R. Tanner found it uncommon but not rare in August, 1966. Otto Buchholz took specimens in the Coastal Region near Sylvania in Screven County in 1946. I collected specimens in the Mountain Region at Lakemont in Rabun County in 1954.

P. ocola has a rapid, darting flight. There are two broods: the adults of the first brood appear in May and June, those of the second brood appear in mid-July, August, and September. Worn specimens have been taken in the latter part of September and in early October.

F. Martin Brown has made a careful study of many of Edwards' types. He has informed me that Edwards' cotype of *P. ocola* came from Georgia.

Genus *Calpodes*

Brazilian Skipper; Canna Skipper. *Calpodes ethlius* Stoll
(Page 129)

Distribution and Records: *C. ethlius* is found mainly in the Coastal Region. It is generally rare, but may be common locally.

Mountain Region—None.
Piedmont Region—*Bibb Co.*: Macon, 11 June 1930 HFS. *Chatham Co.*: Savannah, 5 Aug 1962 JCS. *Richmond Co.*: Augusta, 11 Sept 1941 HWE; Augusta, 5 Oct 1948 HWE.
Coastal Region—*Screven Co.*: Specimens taken May–Sept 1946 OB (AMNH). *Chatham Co.*: Savannah, no dates MHM (CU). *Tift Co.*: Tifton, 11 July 1930 HFS.

This large skipper has a fast flight. The species seems to undergo population explosions, separated by long intervals, and when exceptionally plentiful, it may become common in regions where it is not usually found. I remember when it appeared in Atlanta many years ago. Mary Nichols Mayfield, my sister-in-law, found a freshly emerged skipper on a Canna leaf in front of the house, and brought it in to inquire if I had one in my collection. It was the first that I had ever seen. A quick check was made on the Cannas and there, to my astonishment,

37

were caterpillars in all stages of development, and several pupae. A further investigation of Canna beds in city parks revealed the presence of *C. ethlius* in other parts of the city. In a few years *C. ethlius* vanished following a period of colder winters. Since then, they have reappeared for very brief periods on a few occasions.

The larva is rather large; its body is pale green, with two white lines running lengthways along the back, the spiracles have narrow black rims surrounded by a brownish area, and the head is orange and black. It feeds on Cannas, both cultivated and wild varieties.

Genus *Oligoria*

Twin-Spot Skipper. *Oligoria maculata* Edwards
(Page 136)

Distribution and Records: *O. maculata* occurs locally in the Coastal and Piedmont regions, and is not usually common.

Mountain Region—None.
Piedmont Region—*Richmond Co.*: Augusta, 26 May 1942 HWE. *Coweta Co.*: Madras, 28 May 1950 MES. *Harris Co.*: Callaway Gardens, 6 June 1960 JCS. *Bibb Co.*: Macon, 7 June 1930 HFS (TTRS). *Richmond Co.*: Augusta, 13 Aug 1946 HWE. *Monroe Co.*: Forsyth, 28 Sept 1961 FTN.
Coastal Region—*Glynn Co.*: Jekyll Island, 16 May 1960 JCS. *Grady Co.*: Beachton, Birdsong Plantation, 22 May 1953 LHJ. *Screven Co.*: Sylvania, several taken 4 May–25 June 1946 OB (AMNH). *Charlton Co.*: Folkston, 17 Aug 1949 LHJ (TTRS). *Screven Co.*: Sylvania, several taken 15 Aug–10 Sept 1946 OB (AMNH).

The twin spot on the under side of the hind wing is a distinguishing feature. The larva has a light brown head and a slender, pale green body—the last segments are a deep shade of green. The food plants are various grasses. There are two broods, with adults in May and June, and in August and September.

Genus *Lerodea*

Eufala Skipper. *Lerodea eufala* Edwards (Page 136)

Distribution and Records: *L. eufala* occurs in the Piedmont and Coastal regions and is common throughout its range. It was first described from Apalachicola, Florida.

Mountain Region—None.

Piedmont Region—*Fulton Co.*: Atlanta, Indian Trail Road, 7 Apr 1961 LHJ (TTRS). *Bibb Co.*: Macon, 23 May 1931 HFS. *Coweta Co.*: Madras, May and June 1949 MES. *Clarke Co.*: Athens, rare Aug 1966 LRT. *Fulton Co.*: Atlanta, 2 Aug 1952 LHJ (TTRS); Atlanta, 12 Aug 1960 JCS. *Clarke Co.*: Athens, common Aug–Sept 1931 AGR. *DeKalb Co.*: Avondale Estates, 5 Sept 1952 LHJ (TTRS). *Bibb Co.*: Macon, 10 Sept 1931 HFS. *DeKalb Co.*: Avondale Estates, 28 Sept 1955 LHJ (TTRS); Avondale Estates, 7 Oct 1955 LHJ (TTRS).

Coastal Region—*Charlton Co.*: Folkston, 9 Feb 1952 LHJ (TTRS). *Glynn Co.*: Jekyll Island, 17 Mar 1956 LHJ (TTRS). *Bryan Co.*: Blitchton, 23 May 1962 JCS. *Glynn Co.*: St. Simons Island, 20 Aug 1951 LHJ (TTRS). *Screven Co.*: specimens taken in May and Sept 1946 OB (AMNH). *Chatham Co.*: Savannah, no dates MHM (CU).

In the list of butterflies found on the Oglethorpe College campus that was compiled by J. P. Knudsen (1954), *L. eufala* is listed as "frequent." Under "Remarks" Knudsen states: "More often taken than [*Nastra*] *l'herminieri* which it resembles. Habits same as [*N.*] *l'herminieri.*"

There are two broods, with the adults in the southern part of the state emerging a few weeks earlier than those in the northern part. The adult population of the first brood reaches its peak in March and April, and the second brood reaches its peak in August and September.

The body of the larva is bright green and lightly covered with short hairs; a dark green line bordered with yellowish spots extends along the back; the segmental creases are bright yellow; the head is creamy white with orange brown stripes. The larval food plants are various grasses.

Genus *Amblyscirtes*

Pepper-and-Salt Skipper. *Amblyscirtes samoset* Scudder
(Page 136)

Distribution and Records: *A. samoset* (which has been widely known as *A. hegon*) occurs locally in the Piedmont and Mountain regions. It is generally found in open areas in woods, along roads through woods, and around the edges of woods. It is very rare. The Piedmont Region of Georgia is probably the southern limit of the range of this species.

Mountain Region—*Lumpkin Co.*: Auraria, 15 Apr 1967 JCS. *Murray Co.*: Old Fort Mountain, 21 Apr 1964 JCS. *Rabun Co.*: Coleman River, 4 May 1955 JCS. *Union Co.*: Cooper Creek, 16 July 1961 JCS.

Piedmont Region—*Fulton Co.*: Atlanta, Indian Trail Road, 7 Apr 1961 LHJ (TTRS); Atlanta, Indian Trail Road, 17 Apr 1955 LHJ (TTRS); Atlanta, Indian Trail Road, 18 Apr 1958 LHJ (TTRS); Atlanta, Indian Trail Road, 27 Apr 1957 LHJ (TTRS). *Cobb Co.*: Kennesaw Mountain, 28 Apr 1957 JCS. *DeKalb Co.*: Stone Mountain, 1 May 1952 LHJ (TTRS); Emory University campus, 20 May 1968 JC. *Coweta Co.*: Madras, 28 May 1950 MES.

Coastal Region—None.

The specimen collected at Stone Mountain in DeKalb County on May 1, 1952, was sent to H. A. Freeman for determination, so that we could be certain that Georgia specimens were not being confused with another species.

Apparently, there is only one brood, with adults in April and May.

Cobweb Skipper; Textor Skipper. *Amblyscirtes aesculapius* Fabricius (Page 136)

Distribution and Records: Although generally rare, *A. aesculapius* has a wide range over the state. It occurs chiefly in the Piedmont Region. It is rare in the Coastal Region, but there are records of its being taken as far south as Orlando, Florida (Kimball, 1965, p. 57).

Mountain Region—*Rabun Co.*: Clayton, no date JCBR (see Richards, 1931).
Piedmont Region—*Richmond Co.*: Augusta, 8 Apr 1946 HWE. *Bibb Co.*: Macon, 11 Apr 1930 HFS. *Richmond Co.*: Augusta, 11 May 1945 HWE. *Fulton Co.*: Atlanta, Riverside Drive, 15 May 1956 LHJ (TTRS); Atlanta, Riverside Drive, 18 May 1957 LHJ (TTRS); Atlanta, Mt. Vernon Road, 18 May 1958 LHJ (TTRS). *Bibb Co.*: Macon, 25 May 1959 FTN. *Richmond Co.*: Augusta, 29 May 1961 JCS. *Bibb Co.*: Macon, 5 June 1959 FTN. *Clarke Co.*: Athens, May–July AGR (see Richards, 1931). *Fulton Co.*: Atlanta area, 24 July 1961 JCS; Atlanta, Riverside Drive, 13 Aug 1960 JCS. *Richmond Co.*: Augusta, 13 Aug 1947 HWE. *Fulton Co.*: Atlanta, Harris Trail, 20 Aug 1955 JCS. *Forsyth Co.*: Monroe, 29 Aug 1960 JCS. *DeKalb Co.*: Avondale Estates, 15 Sept 1961 JRH (TTRS).
Coastal Region—*Tift Co.*: Tifton, 24 July 1954 EVK (TTRS).

A. aesculapius is also well known as *A. textor*, a junior synonym published by Hübner.

There are two broods, with the adults emerging from April through May to mid-June, and from mid-July through August to mid-September.

The life history is apparently unknown.

Carolina Skipper. *Amblyscirtes carolina* Skinner
(Page 136)

Distribution and Records: *A. carolina* is widely distributed but of very local occurrence in the Piedmont and Coastal regions.

Mountain Region—None.
Piedmont Region—*Fulton Co.*: Atlanta area, no date (about 1910) WFF (ANSP)*. *Coweta Co.*: Madras, 10 May 1946 MES and RLC*. *Fulton Co.*: Atlanta, Riverside Drive, 18 May 1957 JCS (TTRS); Atlanta, Harris Trail, 19 May 1957 JCS; Atlanta, Harris Trail, 19 May 1957 FTN; Atlanta, Harris Trail,

30 May 1957 LHJ (TTRS); Atlanta, Harris Trail, 16 July 1955 JCS (TTRS); Atlanta area, 29 July 1951 GH (USNM); Atlanta, Harris Trail, 2 Aug 1958 JCS (TTRS).

Coastal Region—*Screven Co.*: near Sylvania, 6 May 1946 OB (AMNH).

A form of the species named *A. carolina* f. *reversa* by F. M. Jones in 1926, also occurs in Georgia. It differs from *A. carolina* chiefly with respect to the underside of the hind wings, which are dark with yellow spots, rather than yellow with darker yellow spots. *A. carolina* f. *reversa* is considered to be a separate species by some lepidopterists.

The earliest Georgia record of *A. carolina* is a specimen collected by W. F. Fiske in Fulton County about 1910, when Fiske was Assistant State Entomologist. The specimen was determined by Dr. Henry Skinner, who described the species in 1892. The specimen was placed in the Academy of Natural Sciences, Philadelphia.

On May 10, 1946, M. Eugene Smith collected *A. carolina* at Madras in Coweta County. This specimen is in the collection of Dr. Ralph L. Chermock. On May 16, 1946, Otto Buchholz collected a specimen in Screven County. This specimen is now in The American Museum of Natural History.

A number of specimens of *A. carolina* f. *reversa* have been taken in Fulton County. A specimen collected in Fulton County on July 29, 1951, by Graham Heid was identified by William D. Field and presented to the U.S. National Museum. John Symmes found a colony of them near his home. The colony was located in a wooded area near a small stream. The food plant, Maiden Cane (*Arundinaria tecta*), was present, and Symmes succeeded in rearing several specimens. Symmes observed that, when the larvae were in the final instar just prior to pupation, the larvae would almost sever the midrib of the leaves in which their cocoons were encased. This allows

* Records followed by an asterisk indicate the species, *A. carolina*. All other records are for *A. carolina* f. *reversa*.

the encased cocoon to rotate freely and it whirls about whenever there is a breeze.

Carolina Skippers are most likely to be found in moist or swampy areas where their food plant grows. These small skippers cruise swiftly back and forth along forest roads and in open areas in places where their colonies are located. They fly with a rapid, darting, zig-zag motion, which makes them difficult to catch.

There are two broods. The spring brood flies in May, and the summer brood in July and early August.

Roadside Skipper. *Amblyscirtes vialis* Edwards
(Page 136)

Distribution and Records: *A. vialis* occurs throughout the state. Although it is local in occurrence, it is usually common where found, except in the Coastal Region.

Mountain Region—*Lumpkin Co.*: Auraria, 15 Apr 1967 JCS and LHJ; Woody Gap, 16 Apr 1967 BMR. *Fannin Co.*: Margaret, 16 Apr 1967 BMR. *Murray Co.*: Old Fort Mountain, 17 Apr 1953 LHJ (TTRS); Old Fort Mountain, 5 May 1951 LHT (TTRS); Old Fort Mountain, 16 May 1950 JRH. *Rabun Co.*: Lake Rabun, 15 July 1928 AGR (see Richards, 1931). *Banks Co.* and *Habersham Co.*: 27 July 1930 RWM (see Montgomery, 1931).

Piedmont Region—*Coweta Co.*: Madras, 21 Apr 1951 MES. *Fulton Co.*: Atlanta, Indian Trail Road, 27 Apr 1957 LHJ (TTRS). *Coweta Co.*: Madras, 29 Apr 1951 MES. *Richmond Co.*: Augusta, 5 May 1941 HWE. *Fulton Co.*: Atlanta, Mt. Vernon Road, 18 May 1958 LHJ (TTRS). *Clarke Co.*: Athens, uncommon July AGR (see Richards, 1931). *DeKalb Co.*: Stone Mountain, 12 Aug 1950 LHT (TTRS); Stone Mountain, 20 and 22 Aug 1950 LHJ (TTRS).

Coastal Region—None. [*A. vialis* is apparently present but rare in this region, and records are needed. Kimball (1965, p. 56) lists several records for Florida.]

A. vialis may easily be overlooked, as it is a small, dark skipper. It occurs in grassy areas of open woods, and also in fields. It visits flowers freely.

There are two broods in Georgia, the first in April and May and the second in July and August.

The larva is pale green, dotted with light green at the base of its short, downy hairs; its head is dull white with reddish stripes. The larval food plants are various grasses; Klots (1951, p. 262) lists *Poa pratensis* (Kentucky Blue-Grass) and *Avena striata* (wild oat).

Bell's Roadside Rambler. *Amblyscirtes celia belli*
H. A. Freeman (Page 138)

Distribution and Records: *A. c. belli* occurs widely in the Piedmont Region. Although very local and rare, at times it may become locally common.

Mountain Region—None.
Piedmont Region—*Richmond Co.*: Augusta, 14 and 17 May 1941 HWE. *Fulton Co.*: Atlanta, Riverside Drive, 18 and 21 May 1957 LHJ (TTRS); Atlanta, Mt. Vernon Road, 18 May 1958 LHJ (TTRS); *Richmond Co.*: Augusta, 29 May 1961 JCS. *Monroe Co.*: Forsyth, 22 May 1959 FTN. *Fulton Co.*: Atlanta, Riverside Drive, 30 May 1955 JCS (TTRS). *Monroe Co.*: Forsyth, 2 June 1959 FTN. *Fulton Co.*: Atlanta, 3 June 1941 PWF (USNM); Atlanta, Harris Trail, 7 June 1959 LHJ (TTRS). *Richmond Co.*: Augusta, 25 June 1945 HWE. *Fulton Co.*: Atlanta, Harris Trail, 20 July 1965 JCS; Atlanta, Harris Trail, 1 Aug 1965 JCS.
Coastal Region—None.

When the subspecies *A. c. belli* was described from Texas by H. A. Freeman in 1941, it was thought to be peculiar to the central United States. However, it was learned that it also occurs in some areas of the southeast when, shortly thereafter, H. W. Eustis collected specimens at Augusta and Professor P. W. Fattig collected it in Atlanta. Their specimens were identified by Austin H. Clark: Professor Fattig's specimen was found by Clark in the U.S. National Museum series of *A. alternata,* and the specimens collected by Eustis were sent to Clark for determination. These specimens were collected in 1941; since that time, a number of specimens have been taken in additional localities by other collectors.

In a series of specimens that he has collected, John C. Symmes found some variations that may indicate either that *A. c. belli* is variable, or that it and some closely related (but as yet unidentified) species or subspecies both occur in Georgia.

This small, rather dark butterfly is easily overlooked as it flies close to the ground, usually in grassy areas in open woods or at the edges of woods. Its life history was recorded by J. Richard Heitzman (1965). He found it to be very local along shaded creek beds, primarily in secluded, undisturbed habitats. He states that adults can be found in grassy areas or sunning themselves on nearby plants.

The larva is pale translucent green with a whitish overcast, with a darker green mid-dorsal line on the back, and a pale greenish-white lateral band along the sides. Its head is creamy white with orange brown bands. The final larval instar is 2.22 cm long.

The larval food plants are various grasses. The host plant found by Heitzman in Missouri is *Uniola latifolia.* He states that the chances are good that a colony of *A. c. belli* will be present near any colony of this grass along a woodland creek.

Least Florida Skipper. *Amblyscirtes alternata*
Grote and Robinson (Page 138)

Distribution and Records: *A. alternata,* which was described from Georgia, is locally common in the Piedmont and Coastal regions.

Mountain Region—None.
Piedmont Region—*Fulton Co.*: Atlanta, Riverside Drive, 18 and

45

21 May 1957 LHJ (TTRS); Atlanta, Harris Trail, 2 June 1956 LHJ (TTRS). *Bibb Co.*: Macon, 11 June 1930 HFS. *Fulton Co.*: Atlanta, 21 and 26 June 1940 LHJ. *Clayton Co.*: Lake Mirror Road, 23 June 1945 JCS. *Fulton Co.*: Atlanta, 14 Aug 1949 LHJ; Atlanta, Harris Trail, 22 Aug 1967 LHJ (TTRS).
Coastal Region—*Screven Co.*: forty-five taken 1 Apr–23 June and 1–15 Aug 1946 OB (AMNH). *Thomas Co.*: Six miles southeast of Metcalf, 20 July 1965 LN.

Even in places where it is common, *A. alternata* is easily overlooked as it is small and inconspicuous. Otto Buchholz collected forty-five specimens in Screven County in the period from April 1 to June 23rd, and August 1st to the 15th, in 1946.

There are two broods, the first in April, May, and June, and the second in July and August. The life history is unknown.

Genus *Atrytonopsis*

Dusted Skipper; Hianna. *Atrytonopsis hianna hianna* Scudder
(Page 138)

Distribution and Records: *A. h. hianna* occurs throughout the state, but is rare and local.

Mountain Region—*White Co.*: Tray Mountain, 4 May 1955 JCS. *Murray Co.*: Old Fort Mountain, 16 May 1950 LHT.
Piedmont Region—*DeKalb Co.*: Stone Mountain, 8 Apr 1945 JCS. *Coweta Co.*: Madras, 15 Apr 1949 MES. *Clarke Co.*: Athens, rare Apr 1967 LRT. *Fulton Co.*: Atlanta, off Harris Trail, 27 Apr 1963 JCS. *Coweta Co.*: Madras, 29 Apr 1951 MES. *Fulton Co.*: Atlanta, off Harris Trail, 2 May 1963 JCS. *Coweta Co.*: Madras, twenty specimens 5–12 May 1940 MES (OB, AMNH). *Cobb Co.*: Kennesaw Mountain, 1 June 1958 JCS; Kennesaw Mountain, 15 July 1965 JCS.
Coastal Region—*Grady Co.*: 6 May 1950 LHJ.

Klots (1951, p. 260) states that he has taken *A. h. hianna* only in dry open fields. Georgia records indicate that it has only one brood in the state, with adults in April and May.

Richard Heitzman has worked out the life history and will

publish it in detail when the illustrations have been completed. He has generously supplied the following life history information: Eggs are laid by the adult female in late April and early May. The larvae, which go through seven instars, feed all summer, except when aestivating during periods of hot summer weather. The larval food plant is Bear Grass (*Andropogon*); the larvae construct tube tents on the host plant above the base (they are higher than the tents of *Hesperia metea*, and never extend into the base of the plant). The mature larvae hibernate until spring.

When mature, the larva averages 32–35 mm long. The color of the body is bright pinkish lavender, except for the next-to-last two segments, which are paler pink, and the last segment, which is pale brown. The underside is grayish white. The body is covered with long, downy, white hair. The head is deep reddish purple, unmarked, and covered with short reddish setal hairs and longer white hairs.

Loammi Skipper. *Atrytonopsis loammi* Whitney
(Page 138)

Distribution and Records: *A. loammi* was described in 1876. The type specimen was taken at Jacksonville, Florida, in the month of March. Although *A. loammi* has a wide range over Florida, as shown by the records compiled by C. P. Kimball (1965, p. 56), it is virtually unknown in Georgia. It may occur as a rare stray or it may be rare and local. Georgia records are wanting, and further collecting is needed to determine its status in the state.

W. J. Holland (1931, p. 394) states that it is known to range from the Carolinas to Florida. A. B. Klots (1951, p. 259) was more specific, stating: "Florida, March, April, October; North Carolina, July."

Informal communications have indicated that some who have studied the *Atrytonopsis* species have doubts that *A.*

47

hianna and *A. loammi* are different species. Mather and Mather (1958, p. 98) have discussed this matter, as it relates to the population (or populations) represented in Mississippi, and have suggested that the question of specific distinctness should be re-examined.

Genus *Euphyes*

Arpa Skipper. *Euphyes arpa* Boisduval and LeConte
(Page 129)

Distribution and Records: *E. arpa* was described from Georgia. It may be very rare and local in the Coastal Region, or it may occur at the present time only as a rare stray from Florida, where, according to Charles P. Kimball (1965, p. 55), it is fairly common in the peninsular area.

The original description was based on a watercolor drawing by John Abbot (Boisduval and LeConte, 1829–1833, pl. 63). It has been assumed that the specimens from which Abbot made his drawing were collected in Screven County. It is not unlikely that *E. arpa* may still be present in Georgia: in 1946, in Screven County, Otto Buchholz established the first state records for two other species in this genus, *E. palatka* and *E. berryi*.

A. B. Klots (1951, p. 254) lists Saw Palmetto (*Serenoa*) as the larval foodplant. Saw Palmetto occurs locally in the Coastal Region, and *E. arpa* would most likely be found in or near a stand of these plants.

The record of a stray specimen taken in Atlanta (no date) reported by me in an earlier publication (Harris, 1950, p. 25) has been omitted here, because not enough information is available to establish it as an authentic record.

Palatka Skipper. *Euphyes palatka* Edwards (Page 129)

Distribution and Records: *E. palatka*, which was described

from St. Augustine, Florida, is known to occur commonly throughout Florida (Kimball, 1965, p. 55). Otto Buchholz, a fine collector, took a single specimen of this species in Screven County, Georgia, on May 25, 1946 (the specimen is now in the collection of the American Museum of Natural History). Buchholz collected other specimens as far north along the Atlantic coast as the southern part of Princess Anne County, Virginia (Clark and Clark, 1951, p. 173).

In Georgia, this large, attractive skipper should occur locally in the Coastal Region, where the larval foodplant, Saw Grass (*Mariscus jamaicensis*), is found.

Alabama Skipper. *Euphyes dion alabamae* Lindsey
(Page 140)

Distribution and Records: *E. d. alabamae*, described from Mobile County, Alabama, occurs widely in the Coastal Region and has been recorded from Bibb and Cherokee counties in the Piedmont Region.

Mountain Region—None.
Piedmont Region—*Bibb Co.*: Macon, 16 June 1931 HFS (TTRS).
 Cherokee Co.: swamp on Cox Road, 21 July 1960 JCS; swamp on Cox Road, 20 Aug 1960 JCS. *Bibb Co.*: Macon, 5 and 15 Sept 1931 HFS.
Coastal Region—*Thomas Co.*: Greenwood Plantation, 14 May 1954 EVK (TTRS). *Bryan Co.*: Blichton, 21 May 1962 JCS; Blichton, 28 May 1960 JCS; Blichton, 30 May 1960 JCS; Blichton, 30 May 1960 LHJ (TTRS). *Screven Co.*: Sylvania, two specimens 1 June 1946 OB (AMNH).

John Symmes and I were enroute to Savannah on US Highway 80 when we stopped to collect on an unpaved forest road a short distance off the highway about one mile west of Blichton in Bryan County. There was a small boggy area near the road, and the drainage ditch along the edge of the road had a diversity of plants and grasses. There, Symmes collected an agile skipper, which he promptly identified as *E. d. alabamae*.

We collected several others in the same limited area. It was the only place we found it, although we explored several other areas along the road for almost a mile. No doubt the food plant was growing in a limited area and the skippers did not stray far from it.

E. d. alabamae should be looked for in wet or boggy areas, in marshes, and along woodland streams having thick growths of tall grasses and sedges.

The life history of *E. dion* has been worked out by Richard Heitzman and we appreciate receiving from him the following information: The mature larva is 45 mm long. Its skin is bluish green and translucent, with yellow intersegmental folds. There are small white flecks over the body, and a dark green dorsal line. The head is orange-brown, with an oval black spot in the center of the face ringed with white. The sutures and the sides of the face are ringed with white. The larva pupates in a tent rather high on the host plant, apparently because the areas in which it occurs are frequently flooded. In Missouri, the larval food plant is *Arex lacustris*. In South Carolina, John Burns found the larva on Wool Grass (*Scirpus cyperinus*).

Berry's Skipper. *Euphyes berryi* Bell (Page 140)

Distribution and Records: *E. berryi* is found in the Coastal Region. It is rare and local.

Mountain Region—None.
Piedmont Region—None.
Coastal Region—*Bryan Co.*: Blichton, 18 May 1963 JCS; Blichton, 21, 22, and 26 May 1962 JCS. *Screven Co.*: near Sylvania, 22 July 1946 OB (TTRS); near Sylvania, 26 July 1946 OB (AMNH). *Effingham Co.*: two miles south of Guyton, 4 and 5 Aug 1962 JCS.

Otto Buchholz found *E. berryi* in Screven County and collected specimens on July 22 and 26, 1946, and again on

August 10, 1946. He sent me the specimen he collected on July 22nd, as it was the first Georgia record; it has now been placed in the Georgia collection at Tall Timbers Research Station. The other two, no doubt, remained in his collection, which is now at the American Museum of Natural History.

John Symmes collected *E. berryi* in Bryan County in May, 1962, and May, 1963, and in Effingham County in August, 1962. Dean F. Berry, for whom this skipper was named, collected the first specimens in Jefferson County, Florida, near Monticello, the type locality. Two Georgia counties, Thomas and Brooks, border on Madison County, thus forming a part of the Georgia–Florida state line. Therefore, it is very likely that *E. berryi* will be found in these counties at some future time, and in other Coastal Region areas also.

H. L. King, Colonel S. S. Nicolay, and John Symmes have collected *E. berryi* in Florida. They found it in wet areas—near ponds and drainage canals, and along the edges of marshes, where it could be taken on the flowers of pickeral weed (*Pontederia*).

There are two broods: the type series from Monticello was collected in March, and there are other Florida records (Kimball, 1965) for May, September, and October. The Georgia specimens were taken in May, July, and August. Based on the above, there is a very likely possibility that the first brood flies in March, April, and May, and the second brood in July, August, and September, with a few adults still on the wing in October.

The life history is unknown.

Two-Spotted Skipper. *Euphyes bimacula* Grote and Robinson
(Page 138)

Distribution and Records: At present, *E. bimacula* is known in Georgia only from one locality—near Blichton, in Bryan County. A new state record and a new southern limit for the species were established by H. L. King and J. C. Symmes when they collected specimens in this area in 1962.

Mountain Region—None.
Piedmont Region—None.
Coastal Region—*Bryan Co.*: Blichton, two males and two females 18 May 1963 JCS; Blichton, seven specimens 20 and 24 May 1962 HLK and JCS.

E. bimacula is a northern species about which little is known (Klots, A.B., 1951: p. 258). The few records available indicate a preference for boggy or marshy meadows, and the Georgia specimens were collected in this type of habitat; they were taken on the flowers of Pickeral Weed. The specimens were examined by Colonel S. S. Nicolay, who confirmed the identification made by Symmes.

Dun Skipper. *Euphyes vestris metacomet* T. W. Harris
(Page 138)

Distribution and Records: *E. vestris metacomet* (formerly known as *Atrytone ruricola metacomet*) occurs throughout the state. It is one of our common species, and may be found on flowers, along roadsides, and also on the ground sipping moisture from a damp spot where other butterflies may also be gathered.

Mountain Region—*Union Co.*: Cooper Creek State Park, 22 June 1951 JCS; Cooper Creek State Park, 29 June 1960 LHJ (TTRS). *Rabun Co.*: Coleman River, 9 July 1961 JCS. *White Co.*: Unicoi Gap, near Helen, 16 July 1961 LHJ (TTRS).
Piedmont Region—*Clayton Co.*: near Hapeville, 29 Apr 1945 JCS. *Fulton Co.*: Atlanta area, 2 June 1956 LHJ (TTRS); off Harris Trail, 4 Aug 1945 JCS; Atlanta area, 5 Aug 1950 LHT (TTRS). *Bibb Co.*: Macon, 8 Sept 1933 HFS (TTRS).
Coastal Region—*Grady Co.*: Beachton, Sherwood Plantation, 3 Mar 1965 LN (TTRS). *Screven Co.*: one specimen 2 July 1946 OB (AMNH). *Lowndes Co.*: Valdosta, 12 July 1936 LHJ (EUM).

The life history of this skipper was unknown until it was carefully worked out by J. Richard Heitzman (1964). There are two broods in Georgia, the first brood appearing in south Georgia in late March and April and flying as late as early May; in middle and north Georgia, the first brood appears in May and flies through June into early July. The second brood appears in late July (earlier in the southern part of the state) and flies through August into early September.

The patience and ingenuity of Heitzman in rearing this species is shown in this excerpt from his 1964 article:

In May 1963, I decided to rear a series [of *E. vestris*] and collected several females for this purpose. Since the host plant was unknown I took several flower pots and planted different species of grasses in each pot. These were covered with nylon netting and a female was placed in each bag with suitable flowers. In every instance I failed to get a single egg although the females lived as long as seven days. After repeated failures with other females and different plants I dissected the abdomens of two worn females and removed the eggs. I might add at this point that I have used this method before in extreme cases with *Hesperiidae* and *Papilio* species. One or two fertile ova can usually be obtained by using this procedure. In this case two fertile ova were secured and the larvae emerged seven days later. Again many grass species were offered but the larvae only wandered aimlessly about refusing to eat. I finally tried a small sedge, *Cyperus esculentus* L., that grows as a weed along roads and ditches in rather damp locations. The larvae fell upon this with relish and were easily reared. Second brood females laid eggs freely when confined with this sedge so it seems certain that this is one of the normal host plants in this area [Independence, Missouri].

Heitzman recorded the emergence of the larvae on June 17. From the records he kept, he found the larvae spent roughly seven days in each of the first four instars. The final instar lasted twelve days, with two days of this time spent spinning the cocoon.

Pupation occurred on July 26 in a white silk-lined tube fashioned from four leaves near the base of the plant. The pupa rests in a vertical position, head up, with a 10 mm topping of foamy silk, and another thinner pad about 5 mm thick beneath. The pupa is very active with abdomen rotating rapidly in a circular motion when disturbed.

The body of the final larval instar is pale translucent green, with a white overcast caused by multiple, horizontal, wavy, white dashes. There are a few hardly noticeable white hairs sprinkled over the body. Each spiracle is indicated with a black dot, a larger dot at the first and anal spiracles. The prothorax is white with the prothoracic shield indicated by a thin black line running into the enlarged first spiracle dot. The back of the head is black, the rest of the head is caramel brown with two cream-colored bands.

The larval food plant, *Cyperus esculentus*, a small sedge, is commonly known as Chufa or Yellow Nutgrass.

Genus *Poanes*

Hobomok Skipper. *Poanes hobomok* T. W. Harris
(Page 140)

Distribution and Records: *P. hobomok* is rare in Georgia. It occurs locally in the Piedmont and Mountain regions; there is a possibility that it may be found in the Coastal Region, but we do not have any records of it there. Clark and Clark (1951, p. 169) record it from the Dismal Swamp in the Coastal Region of Virginia, where it was collected by Otto Buchholz.

Mountain Region—*Murray Co.*: Old Fort Mountain, two males and one female form *pocahontas* 16 May 1950 LHT (TTRS).
Piedmont Region—*Fulton Co.*: Atlanta, Piedmont Road, 20 Apr 1945 JCS; Atlanta, near Harris Trail, 27 Apr 1963 JCS; Atlanta, near Harris Trail, 8 and 12 May 1963 JCS; Atlanta, Riverside Drive, 10 May 1957 JCS; Atlanta, Riverside Drive, 12 May 1956 LHJ (TTRS); Atlanta, near Harris Trail, 15 May 1960 LHJ (TTRS); Atlanta, Riverside Drive, 15 and 18 May 1959 JCS; Atlanta, Riverside Drive, 16 June 1959 JCS.
Coastal Region—None.

The Hobomok Skipper is found in deciduous woods along streams. The males seem to have a regular "beat" that they patrol. They are difficult to catch, and fly rapidly when alarmed.

John Symmes acquainted me with the flight pattern. In Atlanta, in a wooded area near Harris Trail, we observed males of this species patrolling the banks of a small stream. Occasionally, a female would pass by, and the activity of the males would increase. They sometimes were attracted to the fragrant blossoms of wild *Leucothoe* plants that grew near the stream. Most of the skippers that we collected were netted when they stopped to feed.

There are two female forms of *P. hobomok*. One is a yellow form that clearly resembles the male, and the other is a dark form, named *P. hobomok* female form *pocahontas* by Scudder. Klots (1951, p. 250) states that this form seems to occur somewhat later in the season than the normal yellow female. Clark and Clark (1951, p. 169) state: "Both light and dark females, together with various intermediates, occur everywhere in Virginia." Arthur M. Shapiro (1966, p. 58) also found both light and dark *P. hobomok* females in the Delaware Valley flying at the same time, together with intermediates. A Georgia series collected by John Symmes confirms that the same variations occur here.

There is one brood, with adults in April, May, and June. The larva is reported to feed on grasses.

Zabulon Skipper. *Poanes zabulon* Boisduval and LeConte
(Page 140)

Distribution and Records: *P. zabulon*, which was described from Georgia, occurs commonly but locally throughout the state.

Mountain Region—None.
Piedmont Region—*Coweta Co.*: Madras, 3 Apr 1950 MES. *Clay-*

ton Co.: near Hapeville, 27 Apr 1945 JCS. *DeKalb Co.*: Stone Mountain, 1 May 1952 LHJ (TTRS). *Bibb Co.*: Macon, 6 May 1962 FTN. *Fulton Co.*: Atlanta, Harris Trail, 15 May 1960 LHJ (TTRS); Atlanta, Harris Trail, 21 May 1957 FTN. *Bibb Co.*: Macon, 25 May 1963 FTN. *Fulton Co.*: off Harris Trail, near Chattahoochee River, 10 June 1956 JCS; off Harris Trail, 2 Aug 1945 JCS. *Clarke Co.*: Athens, common 1966 Aug LRT. *DeKalb Co.*: Stone Mountain, 20 Aug 1950 LHT (TTRS). *Fulton Co.*: Atlanta, Harris Trail, 22 Aug 1967 LHJ (TTRS). *Cherokee Co.*: swamp on Cox Road, 29 Aug 1960 JCS. *DeKalb Co.*: Stone Mountain, 10 Sept 1950 LHJ (TTRS).
Coastal Region—*Grady Co.*: Beachton, Sherwood Plantation, 8 Apr 1965 LN; Beachton, Susina Plantation, 29 Apr 1965 LN. *Screven Co.*: several collected May and September 1946 OB (AMNH). *Lee Co.*: Leeland Farms, 15 May 1965 LN.

P. zabulon prefers open woodlands, especially the grassy banks of woodland streams. Clark and Clark (1951) observed that the females, and more rarely the males, would stray into fields from the grassy banks of woodland streams, especially in the Piedmont and Mountain regions.

Abbot's drawing of *P. zabulon* was published by Boisduval and LeConte (1829–1833, pl. 76).

More life-history information is needed for this species, as little is known about its early stages of development. The larval food plants are various grasses.

Aaron's Skipper. *Poanes aaroni howardi* Skinner
(Page 129)

Distribution and Records: Several specimens of *P. a. howardi*, which was described from Florida, were collected in Augusta by H. W. Eustis and were determined by A. H. Clark.

Mountain Region—None.
Piedmont Region—*Richmond Co.*: Augusta, 6 Aug 1945 HWE; Augusta, 13 and 28 Aug 1947 HWE.
Coastal Region—None (however, a watercolor drawing of *P. a. howardi* by John Abbot, bearing the date 1827, is presumed to have been based on specimens from this region).

P. a. howardi, which is a little larger and somewhat darker than *P. a. aaroni*, is locally common in coastal salt marshes in Florida. The salt marsh is its chief habitat, but it may also be found near fresh water marshes, ponds, and lakes. The specimens collected by Henry W. Eustis were taken around a small lake near his home.

An unpublished volume of original watercolor drawings of Georgia insects made by John Abbot in 1827 contains a good figure of *P. a. howardi* made long before the species was described. The volume is now in the Emory University Library.

There are two broods, with adults in April and May and in August and September. The life history is not fully known.

Yehl Skipper; Skinner's Skipper. *Poanes yehl* Skinner
(Page 129)

Distribution and Records: *P. yehl*, which was described from Florida, is rare and local in the Coastal and Piedmont regions of Georgia.

Mountain Region—None.

Piedmont Region—*Fulton Co.*: Long Island Creek, off Harris Trail, 27 May 1962 JCS; Atlanta, Harris Trail, 4 June 1958 LHJ (TTRS); Atlanta, Harris Trail, 5 June 1957 JCS. *Meriweather Co.*: Stovall, Harmon Plantation, 6 June 1960 JCS. *Fulton Co.*: Atlanta, Harris Trail, 7 June 1959 LHJ (TTRS). *Richmond Co.*: Augusta, 4 June 1942 HWE. *Bibb Co.*: Macon, 7 June 1962 FTN; Macon, 7, 11, and 18 June 1930 HFS (TTRS). *Monroe Co.*: Forsyth, 6 Sept 1958 FTN. *Richmond Co.*: Augusta, 7 Sept 1945 HWE. *Fulton Co.*: Atlanta, Harris Trail, 10 Sept 1945 JCS; Atlanta, Harris Trail, 10 and 25 Sept 1955 JCS.

Coastal Region—*Thomas Co.*: Metcalf, 18 May 1954 EVK (TTRS). *Chatham Co.*: Savannah, 24 May 1951 HLK (TTRS); Savannah, 24 May 1962 JCS. *Screven Co.*: two females 30 May 1946 OB (AMNH). *Chatham Co.*: Savannah, 20 Aug 1958 GBS.

The habits of this species are similar to those of *P. hobomok* and *P. zabulon*, for it may be found in open deciduous woods along woodland roads, and on flowers in fields and meadows near woods. Clark and Clark (1951) state that it occurs with some frequency in swampy areas. In Virginia, it was found to be abundant in several large swamps, including the Dismal Swamp.

In Thomas County, E. V. Komarek found *P. yehl* on May 18, 1954. Four days later, he collected it in nearby Tallahassee (Leon County), Florida; this was the only record reported by C. P. Kimball (1965), who stated that this species is very rare in Florida, the principal habitat being somewhat more northerly.

Clark and Clark (1951, p. 172) state that this species is unusually variable, with two distinct forms connected by a series of intergrades. In one of the forms, the underside of the hind wings is cinnamon, with the light spots clearly defined and conspicuous. In the other form, the underside of the hind wings is yellow, with the spots vaguely and indefinitely outlined and scarcely contrasting with the light background.

Studies made in Mississippi by Mather and Mather (1958), however, indicate that the variations are seasonal. They found that females of the earlier brood have a larger and lighter area on the underside of the hind wings than those of the later brood, which tend to have the underside of the hind wings dark cinnamon in color.

The variations in the two broods in Georgia are similar to those reported by the Mathers for Mississippi. The first brood appears in May and June, the second in August and September.

The early stages are unknown.

Broad-Winged Skipper. *Poanes viator* Edwards
(Page 142)

Distribution and Records: *P. viator* occurs mainly in the Coastal Region.

Mountain Region—None.

Piedmont Region—*Richmond Co.*: Augusta, 6 May 1948 HWE; Augusta, 28 Sept 1945 HWE; Augusta, 1 and 10 Nov 1944 HWE.

Coastal Region—*Chatham Co.*: Savannah, 12 Apr 1908 (AMNH). *Glynn Co.*: St. Simons Island, 23 Apr 1959 LNH (TTRS). *Chatham Co.*: Savannah, 26 Apr 1949 HLK (TTRS). *Screven Co.*: Sylvania, 15 May 1946 OB (AMNH). *Camden Co.*: White Oak, 24 May 1962 HLK (TTRS). *Chatham Co.*: Savannah, 27 May 1960 JCS; Bonaventure Cemetery, 28 May 1960 LHJ (TTRS); Port Wentworth, 30 May 1964 LHJ (TTRS); Port Wentworth, 1 June 1963 HLK; Port Wentworth, 3 and 16 Aug 1963 HLK; Savannah, 19 Aug 1958 GBS; Savannah, several (no dates) MHM (CU).

Specimens of *P. viator* have been taken along the lower (southeastern) edge of the Piedmont by H. W. Eustis. He collected it regularly, though sparingly, around a lake near his home in Augusta.

In the Coastal Region, *P. viator* is found in or around marshes with a growth of Wild Rice (*Zizania*), its food plant. There are a number of records from the Chatham County area made by H. L. King, Gordon B. Small, Jr., and others, and Otto Buchholz collected a specimen in Screven County, where Abbot lived for many years.

The earliest date on which *P. viator* has been collected in recent years is April 23: Louise Harris collected a specimen on that date in 1959 on St. Simons Island; it was taken at flowers along the edge of the road near Christ Church, not far from Fort Frederica. The latest date recorded is November 1, for a specimen collected by H. W. Eustis in Augusta in 1944.

In Camden County, which is Georgia's southernmost coastal county, H. L. King collected several specimens of *P. viator* near the town of White Oak on US Highway 17.

The Georgia records indicate that *P. viator* is double-brooded, with adults of the first brood flying in April and May, and those of the second in August and September.

Arthur M. Shapiro (1966, p. 58) reported *Zizania* as the larval food plant. He is now gathering biological and distributional information on *P. viator*, which, when published, should add much to the present knowledge of this butterfly.

Genus *Problema*

Byssus Skipper. *Problema byssus* Edwards (Page 142)

Distribution and Records: *P. byssus*, which occurs widely but locally over the Coastal and Piedmont regions, is generally rare.

Mountain Region—None.

Piedmont Region—*Coweta Co.*: Madras, 6 June 1949 MES (TTRS); Madras, 15 June 1951 MES. *Bibb Co.*: Macon, 18 June 1930 HFS (TTRS); Macon, 19 June 1961 FTN. *Fulton Co.*: Atlanta, 21, 24, and 26 June 1940 LHJ (TTRS). *Monroe Co.*: Forsyth, 25 June 1961 FTN. *Cherokee Co.*: Swamp on Cox Road, 20 and 23 Aug 1960 JCS. *Fulton Co.*: Atlanta, Buckingham Circle, 28 Aug 1949 LHT (USNM). *Bibb Co.*: Macon, 3 Sept 1930 HFS (TTRS); Macon, 3 Sept 1956 FTN. *Monroe Co.*: Forsyth, 6 Sept 1958 FTN and JCS.

Coastal Region—*Grady Co.*: Beachton, Birdsong Plantation, 7 May 1950 LHJ (TTRS). *Screven Co.*: Six specimens 29 May–2 June 1946 OB (AMNH). *Grady Co.*: Beachton, Birdsong Plantation, 15 June 1945 LHJ (USNM). *Glynn Co.*: Jekyll Island, 12 and 13 Aug 1960 JCS.

For many years *P. byssus* was confused with the even rarer *P. bulenta*, but it is now known to be distinct.

Although reported to have only one brood farther northward and westward, this species appears to have one full brood with a partial second brood in Georgia, with adults of the first brood in June, and adults of the partial second brood in August and September.

The life history of *P. byssus* has been carefully worked out by Richard Heitzman (1965, pp. 77–81). He found that its range in Missouri was confined to the few remaining areas of virgin prairie. Heitzman reports that, although *P. byssus* is an extremely local species, it is often found to be abundant, once a colony is located. He discovered that the host plant in Missouri is a tall leaved grass *Tripsacum dactyloides*, or Gama Grass (the food plant in Georgia is probably a closely related species). Gama Grass grows in large beds, usually in the dampest part of the prairie. Heitzman observed that *P. byssus* confines its activities to the area of the grass beds, rarely straying farther away than the nearest flowers. Although Gama Grass grows in many locations other than virgin prairie, *P. byssus* seems unable to adjust to another habitat.

Heitzman found that the species is single-brooded in Missouri, with adults flying from early June (males) to late July (stray females).

The larvae hibernate in the fourth instar, according to Heitzman. Shortly after entering the fourth instar, the larvae construct a silk-lined chamber from three to six inches in length within the larval tent. The hibernation stage begins in late August, and is probably triggered by rain and cool nights, which then begin to occur in that area. By late April, the larvae are aroused from their quiescent state. After feeding for seven to ten days, the larvae enter the fifth instar, where they remain for ten to thirteen days, after which they enter the sixth (final) instar. As they near full growth, the larvae construct a tent by drawing two grass blades together and fastening them with strong silken strands, which makes the grass blades appear to be a single leaf. When the larvae are ready to pupate, they each spin a dense cocoon of shiny white silk in the rubbish at the base of the plants among the grass stems. The adult skippers emerge from the pupal stage in thirteen to sixteen days.

Rare Skipper. *Problema bulenta* Boisduval and LeConte
(Page 142)

Distribution and Records: *P. bulenta* is rare in the Coastal Region.

61

Mountain Region—None.
Piedmont Region—None.
Coastal Region—*Chatham Co.*: US 17, on bank of Savannah
River, 5 Aug 1962 JCS; Port Wentworth, 13 Aug 1962 HLK.

John Abbot's first specimens of *P. bulenta* were collected in
the Coastal Region of Georgia. His excellent watercolor
drawing was figured by Boisduval and LeConte (1829–1833,
pl. 67). Dr. Boisduval recognized the butterfly as a new
species, and named it *P. bulenta.*

For many years afterward, *P. bulenta* was either uncollected
or unrecognized, and gradually, many lepidopterists came to
regard Abbot's watercolor as a poor drawing of *P. byssus.*
Fortunately, *P. bulenta* was rediscovered on July 28, 1925, by
Dr. Frank Morton Jones (1926) who recorded the event as
follows:

In July, 1925, the writer made a collecting trip through coastal
Virginia and North Carolina, with Wilmington, North Carolina,
as his southern limit; at this point, crossing the ferry, which at
frequent intervals connects the city with the two mile causeway
through the swamps (old rice lands) to the west, he found here a
most favorable collecting place, especially for the *Hesperiidae;*
the embanked roadway offered firm footing, the broad ditches on
either side were choked with a luxuriant and varied flora; here and
there, abundant blooms on *Pontederia* attracted the larger skippers, among which *viator* Edw. and an unrecognized species of
similar size were frequently noted; at this date (July 28) both
species had been flying for some time and were no longer in prime
condition; five specimens (two males, three females) of the second
species were captured in the course of the morning, and many
others were seen, out of reach.

At Dr. Skinner's suggestion, these insects, which do not belong
to any of recognized species, were compared with the Boisduval–
LeConte plate of *bulenta*, by which comparison it becomes apparent they most probably represent the true *bulenta*—certainly
are much nearer it than are either *byssus* or *palatka.*

After the rediscovery of *P. bulenta* by Jones, a number of
other persons collected specimens of it. One of the first to do

so was Col. S. S. Nicolay. Several years later, John Symmes, H. L. King, and Gordon B. Small, Jr., collected *P. bulenta* at Wilmington, Delaware, and began to search for it farther south.

Symmes, who is a horticulturist, noted that one of the marsh plants in the *P. bulenta* habitat was different from any that he had previously seen and was unknown to him. He began to search for another marshy area with the same unusual plant, and succeeded in finding such a place in South Carolina. There, he found specimens of *P. bulenta*.

On July 29 and August 5, 1962, Symmes collected several specimens near the Georgia–South Carolina border. On August 13, 1962, H. L. King collected specimens near Port Wentworth (Chatham County), Georgia—a locality perhaps not very far from the general area where Abbot found the first specimens more than 100 years earlier. King's record was reported in the "1962 Season Summary" in *Journal of the Lepidopterists' Society* (*J. Lep. Soc.* 17(4):10, 1963).

Genus *Atrytone*

Arogos Skipper. *Atrytone arogos* Boisduval and LeConte
(Page 142)

Distribution and Records: *A. arogos* is distributed locally in the Coastal Region, and may be locally common at times.

Mountain Region—None.
Piedmont Region—None.
Coastal Region—*Screven Co.*: 17 May 1946 OB (AMNH); 19 May 1946 OB (TTRS); 2 June 1946 OB (AMNH); 2 and 12 Aug 1946 OB (AMNH).

A. arogos was figured by Boisduval and LeConte (1829–1833, pl. 76) from an Abbot drawing. Another of Abbot's watercolor drawings of this little butterfly was published by J. E. Smith (1797, pl. 17). Smith thought it might be the skipper that Fabricius had described under the name *vitellius*, but he had some doubts, which he expressed in these words:

Having no mode of determining this fly but by the description of Fabricius, nor any figure to refer to, we have thought it best to affix a mark of doubt, though the characters agree well with Mr. Abbot's drawings; but in so intricate a tribe even the best descriptions, such as those of Fabricius really are, will not always be sufficient.

In addition to Abbot's watercolor drawing of *A. arogos* in Smith (1797), there is also a figure of the species in an unpublished watercolor folio bearing the title *Insects of Georgia, 1827*, by John Abbot. This folio is now in the Emory University Library, Special Collections.

Abbot's specimens were most likely collected in Screven County, where he lived for many years. In 1946, Otto Buchholz spent four months collecting in Screven County, and collected 13 specimens of *A. arogos*. These are the only Georgia records known to me. Mr. Buchholz presented one of his specimens to me, and it is now in the collection at Tall Timbers Research Station.

A. arogos is known to be a species of extremely local distribution. Abbot was aware of this also, when he wrote:

Feeds on the panic-grass figured, and on the buffalo-grass, at length folding the leaves together for protection. It spun itself up July 25, changed 27th, came forth in its winged state August 4. This species has been found only in the pine woods on the north side of Briar Creek, near Mill Town plantation.

Mill Town Plantation, now known as Millhaven Plantation, still exists, and Briar Creek continues to flow nearby.

The life history of *A. arogos* has been carefully worked out by Richard Heitzman (1966; a drawing by William H. Howe accompanies the article). Heitzman found the 1964 season to be exceptionally good for this species, providing ample opportunities for observations and life-history studies. The host plant selection of wild females is Bear Grass (*Andropogon*), and *Andropogon gerardi* is the species on which the larvae were reared.

When the larvae had reached the third instar, each one had constructed a tent about 40 mm long composed of two leaves drawn together and sealed tightly, open only at the bottom. When the sixth (final) instar was reached, the larval tents were, on the average, 50–70 mm long.

Prior to pupation, the cocoon is constructed between two large grass blades near the tops of the leaves, often three to four feet above the ground. The leaves provide the framework for the cocoon, which consists of a lining of thin silk and a cap of fluffy silk that covers the head of the pupa as it rests in a vertical position.

Heitzman found that larvae that completed their development within one summer followed a concise schedule. Instars one through five required eight days each, and the final instar required eighteen days. The adult skippers emerged in twelve days.

Larvae that hibernated in the fourth instar sealed themselves into a small case between two leaves of the host plant. The larvae left their tents open until mid-September, when they sealed them at both ends in preparation for winter.

Heitzman states that the primary flight period occurs during June, with a less numerous second brood in September. In the Coastal Region of Georgia, according to the records of Abbot and Buchholz, the flight periods are about a month earlier.

Delaware Skipper. *Atrytone delaware delaware* Edwards
(Page 142)

Distribution and Records: *A. d. delaware*, formerly known as *A. l. logan*, occurs widely but locally in Georgia, and is generally rare.

Mountain Region—*Fannin Co.*: Cooper Creek, 22 June 1957
JCS; Cooper Creek, 28 June 1958 LHJ (TTRS). *White Co.*:
Unicoi Gap, near Helen, 16 July 1961 LHJ (TTRS). *Fannin
Co.*: Cooper Creek, 26 Aug 1957 JCS.
Piedmont Region—*DeKalb Co.*: Stone Mountain, 9 May 1945
JCS. *Monroe Co.*: Forsyth, 2 June 1959 FTN. *Fulton Co.*:
Atlanta, near Harris Trail, 16 June 1957 JCS; Atlanta, 21 June
1940 LHT (TTRS). *DeKalb Co.*: near Lithonia, 24 July 1959
LHJ (TTRS). *Richmond Co.*: Augusta, 27 July 1945 HWE;
Augusta, 7 Aug 1946 HWE. *Cherokee Co.*: swamp on Cox
Road, 23 Aug 1960 JCS. *Fulton Co.*: Bascomb Swamp, 14 Sept
1955 JCS.
Coastal Region—*Charlton Co.*: Folkston, 7 May 1933 LHJ
(TTRS). *Grady Co.*: Beachton, Birdsong Plantation, 7 May
1950 LHJ (TTRS). *Bryan Co.*: Blichton, 26 May 1963 JCS.
Screven Co.: 21 May and 10 July 1946 OB (AMNH). *Thomas
Co.*: Six miles southeast of Metcalf, 20 and 26 July 1965 LN.
Bryan Co.: Blichton, 29 July 1962 JCS.

There are two broods, the first appearing in May and June,
and the second in July and August.

Specimens of *A. d. delaware* taken by me in White County
and DeKalb County were found at the edges of woods near
small streams; the Charlton County specimens were taken near
a boggy area, and the Grady County specimen was on Button
Bush flowers at the edge of a pond bordered on one side by
deciduous woods and on the other by a pasture.

The food plants are various grasses.

Genus *Atalopedes*

The Sachem. *Atalopedes campestris* Boisduval (Page 142)

Distribution and Records: *A. campestris* is a common species
which occurs throughout the state.

Mountain Region—*White Co.*: Helen, 12 July 1952 LHJ. *Rabun
Co.*: LaPrades, Lake Burton, 18 Aug 1965 LHJ (TTRS); Lake
Burton, ten specimens 29 Aug 1959 LHJ (TTRS). *Banks Co.*
and *Habersham Co.*: 24 Aug and 7 Sept 1930 RWM.

Piedmont Region—*DeKalb Co.*: Avondale Estates, 21 May 1961 LHJ (TTRS); Avondale Estates, 20 June 1957 LHJ (TTRS). *Fulton Co.*: Atlanta, 19 July 1954 LHJ (TTRS). *Clarke Co.*: Athens, common July–Aug 1966 LRT. *DeKalb Co.*: Stone Mountain, 20 Aug 1950 LHT (TTRS); Avondale Estates, 31 Aug 1965 LNH; Avondale Estates, 15 Oct 1956 LHJ (TTRS). Coastal Region—*Grady Co.*: Beachton, Sherwood Plantation, 25 Apr 1965 LN. *Camden Co.*: Coleraine Plantation, 16 July 1944 LHJ. *Thomas Co.*: Metcalf, 21 July 1965 LN. *Grady Co.*: Beachton, Susina Plantation, 23 July 1965 LHJ. *Screven Co.*: several taken May–Sept 1946 OB (AMNH). *Chatham Co.*: no date MHM (CU). *Grady Co.*: Chubb-Baker Plantation, 18 Sept 1964 LN.

A. campestris may be found in grassy areas of fields, meadows, and open woods. It comes freely to flowers. The males have a large, black rectangular stigma on the forewings.

The larva has a pale green body, mottled with a darker green, with a dark dorsal stripe. The body is covered with minute, short hairs. The larval food plant is Bermuda Grass (*Cynodon dactylon*).

Genus *Pompeius*

Southern Little Glassy-Wing. *Pompeius verna sequoyah* H. A. Freeman (Page 146)

Distribution and Records: *P. v. sequoyah*, described from Arkansas, is the southern subspecies of *P. verna*. It occurs throughout the state of Georgia, but is very local.

Mountain Region—*White Co.*: Unicoi Gap, 16 July 1961 LHJ (TTRS). *Fannin Co.*: Cooper Creek, 17 July 1965 JCS. *Rabun Co.*: LaPrades, Lake Burton, 29 Aug 1959 LHJ (TTRS). Piedmont Region—*Fulton Co.*: Atlanta, 21 May 1957 JCS. *Bibb Co.*: Macon, 16 and 23 May 1931 HFS (TTRS); Macon, 25 May 1959 FTN. *Cobb Co.*: Kennesaw Mountain, 1 June 1958 JCS. *Fulton Co.*: Atlanta, Harris Trail, 7 June 1959 LHJ (TTRS). *Richmond Co.*: Augusta, 21 July 1942 HWE; Augusta, 31 July 1948 HWE. *Fulton Co.*: Atlanta, Harris Trail, 2

Aug 1945 JCS; Atlanta, Buckhead area, 5 Aug 1950 LHT (TTRS). *DeKalb Co.*: Stone Mountain, 22 Aug 1950 LHT (TTRS). *Cherokee Co.*: near swamp on Cox Road, 3 Sept 1961 JCS. *Monroe Co.*: Forsyth, 13 Sept 1961 FTN.
Coastal Region—*Screven Co.*: four taken 16–20 May 1946 OB (AMNH). *Grady Co.*: Beachton, Susina Plantation, 18 May 1964 JCS. *Chatham Co.*: Savannah, 29 May 1960 JCS; Savannah, 1 July 1958 GBS.

H. A. Freeman examined a group of Georgia skippers that I sent to him. He found a female *P. v. sequoyah* in the group.

There are two broods, with adults in May and June, and from mid-July to mid-September.

Genus *Wallengrenia*

Broken Dash. *Wallengrenia otho* Smith (Page 146)

Distribution and Records: *W. otho,* which was described from Georgia, probably occurs throughout the state, although records are lacking for the Mountain Region. In the other regions of the state, it is locally common at times.

Mountain Region—None.
Piedmont Region—*Coweta Co.*: Madras, 2 Apr 1950 MES. *Fulton Co.*: Atlanta, Oglethorpe College, common Apr–Sept JPK (see Knudsen, 1954a). *Bibb Co.*: Macon, 25 May 1963 FTN. *Fulton Co.*: Atlanta, Riverside Drive, 4 June 1958 LHJ (TTRS); Atlanta, Harris Trail, 7 June 1959 LHJ (TTRS); Atlanta area, 12 June 1959 JCS. *Clayton Co.*: near Hapeville, 1 and 4 Aug 1945 JCS.
Coastal Region—*Grady Co.*: Beachton, Birdsong Plantation, 19 Mar 1952 LHJ (TTRS). *Screven Co.*: specimens taken Mar–Sept 1946 OB (AMNH). *Grady Co.*: Beachton, Susina Plantation, 29 Apr 1965 LN; Beachton, Sherwood Plantation, 9 May 1965 LN. *Lee Co.*: Leeland Farms, 15 May 1965 LN. *Thomas Co.*: Metcalf, 18 May 1954 LHJ (TTRS). *Grady Co.*: Beachton, Birdsong Plantation, 22 May 1953 EVK (TTRS). *Chatham Co.*: Savannah, 29 May 1960 LHJ (TTRS). *Camden Co.*: Coleraine Plantation, 16 July 1944 LHJ (TTRS). *Chatham Co.*: Savannah, no dates MHM (CU).

Abbot's drawing of this species, published by Smith (1797, pl. 16), is especially interesting because, unlike his other drawings, which usually depict only the butterflies, pupa, caterpillar, and food plant, this one includes a landscape. The food plant, one of the Blue-eyed Grasses (*Sisyrinchium*), is shown in full bloom in the foreground. In the distance, there is a house on a shoreline, with two tall palm trees adjacent to the house.

Abbot (in Smith, 1797) states:

This caterpillar was taken upon the *Sisyrinchium*, but is most frequent on Crab Grass (*Panicum sanguinale*). On the 19th of August it spun the leaves together for a shelter, like the rest of this tribe, changed the next day, and on the 30th the butterfly came forth. It is also a native of Virginia, and the fly is not uncommon on various kinds of blossoms.

We have two broods of *W. otho*; it is possible that there is a partial third brood in the southern areas of the state.

When Dr. C. L. Remington (1950) reviewed *The Butterflies of Georgia, Revised* (Harris, 1950) he stated:

Local lists like this one are of general interest primarily for geographic investigations. Therefore, it is important that the geographic concept of the subspecies be very carefully applied. In the present list one finds such puzzling records as subspecies *flora* flying with subspecies *clyton* of *Asterocampa clyton* and *egeremet* flying with typical race *otho* of *Wallengrenia otho*.

Such criticisms are helpful and appreciated. The specimens in question were subsequently sent to specialists for determination. Some were found to be *W. otho egeremet*. This was indeed puzzling. Fortunately, when Dr. J. M. Burns was in Atlanta on August 22, 1967, he stated that he was studying *W. otho* and *W. egeremet*, that he had found them to be distinct species, and that he was preparing his findings for publication. He suggested that this be stated in this book, which will be in press before his article is published. His article should clear up the puzzling records that others have also encountered with *W. otho* and *W. egeremet* (Mather and Mather, 1958, pp. 95–96; Freeman, 1951, p. 87).

Wallengrenia egeremet Scudder (Page 146)

Distribution and Records: *W. egeremet* is very local and rare, but is widely distributed over the state.

Mountain Region—*Fannin Co.*: Cooper Creek, 7 Aug 1965 JCS. Piedmont Region—*Clarke Co.*: Athens, June–Aug AGR (see Richards, 1931). *Harris Co.*: Pine Mountain, 6 June 1960 JCS. *Fulton Co.*: Oglethorpe College, Apr–Sept JPK (see Knudsen, 1954a); Atlanta, 23 June 1940 JCS; Atlanta, 10 July 1944 JCS; Atlanta, Buckhead area, 5 Aug 1950 LHT (TTRS). *Richmond Co.*: Augusta, 6 Aug 1945 HWE. *Fulton Co.*: Atlanta, Harris Trail, 13 Aug 1960 JCS.
Coastal Region—None.

There are two broods, with adults generally in April and May, and in July and August.

W. egeremet was previously considered to be a subspecies of *W. otho* (see the preceding account). Dr. C. L. Remington (1950) pointed out that records of the two butterflies flying together were puzzling.

It seems appropriate, at this point, to give a brief account of some of the known records of the occurrence of *W. otho* and *W. egeremet* in the same territory. In *The Butterflies of Georgia, Revised* (Harris, 1950), I treated the two as follows:

Wallengrenia otho Smith. This skipper was originally described from Georgia specimens. It is widely distributed over the state, April–August.

(a) *W. o.* var. *egeremet* Scudder, is recorded by Richards from Clarke County June–August. Eustis reports that he gets both forms in Augusta. He has specimens taken on August 6, 1945.

A. G. Richards, Jr. (1931), wrote: "*Catia otho* (A. & S.) Mitchell Co., N. C. (upper Transition) Skinner," and "*C. o. egeremet* (Scud.) Clarke Co., Greenville, River Falls, and Monteagle, June–Aug."

John P. Knudsen (1954) wrote: *"Wallengrenia otho*, April–Sept., common. Both forms of *otho* can be taken on the pickeral weed blossoms behind Lowry and at Lake Phoebe." Henry W. Eustis had previously reported getting both *W. otho* and *W. egeremet* in Augusta. A specimen collected in Atlanta on August 5, 1950, by Lucien Harris III, which was sent to H. A. Freeman for determination, was found to be *W. egeremet*. Clark and Clark (1951, pp. 167–168) found both butterflies present in Virginia and occurring together in the Great Dismal Swamp.

All of this is now of interest in connection with Dr. Burns' studies, which indicate that *W. egeremet* is a distinct species. The presence of these two butterflies in the same area should no longer be puzzling.

Genus *Polites*

Peck's Skipper. *Polites coras* Cramer (Page 146)

Distribution and Records: *P. coras*, formerly known as *P. peckius*, is known at present from only one locality in the mountains of north Georgia. This new state record was added to the Georgia list when Jane and John Symmes collected six specimens (four males and two females) on May 26, 1957. They were taken in a mountain pasture near an old log cabin on the Coleman River, north of Blalock, Rabun County, near the Towns County line. Symmes collected it again at the same locality on September 9, 1960.

Baracoa Skipper. *Polites baracoa* Lucas (Page 146)

Distribution and Records: *P. baracoa* is distributed locally in the Coastal Region.

Mountain Region—None.
Piedmont Region—None.
Coastal Region—*Lowndes Co.*: Valdosta, 31 May 1931 LHJ

(TTRS). *Charlton Co.*: Okefenokee Swamp, three specimens 10 June 1946 OB (AMNH). *Decatur Co.*: Bainbridge, one male July 1912 JCBS (CU); Spring Creek, two females July 1912 JCBS (CU). *Lowndes Co.*: Valdosta, 15 Aug 1930 LHJ (TTRS). *Thomas Co.*: Thomasville, no date (figured by Klots, 1951, pl. 35).

Dr. J. C. Bradley collected *P. baracoa* near Bainbridge, Decatur County, in July 1962. In 1930, a number of these butterflies were found in a city park in Valdosta. The little skippers were in a grassy area near a small stream. The colony persisted in the park for several years.

About twenty years later, a colony was found on Birdsong Plantation in Grady County. The colony was located in a pasture in a rich grassy area near a pond, but existed for only a year or two. Several specimens were collected, but they met an untimely fate on the spreading boards when they were eaten by a mouse.

Tawny-edged Skipper. *Polites themistocles* Latreille
(Page 144)

Distribution and Records: *P. themistocles*, previously known as *P. cernes* and *P. taumas*. It occurs widely but locally in the Piedmont and Coastal regions.

Mountain Region—None.
Piedmont Region—*Bibb Co.*: Macon, 25 May 1963 FTN. *Fulton Co.*: Atlanta, 30 May 1937 LHJ (TTRS). *Bibb Co.*: Macon, 6 June 1931 HFS (TTRS). *Fulton Co.*: Atlanta, Harris Trail, 7 June 1959 LHJ (TTRS). *DeKalb Co.*: 12 Aug 1950 LHT (TTRS); 1 Sept 1955 LHJ (TTRS).
Coastal Region—*Chatham Co.*: Savannah, 30 May 1960 LHJ (TTRS). *Screven Co.*: seven specimens 18–26 Aug 1946 OB (AMNH).

P. themistocles may be found in fields, meadows, and along roadsides. There are two broods, with adults in May and June, and in late July through early September.

Crossline Skipper. *Polites origines* Fabricius
(Page 144)

Distribution and Records: *P. origines*, formerly known as *manataaqua*, is a fairly common skipper of local occurrence that ranges widely over the state.

Mountain Region—*Rabun Co.*: LaPrades, Lake Burton, 29 Aug 1959 LHJ (TTRS).
Piedmont Region—*Clayton Co.*: Lake Mirror Road, 2 May 1945 JCS. *Bibb Co.*: Macon, 31 May 1930 HFS (TTRS). *Fulton Co.*: Atlanta, Riverside Drive, 21 May 1957 LHJ (TTRS). *DeKalb Co.*: Stone Mountain, 5 June 1954 LHJ (TTRS). *Fulton Co.*: Atlanta, Riverside Drive, 10 June 1961 LHJ (TTRS); Atlanta, Riverside Drive, 25 Sept 1960 LHJ (TTRS).
Coastal Region—*Bryan Co.*: Blichton, 24 May 1962 JCS. *Screven Co.*: several taken May–Sept 1946 OB (AMNH). *Bryan Co.*: Blichton, 29 Aug 1962 JCS.

There are two broods: adults of the first brood appear in May and June, and adults of the second brood fly in August and September.

Whirlabout Skipper. *Polites vibex vibex* Geyer
(Page 144)

Distribution and Records: *P. v. vibex*, formerly known as *P. brettus*, is common in the Coastal and Piedmont regions and rare in the Mountain Region.

Mountain Region—None.
Piedmont Region—*Coweta Co.*: Madras, 11 May 1950 MES. *Bibb Co.*: Macon, 23 May 1931 HFS (TTRS). *Monroe Co.*: Forsyth, 2 June 1959 FTN; Forsyth, 11 July 1956 FTN (TTRS). *Fulton Co.*: Atlanta, Riverside Drive, 25 Sept 1960 LHJ (TTRS). *Clarke Co.* common July–Oct AGR (see Richards, 1931).
Coastal Region—*Thomas Co.*: US 19 at Ochlocknee River, 3 May 1965 LN. *Grady Co.*: Beachton, Sherwood Plantation, 7 May 1950 LHJ (TTRS). *Lee Co.*: Leeland Farms, 15 May 1965 LN. *Decatur Co.*: Spring Creek, 17 May 1953 LHJ

(TTRS). *Grady Co.*: Beachton, Susina Plantation, 6 July 1963 LHJ (TTRS); Beachton, Susina Plantation, 27 Aug 1967 LHJ. *Screven Co.*: thirty specimens 20 Apr–30 May and 4–27 Aug 1946 OB (AMNH). *Chatham Co.*: Savannah, many specimens (no dates) MHM (CU).

There are two broods, with adults of the first brood flying from May through mid-July, and those of the second in August and September.

Klots (1951) succinctly dealt with the problem of nomenclature. He stated that *P. vibex* and *P. brettus* have usually been considered separate species, with the latter name used for the eastern population; he was assured by specialists, however, the two are racially distinct at best and should be considered a single species.

Genus *Hesperia*

Cobweb Skipper. *Hesperia metea* Scudder (Page 144)

Distribution and Records: *H. metea* is widely distributed over the state but is very local in occurrence.

Mountain Region—*Lumpkin Co.*: Auraria, 15 Apr 1967 BMR and JCS. *Union Co.*: Woody Gap, 15 Apr 1967 BMR. *Fannin Co.*: Blue Ridge Wildlife Area, 16 Apr 1967 LHJ (TTRS). *Gilmer Co.*: four miles east of Old Fort Mountain, 6 May 1964 JCS.

Piedmont Region—*Coweta Co.*: Madras, twenty-seven specimens 1–16 Apr 1946 MES (OB, AMNH); Madras, 3 Apr 1950 MES. *Clayton Co.*: near Hapeville, 4 Apr 1945 JCS. *Monroe Co.*: Forsyth, 4 Apr 1955 FTN. *DeKalb Co.*: Stone Mountain, 19 Apr 1955 JCS. *Fulton Co.*: Indian Trail Road, 24 Apr 1960 JCS. *Coweta Co.*: Madras, 29 Apr 1951 MES.

Coastal Region—None.

Arthur M. Shapiro (1965) states:

In Pennsylvania, *metea* is very closely associated with the grass *Andropogon scoparius* Michx. This grass, commonly known as bunchgrass, bluestem beard grass, or fire grass, is a characteristic species of dry hillsides, woodland clearings, burn scars, and denuded or sterile sites. Its aerial method of distribution facilitates its occupying such situations rapidly. It reaches its greatest abundance on dry open hillsides surrounded by woods; hills which open above the trees on at least one side. This is the typical situation for *metea*. The butterfly is never found where the *Andropogon* is less than the dominant element of the herbaceous vegetation, nor where it is only a short-term component.

Shapiro observed that adults of *H. metea* do not wander far from the *Andropogon* plants. He also found that the males seemed to have a definite, though transient, territory. He observed that the males feed early in the morning and extend their range in the late morning, each occupying a specific site and, normally, returning to it when disturbed. The resting sites were usually open spots of bare ground and tufts of *Andropogon*, but occasionally were projecting clumps of low vegetation.

Shapiro also observed that the females fly low, and rest during the heat of the day.

In the New Jersey pine barrens, the ecology of *H. metea* is necessarily somewhat different from what it is in Pennsylvania: Shapiro found it associated with *Andropogon scoparius* var. *glomeratus*, a grass found locally in sandy barrens. In clearings in the pine forests, *H. metea* exists under conditions not unlike those in Pennsylvania, although rarely in large numbers.

Shapiro's studies indicate that *H. metea* may occur in areas from which it is unknown at present. It seems likely that it may be found in the Coastal Region of Georgia. C. P. Kimball (1965, p. 53) lists two Florida records: Orlando, April 20, 1940; and May 17 (the year and place of capture is not given, but the specimen is in the Los Angeles County Museum).

John M. Burns has worked out the life history of *H. metea* and has supplied the following data from his notes:

Larva: 7 instars, egg laid in April, larvae feeding all summer aestivating for periods of hot weather in July and August. Living in tube tent on plant and in base of plant below ground level.

Mature larvae hibernates. Length 35 mm. Pale grayish brown with lavender overcast slightly paler on the underside. Head dark purple, almost black with orange lines along the suture lines and frous lines and an orange raised dot above the base of each jaw. Markings tend to become obscure near end of instar.

The larval food plant is *Andropogon* (Beard Grass).

Indian Skipper. *Hesperia sassacus sassacus* Harris
(Page 144)

Distribution and Records: *H. sassacus* was originally recorded from the Coastal Region of Georgia by Abbot, according to S. H. Scudder (1889, vol. 2). Scudder stated that ". . . it has been reported but from a single locality in Georgia, where Abbot says it is common and from which state I have seen specimens. . . ."

C. P. Kimball (1965, p. 54) gives a record for Jacksonville, Florida, listed by J. A. Grossbeck (1917, p. 32). Kimball states: "Since dos Passos has not seen this south of Virginia and Tennessee, and it is very rare in Tennessee, the Florida record needs to be duplicated."

There is an unconfirmed record of one specimen of *H. sassacus* being taken near the base of Stone Mountain (DeKalb County) by Paul Kight.

W. J. Holland (1931, p. 373) and A. B. Klots (1951, p. 238) each include Georgia in the southward range of *H. sassacus*, but this may have been on the basis of the Scudder and Grossbeck references. New records are needed to establish the present range of the species in Georgia.

Klots (1951, p. 238) gives mid-April as the flight period for adults. The habitat is reported to be open fields and meadows. The larval food plant is recorded as "Grasses."

Meske's Skipper. *Hesperia meskei* Edwards
(Page 144)

Distribution and Records: *H. meskei* is widely distributed over the state but is local and rare. We have records for the Coastal and Piedmont regions, but none for the Mountain Region.

Mountain Region—None.

Piedmont Region—*Monroe Co.*: Stewart's Mill, 27 May 1959 FTN; Forsyth, 2 June 1959 FTN. *Fulton Co.*: dirt road in northern section, seven specimens 5 June 1957 JCS. *DeKalb Co.*: Stone Mountain, 8 June 1958 LHJ. *Fulton Co.*: Indian Trail Road, June 1957 JCS; Atlanta, Buckhead area, 13 June 1937 LHT; Atlanta, Indian Trail Road, June 1957 JCS. *Coweta Co.*: Madras, 14 June 1949 MES. *Monroe Co.*: Forsyth, 18 June 1956 FTN. *Cobb Co.*: Tilly Mill Road, 24 Sept 1960 JCS. *Fulton Co.*: dirt road in northern section, 25 and 30 Sept 1955 JCS. *Monroe Co.*: Forsyth, 29 Sept 1956 FTN. *Fulton Co.*: Riverside Drive, 1 Oct 1960 LHJ (TTRS); dirt road in northern section, 3 Oct 1955 JCS; Riverside Drive, 6 Oct 1960 JCS. *Cobb Co.*: Terrell Mill Road, 25 Sept 1960 LHJ (TTRS).

Coastal Region—*Screven Co.*: one each on 30 May and 4 June 1946 OB (AMNH).

In September, 1955, John Symmes found a colony of *H. meskei* in an area along a dirt road in the northern part of Fulton County. The skippers would fly out of some sparse open woods and alight on a few scattered fall flowers. Occasionally, one or two would sit on a sunlit rock, and would partly spread its wings as though warming them, for the weather was cool. The skippers were still active in the area in the first half of October.

John Symmes observed that *H. meskei* is attracted to yellow flowers; he collected a number of specimens on them along Indian Trail Road in Fulton County in June, 1957.

Our oldest record is a pair taken in Atlanta by Lucien Harris III, on June 13, 1937.

Although we have a number of records for middle Georgia, we have only two records for the Coastal Region. Two specimens were collected by Otto Buchholz in Screven County, one May 30, and the other June 4, 1946.

There are two broods, with adults in late May and June, and in September and October. Life-history information is needed.

Dotted Skipper. *Hesperia attalus seminole* Scudder
(Page 144)

Distribution and Records: *H. a. seminole* was described from
Florida; in Georgia, it is probably found only in the Coastal
Region. The only Georgia specimens were taken in July, 1912,
in Decatur County, near Bainbridge, by Dr. J. C. Bradley. Dr.
Bradley's specimens are presently in the collection of Cornell
University.

A. B. Klots (1951, p. 239) states that the Florida race of
H. attalus is fairly distinctive, but data about its northern extent are badly needed. Forbes (1960, p. 94) gives the range
of *H. a. seminole* as "Florida straggling north to Massachusetts."

C. P. Kimball (1965, p. 53) states that Col. S. S. Nicolay
found it in pine flats in the Pensacola area in February, April,
and August. It should be found in a similar habitat in south
Georgia, and possibly in the same months. The flight periods
may be brief, lasting only three or four weeks.

H. a. seminole visits flowers: John Symmes and Gordon
Small collected them on thistles near Weeki-Wachee Springs,
and Colonel Nicolay found them on small flowers near
Pensacola.

Information about the life history is needed.

Genus *Hylephila*

Fiery Skipper. *Hylephila phyleus* Drury (Page 144)

Distribution and Records: *H. phyleus* is common throughout
the state.

Mountain Region—*Rabun Co.*: Dick's Creek Road, Lake Burton,
18 Aug 1965 LNH; LaPrades, Lake Burton, 29 Aug 1959 LHJ
(TTRS); Lakemont, 3 Oct 1954 LHJ (TTRS).
Piedmont Region—*Coweta Co.*: Madras, 15 June 1951 MES.
Clarke Co.: Athens, common Aug 1966 LRT. *Fulton Co.*:
Atlanta, 2 Aug 1952 LHJ (TTRS); Atlanta, Symmes Field, 22

Aug 1967 LHJ. *DeKalb Co.*: Stone Mountain, 10 Sept 1950
LHJ (TTRS). *Bibb Co.*: Macon, 11 Sept 1952 LHJ (TTRS).
DeKalb Co.: Avondale Estates, 4 Oct 1967 LNH (TTRS).
Fulton Co.: Atlanta, 8 Oct 1960 JCS. *Coweta Co.*: Madras,
20 Oct 1950 MES.
Coastal Region—*Charlton Co.*: Folkston, 9 Feb 1952 LHJ
(TTRS). *Grady Co.*: Beachton, Sherwood Plantation, 21 May
1965 LN; Beachton, Birdsong Plantation, 22 May 1953 EVK
(TTRS). *Bryan Co.*: Blichton, 22 May 1962 JCS. *Chatham
Co.*: Savannah, 22 May 1962 HLK. *Screven Co.*: Sylvania,
May–Aug 1946 OB (AMNH). *Camden Co.*: Coleraine Plan-
tation, 16 July 1944 LHJ. *Glynn Co.*: St. Simons Island, 20
Aug 1951 LHJ (TTRS). *Grady Co.*: Beachton, Susina Planta-
tion, 16 Nov 1966 LHJ (TTRS). *Chatham Co.*: Savannah,
Many specimens (no dates) MHM (CU).

A. B. Klots (1951, pl. 34, fig. 7) figures, in color, a specimen of *H. phyleus* taken at Bainbridge, in southwest Georgia.

H. phyleus has a rapid, darting flight, but is easily taken at
flowers. There are two broods in the northern regions of the
state and possibly three in the southern.

The pale green body of the larva is lightly mottled with
darker green, except in a lighter lateral stripe. The larval food
plants are various grasses.

Genus *Copaeodes*

Southern Skipperling. *Copaeodes minima* Edwards
(Page 146)

Distribution and Records: *C. minima* is found in the Piedmont
and Coastal regions of Georgia.

Mountain Region—None.
Piedmont Region—*Monroe Co.*: Forsyth, 12 June 1956 FTN.
Coweta Co.: Madras, 24 Aug 1951 MES. *Monroe Co.*: Forsyth, abundant 24 Aug 1956 FTN. *Bibb Co.*: Macon, 25 Aug
1960 FTN. *Clarke Co.*: Athens, thirty-eight specimens 12 Sept
1928 AGR (see Richards, 1931). *Bibb Co.*: Macon, 16 Sept
1928 HFS (TTRS). *Clarke Co.*: Athens, uncommon Aug 1966
LRT.

Coastal Region—*Glynn Co.*: St. Simons Island, 19 May 1965 LNH. *Screven Co.*: several taken May–Sept 1946 OB (AMNH). *Chatham Co.*: Savannah, no dates MHM (CU).

On September 12, 1928, Dr. A. Glenn Richards, Jr., collected thirty-eight specimens in one morning on the flowers of Bitterweed (*Helenium tenuifolium*) on an open hillside on the University of Georgia campus at Athens. Prior to that date, it was usually rare and only isolated captures were made (Richards, 1931).

In August 1966, *C. minima* was collected on the University of Georgia campus by L. R. Tanner, but he reported it to be uncommon at that time.

C. minima is smaller than *Ancyloxypha numitor*. Its bright, light orange color makes it easy to see in the low grasses where it is found. It is an active little butterfly, and seems to prefer open fields and meadows where the grasses are not very tall.

There are two broods, with adults in May and June, and in August and September. The early stages are unknown. The larval food plants are presumed to be grasses.

Genus *Ancyloxypha*

Least Skipper. *Ancyloxypha numitor* Fabricius
(Page 146)

Distribution and Records: *A. numitor* is found locally throughout the state in favorable localities.

Mountain Region—*Banks Co.* and *Habersham Co.*: 7 Sept 1930 RWM (see Montgomery, 1931).
Piedmont Region—*Fulton Co.*: Atlanta, Oglethorpe College, Apr–Sept JPK (see Knudsen, 1954). *Bibb Co.*: Macon, 6 May 1962 FTN. *Clarke Co.*: Athens, May 1967 LRT. *Fulton Co.*: Wayte's Farm, Roswell, 10 July 1965 LHJ (TTRS). *Clarke Co.*: Athens, Sept 1966 LRT.
Coastal Region—*Mitchell Co.*: Camilla, 17 May 1965 JCS (TTRS). *Grady Co.*: Beachton, Birdsong Plantation, 6 June 1960 LHJ (TTRS). *Dougherty Co.*: Gillionville Plantation, 7

Sept 1964 LN. *Screven Co.*: several taken May–Sept 1946 OB (AMNH).

This is one of our smallest butterflies; it may easily be overlooked, as it flies low in grassy areas, usually among tall grasses.

There are at least two broods (perhaps three in the Coastal Region), with adults emerging from May through mid-September.

The larva is small. Its body is green and covered with very short, light hairs, and the head is mottled with light markings. The larval food plants are various grasses.

Abbot figures a male in "Insects of Georgia" (1827). This unpublished original sketchbook is now in the Emory University Library.

Genus *Lerema*

Clouded Skipper. *Lerema accius* J. E. Smith (Page 148)

Distribution and Records: *L. accius* occurs locally throughout the state. Where it occurs, it is generally common.

Mountain Region—*Rabun Co.*: LaPrades, Lake Burton, 3 Sept 1952 LHJ (TTRS).
Piedmont Region—*Richmond Co.*: Augusta, 9 May 1942 HWE. *Fulton Co.*: Atlanta, Riverside Drive, 21 May 1957 LHJ (TTRS). *Richmond Co.*: Augusta, 14 June 1945 HWE. *De-Kalb Co.*: Stone Mountain, 20 Aug 1950 LHT (TTRS). *Fulton Co.*: Atlanta, Harris Trail, 22 Aug 1967 LHJ. *Monroe Co.*: Forsyth, 24 Aug 1956 FTN. *Clarke Co.*: Athens, common Aug–Sept AGR (see Richards, 1931); Athens, rare Sept 1966 LRT. *DeKalb Co.*: Stone Mountain, 10 Sept 1950 LHJ (TTRS). *Bibb Co.*: Macon, 11 Sept 1952 LHJ (TTRS). *Richmond Co.*: Augusta, 11 Nov 1944 HWE.
Coastal Region—*Grady Co.*: Beachton, Melton Place, 9 Jan 1965 LN; Beachton, Sherwood Plantation, 19 Mar 1952 LHJ (TTRS); Beachton, Sherwood Plantation, 27 Mar 1965 LN. *Screven Co.*: specimens taken 14 Apr–5 June 1946 OB (AMNH). *Chatham Co.*: Savannah, no date MHM (CU).

Abbot's drawing of the life history of *L. accius* was published in Smith (1797, pl. 23). Abbot's observations are quoted in the text:

This was taken in June on the beautiful climbing shrub here delineated, but is most commonly to be met with in the chrysalis state on the blades of Indian corn, *Zea Mays*, in which it enfolds itself. It changed the 21st of June, and came out the 29th. It is also found in Virginia, but is not near so common as the last described.

The "last described" referred to by Abbot is *Thorybes bathyllus*, and "the beautiful climbing shrub" is Wisteria.

J. E. Smith (1797) wrote: "The tribe of butterflies to which this and the neighboring ones belong is remarkable for the slender neck of the *larva*, and a certain similitude between the different species runs through all their states, particularly the pellucid spots on the upper wings."

There are two broods of *L. accius* in Georgia.

The head of the larva is small, flattened in front, white with a black band around the top and sides, with a black streak down the front and one on each side. The body is slender, almost white, with a number of thin dark lines running lengthwise. The larval food plants are various grasses, including Indian Corn (*Zea mays*).

Genus *Nastra*

Swarthy Skipper; Fusca Skipper. *Nastra lherminier* Latreille
(Page 148)

Distribution and Records: *N. lherminier* occurs widely in the Piedmont and Coastal regions.

Mountain Region—None.
Piedmont Region—*Richmond Co.*: Augusta, 22 Apr 1945 HWE. *Coweta Co.*: Madras, 11 May 1950 MES. *Forsyth Co.*: Lake Lanier, near Cumming, 2 June 1962 JRH (TTRS). *Richmond Co.*: Augusta, 8 June 1941 HWE. *Clarke Co.*: Athens, rare July AGR (see Richards, 1931). *DeKalb Co.*: Stone Mountain, 12

Aug 1950 LHT (TTRS). *Fulton Co.*: Atlanta, Buckhead area, 19 Sept 1949 LHT (TTRS). *Richmond Co.*: Augusta, 28 Sept 1945 HWE.

Coastal Region—*Screven Co.*: specimens taken Apr–June and Aug 1946 OB (AMNH). *Thomas Co.*: Ochlocknee River, near US 19, 3 May 1965 LN. *Charlton Co.*: Folkston, 6 July 1944 LHJ (TTRS). *Thomas Co.*: Metcalf, 22 July 1965 LN. *Charlton Co.*: Folkston, 7 Aug 1949 LHJ (TTRS).

N. lherminier is a small, inconspicuous skipper that has been widely known as *Lerodea fusca*. However, this little butterfly continues to skip merrily about in open fields and in thick grassy areas unmindful of the names that have been applied to it.

Klots' (1951) description has made it easy for me to remember this little skipper. He wrote: "If you have a specimen that looks as neutral dull, drab, and undistinguished as possible, think of *l'herminieri*!" (The differences in the spelling of the name is due to an error that occurred many years ago. The current spelling follows dos Passos, 1964.)

The life history of *N. lherminier* is unknown.

Genus *Pholisora*

Common Sooty-Wing; Pigweed Skipper. *Pholisora catullus* Fabricius (Page 146)

Distribution and Records: *P. catullus*, a small, dark skipper that may easily be overlooked, is widely but locally distributed throughout the state. It may be common in the vicinity of its food plants, *Chenopodium album* (Pigweed or Lamb's Quarters), *Monarda punctata* (Horse Mint), and *Origanum vulgare* (Wild Marjoram).

Mountain Region—*Banks Co.* and *Habersham Co.*: 26 Aug 1930 RWM (see Montgomery, 1931).

Piedmont Region—*Clarke Co.*: Athens, common Apr 1967 LRT. *Coweta Co.*: Madras, 28 Apr 1951 MES; Madras, 29 Apr 1950 MES. *Fulton Co.*: Atlanta, 30 May 1937 LHJ (TTRS). *Clayton*

Co.: Ellenwood, 15 June 1969 JC (TTRS). *Monroe Co.*: Forsyth, 13 July 1958 FTN. *Fulton Co.*: Atlanta, 18 July 1958 LHJ (TTRS). *Clarke Co.*: Athens, common Aug 1966 LRT. *Fulton Co.*: Atlanta, 5 Aug 1950 LHJ. *Clarke Co.*: Athens, common early Apr–Sept AGR (see Richards, 1931). Coastal Region—*Screven Co.*: several taken summer of 1946 OB (AMNH). *Baker Co.*: Blue Springs Plantation, 4 Aug 1964 LN. *Grady Co.*: Beachton, Birdsong Plantation, 2 Sept 1956 LHJ (TTRS). *Chatham Co.*: Savannah, no dates MHM (CU).

In Abbot's excellent drawing (in Smith, 1797, pl. 24), the life cycle is illustrated in detail, showing the larva, pupa, adults, and a food plant. Abbot's accompanying observations state:

Feeds on *Monarda punctata*, etc., spinning itself up in the folded leaves, in which state one of these caterpillars changed the 18th of June, and appeared on the wing the 26th; another spun and changed July 29, and came out the 5th of August, and a third which enclosed itself September 14, appeared in the middle of March. The butterfly frequents gardens and fields among melon blossoms, and is also found in Virginia.

Because he could not identify the food plants listed by Abbot in the common or vernacular names of his day, Smith added the following note:

Mr. Abbot mentions origanum, common and red careless, and lamb's quarters, as the food of this insect, plants whose scientific names we cannot certainly determine, though they may be guessed at. Perhaps the first may be the pretty *Monarda punctata*, on which he has drawn the caterpillar.

Smith guessed incorrectly that the plant illustrated, *Monarda punctata*, was the "origanum" to which Abbot referred— Wild Marjoram (*Origanum vulgare*) was the plant Abbot intended. The common name "careless" has been applied to several weeds of the genera *Amaranthus* and *Chenopodium*; perhaps Abbot intended *C. album* and a closely related species when he referred to "common and red careless."

The larva of *P. catullus* has a black head. Its first body segment is small, but the body gradually enlarges in the central portion and tapers at the end. The body is pale olive-green and is covered with many, very small, yellowish granulations and a short down; there are two greenish lateral stripes on each side.

Genus *Pyrgus*

Checkered Skipper. *Pyrgus communis communis* Grote
(Page 148)

Distribution and Records: *P. c. communis*, which was described from central Alabama, is one of our most abundant skippers, and is found throughout the state.

Mountain Region—*Banks Co.* and *Habersham Co.*: 24 Aug and 1 Sept 1930 RWM (see Montgomery, 1931).

Piedmont Region—*Monroe Co.*: Forsyth, 19 Mar 1957 FTN. *Fulton Co.*: Atlanta area, 11 June 1937 LHJ (TTRS). *Coweta Co.*: Madras, 17 June 1951 MES. *Bibb Co.*: Macon, 3 July 1934 HFS (TTRS). *Clarke Co.*: Athens, common Aug 1966 LRT.

Coastal Region—*Charlton Co.*: Folkston, 9 Feb 1952 LHJ (TTRS). *Grady Co.*: Beachton, Sherwood Plantation, 18 Mar 1966 LN; Beachton, Sherwood Plantation, 11 Apr 1965 LHJ (TTRS); Beachton, Birdsong Plantation, 16 Apr 1953 EVK (TTRS); Beachton, Birdsong Plantation, 16 Apr 1954 EVK (TTRS). *Baker Co.*: Blue Springs Plantation, 14 Aug 1964 LN. *Chatham Co.*: Savannah, no dates MHM (CU). *Screven Co.*: Sylvania, summer 1946 OB (AMNH). *Dougherty Co.*: Gillionville Plantation, 7 Sept 1964 LN.

This species has a fast flight, usually more direct than many skippers. It will rest, at times, on a leaf or other suitable perch in a sunny place and expand its wings. It visits flowers freely, and may sometimes be seen in flower gardens.

There are two broods in north Georgia, and possibly three in south Georgia.

Specimens of *P. communis* collected by R. W. Montgomery on August 24 and September 1, 1930, were erroneously identified as *P. centaureae* and so recorded in his 1931 list. A correction was made later (Harris, 1950), after Montgomery sent the specimen to R. A. Leussler for his expert opinion. (There is a slight possibility that *P. centaureae* may yet be found at the highest elevations in the mountains of north Georgia. It has been found at Tryon and Westval in North Carolina.)

The larva of *P. c. communis* is greenish, except for the head and first thoracic segment, which are brownish black. The body is enlarged at the middle, tapering toward the end, and is covered with many short, whitish hairs. There are four rather indistinct whitish lines, two lengthwise along the back and two along the sides. The larval food plants are various mallows (family Malvaceae), including Hollyhocks (*Althaea*), Indian Mallow or Flowering-Maple (*Abutilon*), and Wild Tea (*Sida*).

Genus *Erynnis*

The scholarly treatise *Evolution in the Skipper Butterflies of the Genus Erynnis* by John M. Burns, published in 1964, was the result of a study in which more than 11,000 adult specimens of *Erynnis* were critically examined. This excellent monograph contains a wealth of information on this complex genus.

John Symmes of Atlanta and I were among many who sent specimens to Burns for determination. These and other records listed by Burns are given in the appropriate species accounts; Burns' determinations insure their accuracy: many specimens in this group had been incorrectly identified in the past because of the great similarity of several species of the genus. Dr. Burns was in Atlanta on August 22, 1967, and checked the *Erynnis* section of this manuscript. He made a field trip with John Symmes and they collected larvae of *E. martialis*, *E. horatius*, and *E. zarucco*.

Life-history data gathered by Dr. Burns indicate the following: *Erynnis* species overwinter as full-grown larvae. The larvae pupate with the advent of spring. Adults emerge in a very few weeks. Eggs are oviposited singly, directly upon the larval food plant. The new larvae may emerge in less than a week, or as much as two weeks later. During their slow subsequent development, they go through five or six instars, depending upon the species. The larvae construct a series of progressively larger shelters from one or more of their host's leaves. At first, the young larvae feed on tender young leaves, but later instars eat mature leaves. The larvae stop feeding when full grown and become quiescent. They may then pupate promptly to produce, in the same year, at least a partial second generation (which may, in turn, yield a complete or partial third), or the larvae may remain quiet, even through many weeks of summer, until the following spring. Dr. Burns points out that, presumably, cold-hardiness is limited to one stage, so that prolonged cold weather drains all other stages (both adult and immature) from a population, while damming up a reservoir of full-grown larvae, which give rise to a relatively synchronous spring flight of adults. However, in areas with relatively mild winters, overwintering may sometimes take place in the pupal stage as well as in the mature larval stage.

Dr. Burns found that most species of *Erynnis* having two or more broods produce two forms, or temporal phenotypes. The average differences between these phenotypes involve variation in forewing characters that also show sexual dimorphism. Thus, "phenotype I" of spring generally has shorter wings, more numerous gray scales, altered spot frequencies, and greater contrast between dark markings and ground color, relative to "phenotype 2" of summer; and males, relative to females, usually have shorter wings, some distinctively formed and distinctively oriented gray scales, lower spot frequencies, and less contrast. He found that recognizing these aspects of nongeographic variation promoted a meaningful analysis of geographic variation.

Six members of the genus *Erynnis*, representing the subgenera *Erynnis* and *Erynnides,* are found in Georgia: *E. (Erynnis) icelus, E. (Erynnis) brizo brizo, E. (Erynnides) baptisiae, E. (Erynnides) zarucco, E. (Erynnides) martialis, E. (Erynnides) horatius,* and *E. (Erynnides) juvenalis.*

It should be noted that Burns treats *E. lucilius* and *E. baptisiae* as separate, but closely related, species, while W. H. Evans treats the latter as a subspecies of the former. The former is the northern species, and the latter is the southern species. They are sympatric in a narrow band stretching from southern New England, New York, and New Jersey to southern Minnesota. Former Georgia records of *E. lucilius* would be referrable to *E. baptisiae* on the basis of presently available data.

E. persius has also been omitted from the Georgia list, at least for the present, as Burns' studies have shown that it is essentially a boreal species. Its present range southward follows the Appalachian Mountains, and the southernmost records are of specimens taken in the Great Smoky Mountains. It is possible that old records for this species in Georgia may be referrable to *E. baptisiae*; they should be confirmed by an expert on this difficult group.

Dreamy Dusky-Wing. *Erynnis (Erynnis)icelus* Scudder and Burgess (Page 148)

Distribution and Records: *E. icelus* is found in the mountains of north Georgia, which seem to be the southernmost limit of its range. It is local and not as common as other species of *Erynnis* in Georgia.

Mountain Region—*Murray Co.*: Old Fort Mountain, one male 17 Apr 1953 LHJ (TTRS).* *Fannin Co.*: Margret, 26 Apr 1959 LHJ (TTRS). *Murray Co.*: Fort Mountain State Park, one male and one female 2 May 1950 LHT (TTRS)*; Old Fort Mountain, one female 5 May 1951 LHJ (TTRS)*; Old Fort Mountain, one male 5 May 1951 LHT (TTRS)*. *Rabun Co.*: LaPrades Camp, 16 May 1964 LNH (TTRS). *Murray Co.*: Old

Fort Mountain, one female 22 May 1951 PWF (TTRS)*.
White Co.: Unicoi Gap, three males 4 June 1951 LHJ (TTRS)*.
Rabun Co.: two males 15 and 17 July 1928 AGR (AMNH)*.
Piedmont Region—None.
Coastal Region—None.

Adults fly in April, May, and early June, with a partial
second brood in July.
The larva overwinters in its final instar. The larval food
plants are chiefly of the genera *Salix* and *Populus*, according to
Burns (1964, pp. 34–35): he noted that it had been reared
on poplar, willow, aspen, and black locust. In 1965, he re-
peatedly collected and reared larvae of this species on black
locust in the vicinity of the Mountain Lake Biological Station
in the Appalachian Mountains of southwestern Virginia.

Sleepy Dusky-Wing. *Erynnis (Erynnis) brizo brizo*
Boisduval and LeConte (Page 148)

Distribution and Records: The type locality of *E. b. brizo* was
given as "L'Amerique septentrionale"; most likely, the specimen was from Georgia, because the name was based on a
figure drawn by Abbot (Boisduval and LeConte, 1829–1833,
pl. 66). It is found throughout the state, but is of local
occurrence.

Mountain Region—*Murray Co.*: Old Fort Mountain, 28 Mar
1963 LHJ (TTRS)*. *Lumpkin Co.*: Auraria, 15 Apr 1967
BMR and JCS. *Fannin Co.*: near Margret, 16 Apr 1967 BMR
and JCS. *Murray Co.*: Old Fort Mountain, 16 Apr 1955 LHJ
(TTRS)*; Old Fort Mountain, 19 Apr 1964 LHJ (TTRS)*;
Old Fort Mountain, 26 Apr 1959 LNH (TTRS)*; Old Fort
Mountain, 5 May 1951 LHT (TTRS)*.
Piedmont Region—*Clarke Co.*: Athens, one male 28 Mar 1939
AGR (AMNH)*. *DeKalb Co.*: Avondale Estates, one male
1 Apr 1945 LHJ (TTRS)*. *Fulton Co.*: Atlanta, one male 2
Apr 1950 LHJ*. *Coweta Co.*: Madras, one male 3 Apr 1947
MES*. *Cobb Co.*: Blackjack Mountain, 6 Apr 1952 LHT*.

* Records followed by an asterisk indicate specimens determined by J. M.
Burns.

Coastal Region—*Thomas Co.*: Thomasville, one male 20 Mar 1903 (LACM)*; Thomasville, one male 21 Mar 1903 (LACM)*; Thomasville, one male 29 Mar 1904 (ANSP)*. *Screven Co.*: one female 31 Mar 1946 OB (AMNH)*; two females and one male 1 Apr 1946 OB (AMNH)*; two males 8 and 9 Apr 1946 OB (AMNH)*; one female 10 Apr 1946 OB AMNH)*.

There is only one brood. Adults first appear in south Georgia in late February, increasing in numbers in March and April. In middle and north Georgia, they appear about two weeks later.

Studies made by Burns have established that the subspecies *E. b. somnus* does not occur in Georgia. It is confined to the peninsular area of Florida. Burns examined the specimens from Georgia in the Los Angeles County Museum that had been listed by Martin and Truxal (1955) as *E. b. somnus*, but he found them to be *E. b. brizo*.

The larva overwinters in the last instar, and pupates in early spring. The larval food plants are various oaks (*Quercus*). Burns examined and confirmed the identification of a specimen of *E. b. brizo* that was reared on *Quercus ilicifolia* (Bear Oak), one of the scrub oaks. Other authors have observed that it is common in scrub-oak regions.

A reference made by John Abbot to Wild Indigo (*Baptisia tinctoria*) as a food plant may have been due to his confusing this with another *Erynnis* species, such as *E. baptisiae*.

Wild-Indigo Dusky-Wing. *Erynnis* (*Erynnides*) *baptisiae* Forbes (Page 148)

Distribution and Records: *E. baptisiae* is somewhat rare in Georgia. It is distributed locally throughout the state, but records for the Mountain Region are lacking.

Mountain Region—None.

* Records followed by an asterisk indicate specimens determined by J. M. Burns.

Piedmont Region—*Bibb Co.*: Macon, 21 June 1934 HFS (TTRS)
(determined by W. T. M. Forbes and J. M. Burns).
Coastal Region—*Screven Co.*: Sylvania, 5 Apr 1946 OB (AMNH);
Sylvania, 19 May 1946 OB (AMNH). *Grady Co.*: Beachton,
Susina Plantation, 10 June 1964 LHJ (TTRS) (determined by
J. M. Burns).

This species was described in 1936 by Prof. W. T. M.
Forbes. The type and allotype were taken in close association
with the food plant, *Baptisia tinctoria* (Wild Indigo).

Many old Georgia records of *E. persius* taken in the Mountain Region may be referrable to this species; it is very likely
that all specimens labeled *E. persius* from the Piedmont and
Coastal regions are referrable to this species also.

Burns (1964, p. 190) states that *E. baptisiae* shows a strong
tendency to have more than one brood.

Zarucco Dusky-Wing. *Erynnis* (*Erynnides*) *zarucco* Lucas
(Page 148)

Distribution and Records: *E. zarucco* is a common species and
is found throughout the state. It is usually local in occurrence,
and is not as common in the mountains as it is elsewhere in
the state.

Mountain Region—*White Co.*: Tray Mountain, 4 May 1955 JCS*.
Fannin Co.: Cooper Creek State Park, 9 July 1960 LHJ
(TTRS)*; Cooper Creek State Park, 1 Aug 1965 JCS. *Rabun
Co.*: Dick's Creek Fish Hatchery, 18 Aug 1965 LHJ; Dick's
Creek Fish Hatchery, 12 Sept 1953 LHJ (TTRS)*.
Piedmont Region—*Richmond Co.*: Augusta, 1 Apr 1944.*
Coweta Co.: Madras, 7 Apr 1947 MES*. *DeKalb Co.*: Brook-
haven, 13 Apr 1952 ELT*; Stone Mountain, 14 Apr 1951 LHT
(TTRS)*. *Richmond Co.*: Camp Gordon, 13, 19, and 27 May
1951 RWP (PMNH)*. *Fulton Co.*: Atlanta, 20 May 1957.*
Richmond Co.: Camp Gordon, 2 and 9 June 1951 RWP
(PMNH)*; Camp Gordon, 8 July 1951 RWP (PMNH)*.
DeKalb Co.: Stone Mountain, 15 July 1950 LHT (TTRS)*;
Stone Mountain, 12 Aug 1950 LHT (TTRS)*.
Coastal Region—*Grady Co.*: Beachton, 19 Mar 1952 LHJ

(TTRS)*; *Thomas Co.*: Thomasville, 20 Mar 1955 LHJ (TTRS)*; Thomasville, 21 Mar 1903 (ANSP)*. *Chatham Co.*: Savannah, 13 Apr 1908 (AMNH)*. *Screven Co.*: Sylvania, 1 and 19 Apr 1946 OB (AMNH)*; Sylvania, 5, 10, 16, 18, 29, and 30 May 1946 OB (AMNH)*. *Baker Co.*: Newton, Blue Springs Plantation, 9 Feb 1965 LN*. *Grady Co.*: Beachton, Susina Plantation, 10 June 1964 LHJ. *Ware Co.*: Deenwood, Waycross, 16–18 July 1916 (AMNH)*. *Lowndes Co.*: Valdosta, 20 or 21 July 1916 (AMNH)*. *Screven Co.*: Sylvania, 23 and 29 July 1946 OB (AMNH)*. *Decatur Co.*: between Climax and Bainbridge, 28 July 1916 (AMNH)*. *Chatham Co.*: Savannah, no dates MHM (CU) (determined by W. T. M. Forbes). *Baker Co.*: Newton, Blue Springs Plantation, 26 Aug 1964 LN*.

E. zarucco is multiple-brooded. Each brood appears somewhat earlier in the Coastal Region than it does in the Piedmont and Mountain regions. The average months for the state are April and May for the spring brood, and July and August for the summer brood.

The larva has been described by Roy O. Kendall (1960, p. 176): The color of the mature larva is cream, with a dorsolateral yellow line segmentally punctuated with squarish yellow spots; there are distinct whitish granulations on the body. The angled head is black with six distinct yellow spots.

Mottled Dusky-Wing. *Erynnis* (*Erynnides*) *martialis* Scudder
(Page 148)

Distribution and Records: *E. martialis* is a common species throughout the state.

Mountain Region—*Lumpkin Co.*: Auraria, 15 Apr 1967 BMR and JCS. *White Co.*: Unicoi Gap, 4 June 1951 LHJ (TTRS)*. *Rabun Co.*: one male 30 June 1927 (AMNH)*; one female 30 June 1927 (ANSP)*.
Piedmont Region—*Coweta Co.*: Madras, 27 Mar 1935 MES (PMNH)*; Madras, 25 Apr 1935 MES (PMNH)*; Madras, 28, 29, and 30 Apr 1935 MES (AMNH)*; Madras, 5, 10, and

* Records followed by an asterisk indicate specimens determined by J. M. Burns.

12 May 1940 MES (AMNH)*. *Fulton Co.*: Atlanta, 8 Apr 1956 JCS*. *Richmond Co.*: Camp Gordon, 16 and 24 June 1951 RWP (PMNH)*. *Coweta Co.*: Madras, 5 July 1934 MES (PMNH)*. *Richmond Co.*: Camp Gordon, 8 July 1951 RWP (PMNH)*. *Fulton Co.*: 14 July 1904 (ANSP)*; Atlanta, 15 July 1928.* *DeKalb Co.*: 5 Aug 1950 LHJ (TTRS)*.
Coastal Region—*Screven Co.*: Sylvania, 26 Apr 1946 OB (AMNH)*.

Because of its mottled appearance, this is one of the easiest Dusky-Wings to identify.

There are two broods, with a partial third brood. The first brood appears in March and April, the second in June and July, and the partial third in late August and early September.

The larva was originally known only from a drawing by Abbot; the life history was not fully known until it was worked out by J. M. Burns (1964). Burns (1964, p. 148) confirmed Abbot's statement, quoted by Scudder (1889, p. 1497) that the caterpillar feeds upon "red shank" (*Ceanothus americanus*). In 1961, Burns suggested that *Ceanothus* seemed the most likely candidate as the possible food plant out of a group of nine that had been suggested by various authors over a period of years. Burns' footnote (1964, p. 148) states:

This prediction (made in 1961) was verified May 16, 1964, when I saw a female *Erynnis martialis* oviposit on *Ceanothus americanus* in the Karner pine barrens and oak scrub, Albany County, N.Y. I got the female and her egg, and successfully reared on *C. americanus* the larvae eclosing from her egg and from eggs laid by a caged *martialis* female.

Horace's Dusky-Wing. *Erynnis* (*Erynnides*) *horatius* Scudder and Burgess (Page 150)

Distribution and Records: *E. horatius* is a common species that occurs throughout the state.

* Records followed by an asterisk indicate specimens determined by J. M. Burns.

Mountain Region—*Lumpkin Co.*: Auraria, 15 Apr 1967 BMR and JCS. *Fannin Co.*: near Margret, 16 Apr 1967 BMR and JCS. *Murray Co.*: Old Fort Mountain, 16 Apr 1955 LHJ (TTRS)*. *Rabun Co.*: Lake Burton, 24 June 1950 LHT (TTRS)*.

Piedmont Region—*Fulton Co.*: Atlanta, 3 Mar 1957 LHJ (TTRS)*. *Coweta Co.*: Madras, 22 Mar 1935 MES (LACM)*. *Fulton Co.*: Hapeville, 19 Apr 1950 LHT (TTRS)*. *Clarke Co.*: Athens, 20 Sept 1927 AGR (AMNH)*. *DeKalb Co.*: Stone Mountain, 17 June 1950 LHT (TTRS)*. *Fulton Co.*: Atlanta, 1 and 3 Aug 1945 JCS*.

Coastal Region—*Chatham Co.*: Savannah, 12 Mar 1926 WJC (ANSP)*. *Screven Co.*: near Sylvania, 12 May 1946 OB (AMNH)*. *Decatur Co.*: near Bainbridge, 17 May 1953 EVK (TTRS)*. *Chatham Co.*: Savannah, 24 May 1951 HLK (TTRS)*; Savannah, no dates MHM (CU) (determined by W. T. M. Forbes). *Grady Co.*: near Thomasville, 6 July 1957 LHJ (TTRS)*. *Camden Co.*: Coleraine Plantation, 15 July 1944 LHT (TTRS)*. *Ware Co.*: Waycross, 16–18 July 1916(?) (AMNH)*. *Decatur Co.*: near Bainbridge, 28 July 1916 (AMNH)*. *Glynn Co.*: St. Simons Island, 1 Aug 1958 JRH (TTRS)*. *Screven Co.*: near Sylvania, 19 Aug 1946 OB (AMNH)*. *Glynn Co.*: St. Simons Island, 19 and 20 Aug 1951 LHJ (TTRS)*.

E. horatius can easily be confused with *E. juvenalis*. For example, Burns (1964, p. 123) states that Klots' illustration (1951, pl. 29, fig. 9) designated as the former is actually the latter. Burns made the determination after examining the original specimen used for the illustration.

The larval food plants are various species of Oaks (*Quercus*). R. W. Pease, Jr., while stationed at Camp Gordon in Richmond County, near Augusta, found larvae on a Willow Oak (*Q. phellos*), according to Burns (1964, p. 123). Pease offered other types of oak leaves. They ate the leaves of White Oak (*Q. alba*) but refused those of Red Oak (*Q. falcata*). The larvae were reared, and the skippers emerged on Septem-

* Records followed by an asterisk indicate specimens determined by J. M. Burns.

ber 3, 1951. The two reared specimens are now located in the Peabody Museum of Natural History at Yale University.

Juvenal's Dusky-Wing. *Erynnis* (*Erynnides*) *juvenalis*
Fabricius (Page 150)

Distribution and Records: *E. juvenalis* is fairly common over most of the state.

Mountain Region—*Fannin Co.*: near Margret, 16 Apr 1967 BMR. *Murray Co.*: Old Fort Mountain, 17 Apr 1953 LHJ (TTRS)*; Old Fort Mountain, 5 May 1951 LHT (TTRS)*.
Piedmont Region—*Clarke Co.*: Athens, 28 Mar 1929 AGR*. *Dawson Co.*: Dawsonville, 31 Mar 1957.* *DeKalb Co.*: Avondale Estates, 1 Apr 1945 LHJ (TTRS)*. *Cobb Co.*: Blackjack Mountain, 6 Apr 1952 LHT (TTRS)*. *Richmond Co.*: Augusta, 8 Apr 1951 RWP (PMNH)*. *DeKalb Co.*: Stone Mountain, 14 Apr 1951 LHT (TTRS)*. *Fulton Co.*: Atlanta, 19 Apr 1950 LHJ (TTRS)*.
Coastal Region—*Grady Co.*: Sherwood Plantation, 19 Mar 1952 LHJ*. 31 Mar 1946 OB (AMNH)*. *Screven Co.*: Sylvania area, 2 and 4 Apr 1946 OB (AMNH)*.

This species has only one brood, the adult skippers appearing in March and April, with the peak population in mid-April, decreasing rapidly in May. A few worn specimens may be found in early June.

E. juvenalis is sometimes confused with *E. horatius*, which has more than one brood: the first brood of the latter appears at the same time as the single brood of the former.

A life-size drawing by Abbot of the caterpillar, pupa, and three adults (the upper sides of a male and a female and the lower side of a third adult) was published in Boisduval and LeConte (1829–1833, pl. 65).

The larva, which overwinters in the last instar and pupates in the early spring, feeds on several species of Oak (*Quercus*).

* Records followed by an asterisk indicate specimens determined by J. M. Burns.

Genus *Staphylus*

Southern Sooty-Wing; Hayhurt's Sooty Wing.
Staphylus mazans hayhurstii Edwards (Page 146)

Distribution and Records: *S. m. hayhurstii* has a wide range over the state. It is very local, usually being found in or near the areas with growth of the larval food plants, *Chenopodium* and *Alternanthera*.

Mountain Region—*Fannin Co.*: Cooper Creek State Park, 28 June 1958 LHJ. *Rabun Co.*: Lake Burton, July AGR (see Richards, 1931).
Piedmont Region—*Richmond Co.*: Augusta, Apr–Sept HWE. *Coweta Co.*: Madras, 11 May 1950 MES. *Fulton Co.*: Atlanta, Oglethorpe College, infrequent June–Aug JPK (see Knudsen, 1954). *Coweta Co.*: Madras, 5 July 1951 MES. *Fulton Co.*: Atlanta, 9 July 1950 LHJ (TTRS); Atlanta, 11 July 1958 LHJ (TTRS). *Monroe Co.*: Forsyth, 13 July 1958 FTN. *DeKalb Co.*: Avondale Estates, 15 July 1952 LHJ (TTRS). *Clarke Co.*: Athens, May and Aug AGR (see Richards, 1931); Athens, rare Aug 1966 LRT.
Coastal Region—*Screven Co.*: Sylvania, 15 May and 22 Aug 1946 OB (AMNH). *Chatham Co.*: Savannah, no dates MHM (CU).

J. R. Heitzman (1963) states that one of the peculiarities of this skipper is its mothlike habit of spreading its wings out flat against the surface upon which it alights. Heitzman also found that it is strongly attracted to certain flowers; at times, he has found a dozen or more specimens clustered about a bed of Spearmint flowers (*Mentha picta*). Sweet Clover (*Meliflorus*) was also found to have a particular attraction for this species.

S. hayhurstii is a small, dark skipper that may easily be overlooked. It should be looked for in moist and rather shady areas. A good place to find it is near a small creek running through a wooded area. Another good place is along the weedy edges of an old railroad track. In urban areas, it may be found in weedy vacant lots where the host plants are growing.

There are two broods in Georgia with, perhaps, a partial third brood in the Coastal Region. The first brood appears in May and June, the second brood in July and August. The larvae produced by the second brood normally hibernate in the third instar.

The life history has been carefully worked out by Heitzman (1963). The larva, which is 20–23 mm long in the final instar, is mainly deep green with a rosy overcast. Its intersegmental folds are pinkish green, its legs are cream, and the ventral port of the abdomen and the prolegs are deep green. The body is covered with fine white hairs, those on the last segment slightly longer. The spiracles are pale creamy white and slightly raised. The skin is quite translucent, and the heart is visible as a deep green middorsal line. The prothoracic shield in the final instar is a very pale brown. The head is deep purple, almost black, thickly covered with white hair, and deeply cleft vertically at the epicranial suture.

The tent the caterpillar constructs in the final instar consists of an entire leaf folded together. Pupation occurs in the tent within a very thin lining of silk. There is also a silken pad to which the cremaster is attached.

Genus *Thorybes*

Southern Cloudy-Wing; Southern Dusky-Wing.
Thorybes bathyllus Smith (Page 150)

Distribution and Records: *T. bathyllus*, described from Georgia, occurs commonly throughout the state.

Mountain Region—*Towns Co.*: Brasstown Bald (alt. 4700 ft), 12 Aug 1951 LHJ (TTRS). *Banks Co.* and *Habersham Co.*: 27 July and 7 Sept 1930 RWM (see Mongomery, 1931).
Piedmont Region—*Coweta Co.*: Madras, 26 Mar 1950 MES. *Monroe Co.*: Forsyth, 30 Mar 1957 FTN. *Coweta Co.*: Madras, 1 Apr 1951 MES. *Fulton Co.*: Atlanta, Indian Trail Road, 17 Apr 1955 LHJ (TTRS). *DeKalb Co.*: Stone Mountain, 1 May 1952 LHJ (TTRS). *Fulton Co.*: Atlanta area, 20 May 1950

LHJ (TTRS). *Monroe Co.*: Forsyth, 22 May 1959 FTN. *De-Kalb Co.*: Stone Mountain, 24 May 1952 LHJ (TTRS); Stone Mountain, 15 July 1950 LHT (TTRS). *Clarke Co.*: Athens, common July 1966 LRT.

Coastal Region—*Grady Co.*: Beachton, Susina Plantation, 28 Mar 1964 LHJ (TTRS); Beachton, Sherwood Plantation, 25 Apr 1965 LN; Beachton, Susina Plantation, 6 July 1963 LHJ (TTRS). *Thomas Co.*: Thomasville, 10 July 1944 LHJ (TTRS). *Chatham Co.*: Savannah, no date MHM (CU). *Screven Co.*: summer of 1946 OB (AMNH). *Baker Co.*: Newton, Blue Springs Plantation, 14 Aug 1964 LN. *Grady Co.*: Beachton, Susina Plantation, 27 Aug 1967 LHJ.

There are two broods, the first appearing from mid-March through mid-June, the second appearing in late June, July, and August, and flying in September and perhaps early October in south Georgia.

Abbot's excellent drawing (in Smith, 1797, pl. 22) shows the adult skippers, the larva, pupa, and a food plant. His accompanying note states:

This caterpillar feeds on the wild bean here represented, and folds the leaves together for a retreat. The skipper caterpillars, to conceal themselves the better, generally attach together with a web the leaves of some other plant growing next to that they feed on, which renders them difficult to be met with. This species changed the 11th of June. The butterfly liberated itself the 24th. It occurs also in Virginia, and is one of the most common of its tribe.

A Georgia specimen of the species was figured by Klots (1951, pl. 27, fig. 3).

The body of the larva is brown with a slight tinge of olive green, and is covered with many tiny, pale wartlets, each bearing a short hair. The head of the larva is black. The larval food plants are Netted-leaved Glycine (*Glycine reticulata*), according to Abbot; Wild Bean (*Strophostyles*); Butterfly Pea (*Bradburya virginiana*); Goats Rue (*Cracca ambigua*); and, possibly, other related plants.

Northern Cloudy-Wing; Northern Dusky-Wing.
Thorybes pylades Scudder (Page 150)

Distribution and Records: *T. pylades* seems equally at home in the south as it is in the north. It is found throughout Georgia.

Mountain Region—*Banks Co.* and *Habersham Co.*: 21 July and 29 Aug 1930 RWM (see Montgomery, 1931).

Piedmont Region—*Richmond Co.*: Augusta, Apr 1941 HWE. *DeKalb Co.*: Stone Mountain, 14 Apr 1951 LHT (TTRS). *Coweta Co.*: Madras, 19 Apr 1950 and 29 Apr 1951 MES. *Clarke Co.*: Athens, common May 1967 and Sept 1966 LRT. *DeKalb Co.*: Stone Mountain, 5 May 1952 LHJ (TTRS). *Monroe Co.*: Forsyth, 6 and 7 May 1962 FTN. *Fulton Co.*: Atlanta area, 20 May 1950 LHT (TTRS); near Chattahoochee River, off Harris Trail, 27 May 1962 JCS; Atlanta, Indian Trail Road, 6 June 1957 LHJ (TTRS); Atlanta, Indian Trail Road, 7 June 1959 LHJ (TTRS).

Coastal Region—*Grady Co.*: Beachton, Susina Plantation, 28 Mar 1964 LHJ (TTRS); Beachton, Susina Plantation, 12 Apr 1965 LHJ (TTRS). *Screven Co.*: Sylvania, summer of 1946 OB (AMNH). *Chatham Co.*: Savannah, no dates MHM (CU).

T. pylades is not as common as *T. bathyllus*, but it may be locally common at times. In Athens, Clarke County, L. R. Tanner found *T. bathyllus* common in July, 1966, and *T. pylades* in September, 1966, and May, 1967.

To the north, in Banks and Habersham counties, R. W. Montgomery collected specimens on July 21 and August 29, 1930.

In the Atlanta area, I have taken it in April, May, and June. It has also been collected by John Symmes in the Atlanta area, near the Chattahoochee River off Harris Trail, on May 27, 1962.

In the Coastal Region, I have collected it in March, Leon Neel and I have collected it in April, and Otto Buchholz has taken it in the summer.

There are two broods of *T. pylades*, possibly three.

The head of the larva is black; its body is green with a broken, dark green stripe along the back, a dull pinkish stripe along each side, and a similar, less distinct one below this. The body is covered with many tiny wartlets bearing short hairs. The larval food plants are various members of the family Fabaceae, such as Beggar's Ticks (*Desmodidium*), Bush Clover (*Lespedeza*), and Clover (*Trifolium*).

Confused Cloudy-Wing; Confused Dusky-Wing.
Thorybes confusis Bell (Page 150)

Distribution and Records: *T. confusis*, which was described from Florida, occurs widely in the Coastal and Piedmont regions of Georgia. We do not have records of its occurrence in the Mountain Region as yet. It is rather local in occurrence and is generally rare, but it may be common at times. For example, in 1946, Otto Buchholz found it common in Screven County from March 30 to June 10 and during the month of July: his total catch was eighty specimens!

Mountain Region—None.
Piedmont Region—*Bibb Co.*: Macon, 11 and 13 Mar 1915 FWW and RAL. *Clarke Co.*: Athens, 14 Apr 1926 AGR (see Richards, 1931). *Fulton Co.*: Atlanta, Riverside Drive, 18 May 1957 LHJ (TTRS). *DeKalb Co.*: Stone Mountain, 1 and 24 May 1952 LHJ (TTRS). *Clarke Co.*: Athens, rare Sept 1966 LRT.
Coastal Region—*Screven Co.*: Sylvania, 10 and 19 Apr 1946 OB (TTRS). *Grady Co.*: Beachton, Sherwood Plantation, 25 Apr 1965 LN. *Thomas Co.*: Greenwood Plantation, 16 May 1953 LHJ (TTRS). *Chatham Co.*: Savannah, 18 July 1934 FMJ (TTRS); Savannah, no dates MHM (CU).

T. confusis has an appropriate name, for it is easily confused with *T. pylades*. The male of *T. confusis* may be distinguished from the male of *T. pylades* by the lack of a costal fold on the forewing.

Skinner and Williams (1922, p. 124) state that specimens

of this species from Georgia are in the Academy of Natural Sciences of Philadelphia.

Two of the oldest Georgia records are the specimens collected in Macon on March 11 and 13, 1915, by Fred W. Walker. These specimens were placed in the collection of R. A. Leussler of Omaha. Another early record was a specimen taken in Athens by A. G. Richards, Jr., on April 14, 1926. This specimen was compared with the type by F. E. Watson.

Specimens that I collected on Stone Mountain on May 1 and 24, 1952, were determined by H. A. Freeman. Frank M. Jones thoughtfully sent me a specimen that he had collected in Savannah, so that I might have it for comparative use when I was unfamiliar with this species.

Information is needed about the larva and its food plants.

Genus *Achalarus*

Hoary-Edge. *Achalarus lyciades* Geyer (Page 128)

Distribution and Records: *A. lyciades* is widely distributed over the state. Although uncommon in the mountains, it is common elsewhere in the state.

Mountain Region—*Rabun Co.*: Lake Burton, 21 May 1911 JCBS (see Richards, 1931); Clayton, 18 and 26 May 1911 JCBS (see Richards, 1931). *Banks Co.*: 10 July 1930 RWM (see Montgomery, 1931). *Habersham Co.*: 7 Sept 1930 RWM (see Montgomery, 1931).

Piedmont Region—*Coweta Co.*: Madras, 19 Apr 1950 MES. *Clarke Co.*: Athens, Apr 1967 LRT. *Coweta Co.*: Madras, 19 Apr 1950 MES. *Clarke Co.*: Athens, common Apr 1967 LRT. *Fulton Co.*: Atlanta, 13 and 15 May 1950 LHT (TTRS). *Monroe Co.*: Forsyth, 17 May 1956 FTN. *DeKalb Co.*: Stone Mountain, 24 May 1952 LHJ (TTRS). *Fulton Co.*: Atlanta, 9 July 1955 LHJ (TTRS); Atlanta, Harris Trail, 22 Aug 1967 LHJ.

Coastal Region—*Colquitt Co.*: Moultrie, 1 and 9 Apr 1945 HVAV (UWO). *Grady Co.*: Beachton, Sherwood Plantation,

10 and 25 Apr 1964 LN. *Thomas Co.*: Thomasville, 10 July 1944 LHJ (TTRS). *Lowndes Co.*: Valdosta, 12 July 1930 LHJ. *Screven Co.*: several specimens summer 1946 OB (AMNH). *Baker Co.*: Newton, Blue Springs Plantation, 26 Aug 1964 LN. *Grady Co.*: Chubb-Baker Plantation, 10 Sept 1964 LN.

A. lyciades was described under the name "*lycidas*" by Dr. James Edward Smith (1797, pl. XX), and the name was erroneously attributed to Cramer.

Abbot's watercolor drawing (in Smith, 1797) figures the upper and under side of the adults, a mature larva, a pupa, and a food plant, *Hedysarum*. Abbot states:

Feeds on the Hedysarum called Beggar's Lice, from the seeds sticking to the people's clothes. It changed to a chrysalis July 10, and to a butterfly the 23rd. This is a common species and continues breeding most of the summer.

According to J. Richard Heitzman (personal communication), the larva is 37 mm long; its body is pinkish buff with gray blotches showing through, with a gray dorsal line and two pale subdorsal lines. The body is thickly covered with minute warts and short pale setae. The head is deep reddish purple, without marks, and covered with stiff white setae. The cocoon is made in loose leaves at the base of the host plant.

The larval food plants are various wild bean species according to Heitzman. Other host plants are Beggar's Lice (*Hedysarum*), Beggar's Ticks (*Desmodium*), and possibly other legumes.

Genus *Autochton*

Golden-banded Skipper. *Autochton cellus*
Boisduval and LeConte (Page 129)

Distribution and Records: The type locality of *A. cellus* is Screven County, Georgia. This species occurs throughout the state, but it is rare and local.

Mountain Region—*Murray Co.*: Old Fort Mountain, 16 May 1950 JRH. *White Co.*: Helen, 15 June 1952 LHT (TTRS).
Piedmont Region—*Fulton Co.*: Atlanta, 1 May 1937 LHJ. *Richmond Co.*: Augusta, 3 May 1897 FMJ. *Fulton Co.*: Atlanta, Riverside Drive, 12 May 1956 LHJ (TTRS). *Bibb Co.*: Macon, 13 May 1933 HFS. *Fulton Co.*: Atlanta, Riverside Drive, 18 May 1958 LHJ (TTRS). *Bibb Co.*: Macon, Arkwright Road, 19 May 1962 FTN. *Fulton Co.*: Atlanta, Oglethorpe College, May 1953 JPK (see Knudsen, 1954a); Atlanta, Riverside Drive, 1, 13, and 21 May 1956 FTN. *Bibb Co.*: Macon, 23 May 1930 HFS. *Fulton Co.*: Atlanta, Riverside Drive, 25 May 1959 FTN. *Richmond Co.*: Augusta, 8–23 July 1942 HWE. *Fulton Co.*: Atlanta, 12 Aug 1933 LHJ.
Coastal Region—*Grady Co.*: Beachton, Sherwood Plantation, 10, 11, and 12 Apr 1965 LN; Beachton, Sherwood Plantation, 12 Apr 1965 LHJ (TTRS); Beachton, Sherwood Plantation, 7 Sept 1967 LN (TTRS).

A. cellus is always a good catch for, in addition to being rare, it flies rapidly and is wary.

On May 16, 1950, J. R. Harris netted a fresh specimen feeding on blackberry blossoms near the entrance marker to Old Fort Mountain State Park in Murray County. In another mountain area—in White County, at Helen—Lucien Harris III, collected a specimen on June 15, 1952.

In the Atlanta area, near Riverside Drive, an active colony was found by John Symmes. The females were ovipositing on a vine, Hog-Peanut (*Falcata pitcheri*), which was common in the area. In the Macon area, Fred Naumann collected *A. cellus* in the vicinity of Arkwright Road on May 19, 1962.

In the Augusta area, Frank Morton Jones collected it on May 3, 1897, on the flowers of Trailing Arbutus (*Epigaea repens*)—a very rare experience indeed. Many years later, Henry W. Eustis also found *A. cellus* in Augusta. On May 30, 1942, he took several on the flowers of Hollyhock (*Althaea*), and from July 6 to July 23, 1942, he collected several more on the flowers of *Abelia*.

In Grady County, a few miles from the Georgia-Florida

state line, Leon Neel found an active colony of *A. cellus* just a short distance—in fact, practically a "stone's throw"—from his home on Sherwood Plantation. He collected his first specimens on April 10, 1965. His latest record is September 6, 1967.

There are two broods. The spring brood appears as early as April in south Georgia, and in May in the northern part of the state. The summer brood appears mainly in July and August, with a few individuals flying later.

This butterfly was first known from a drawing by John Abbot reproduced by Boisduval and LeConte (1829–1833, pl. 73) with their original description of the species.

The early stages of *A. cellus* were almost unknown until Austin H. Clark found it near Great Falls, Maryland, and studied its life history and habits. His account of the life history of this skipper in *National Geographic* (Clark, 1936c) was a portion of a longer, more complete report published by the Smithsonian Institution (Clark, 1936b), in which he tabulated all records then known to him, including the following:

Georgia: no further data; Henry Edwards (1 male, British Mus.) near Jacksonboro, a town formerly existing about 8 miles north of Sylvania, Screven County, John Abbot, April 25, (Boisduval and LeConte, without locality, 1833; Scudder, as Georgia, 1889; Skinner, as Georgia, 1911.) Macon, Bibb County, in the central part of the State; Strohecker (Harris, 1931, Richards, 1931).

Clark (1936b) stated that the Abbot painting published with the original description shows the caterpillar "on one end of the leaves of a sprig of *Breweria aquatica*." Clark further noted that the caterpillar shown in this painting was the only one known until those he found in Maryland in 1934.

The larva is green or yellowish, with a broad yellow stripe along each side. The head is brown with two yellow spots resembling eyes. The larval food plant is Hog-Peanut (*Falcata pitcheri*). Klots (1951, p. 211) also lists *Breweria aquatica* (Convolvulaceae) as a probable food plant.

Clark (1936b) reared the larvae on Hog-Peanut. He found that the caterpillars feed only at night, hiding during the day in little tents they make for themselves. As they grow, they are continually making new homes for themselves. When they leave an old one, they always partly destroy it by cutting the silk threads that hold it together.

The pupa is black and very highly polished, but is completely covered with fluffy white wax, which protects it from too much moisture. It lies in a flimsy cocoon formed by binding together dead leaves or other rubbish on the ground.

Genus *Urbanus*

Long-tailed Skipper. *Urbanus proteus* Linnaeus
(Page 129)

Distribution and Records: *U. proteus* is common in the Coastal Region, uncommon in the Piedmont Region (although it may be locally common at times in some areas), and absent in the Mountain Region—except, perhaps, as a rare stray.

Mountain Region—None.

Piedmont Region—*Monroe Co.*: Forsyth, 25 May 1963 FTN. *Coweta Co.*: Madras, 20 Aug 1951 MES. *DeKalb Co.*: Stone Mountain, 10 Sept 1950 LHJ (TTRS). *Bibb Co.*; Macon, 13 Sept 1953 LHJ (TTRS). *Coweta Co.*: Madras, 27 Oct 1950 MES.

Coastal Region—*Grady Co.*: Beachton, Sherwood Plantation, 2 Jan 1965 LN; Beachton, Susina Plantation, 2 Jan 1965 LHJ (TTRS). *Colquitt Co.*: Moultrie, 12 Mar 1945 HVAV (UWO). *Thomas Co.*: Thomasville, 11 July 1944 LHJ (TTRS). *Grady Co.*: Beachton, Susina Plantation, 20 July 1965 LHJ (TTRS). *Screven Co.*: Sylvania, summer 1946 OB (AMNH). *Grady Co.*: Beachton, Susina Plantation, 27 Aug 1967 LNH.

U. proteus comes freely to flowers and at times may be seen in flower gardens.

This skipper was given the descriptive name Swallow-tailed Skipper Butterfly by James Edward Smith (1797), but the present common name is Long-tailed Skipper. John Abbot (in Smith, 1797) states:

The caterpillar of this rare species I discovered by seeing the butterfly lay eggs upon the wild pea-vine, for the caterpillars of *Skippers* fold the leaves together for safety which makes them not easy to be discovered. On the 2'd of July it spun itself up in the leaves, and on the 4th changed to a chrysalis covered with a bluish white powder, as in the Red Underwing. The fly appeared August 18. It breeds in autumn only. I afterwards discovered some of these caterpillars on another plant of the pea or bean tribe. This butterfly was plentiful in the year 1782, but I have not since met with it.

Smith (1797) added this nomenclatural comment: "This being one of the most variable species in the length of the hind wings as well as general colour, is aptly named *Proteus* by Linnaeus; yet it is not really so variable as he thought, some of his supposed varieties being unquestionably distinct species."

The body of the larva is green, with a narrow, dark, mid-dorsal line. On each side of the middorsal line, there is a yellow lateral stripe, and below these, a pair of pale green stripes; the area between the stripes is gray-green dotted with black and yellowish spots.

The food plants are Pea (*Pisum sativum*), Butterfly Pea (*Clitoria mariana*), Wisteria (*Wisteria frutescens*), Cultivated Beans (*Phaseolus* spp.), Beggar's Ticks (*Desmodium*), and other plants of the Pea family.

Genus *Epargyreus*

Silver-spotted Skipper. *Epargyreus clarus clarus* Cramer
(Page 129)

Distribution and Records: This attractive skipper—known for many years as *E. tityrus* Fabricius—is common throughout the state.

Mountain Region—*Lumpkin Co.*: Woody Gap, 15 Apr 1967 BMR. *Banks Co.*: 10 May 1930 RWM (see Montgomery, 1931). *Towns Co.*: Brasstown Bald, 12 Aug 1951 LHJ (TTRS). *Habersham Co.*: Cornelia area, 1 Sept 1930 RWM (see Montgomery, 1931).

Piedmont Region—*Clarke Co.*: Athens, common Apr 1967 LRT. *Coweta Co.*: Madras, 11 Apr 1950 MES. *Fulton Co.*: Atlanta, Mt. Vernon Road, 15 May 1956 LHJ (TTRS). *Monroe Co.*: Forsyth, 25 May 1963 FTN.

Coastal Region—*Grady Co.*: Beachton, Sherwood Plantation, 7 and 11 Apr 1965 LN. *Thomas Co.*: Thomasville, 10 July 1944 LHJ (TTRS). *Screven Co.*: Sylvania, several specimens summer 1946 OB (AMNH). *Chatham Co.*: Savannah, no dates MHM (CU).

There appear to be several broods: adults are on the wing from March through October.

The Silver-spotted Skipper visits many types of flowers and is frequently seen in flower gardens around homes. It is a strong flier and has a rapid, erratic flight. It is easily identified by the central patch on the underside of the hindwings. When feeding or resting, the wings are held upright and the "silver spot" is easily seen.

The head of the larva is large, with two orange, oval, eyelike spots; the body is yellow or greenish yellow. It makes a nest by fastening leaves of the foodplant together with silk, and remains concealed within it. It hibernates as a pupa.

Abbot's life-size drawing in Smith (1797, pl. 19) illustrates the life history. Abbot wrote:

This caterpillar was taken feeding on the wild locust tree the latter end of August. It spins the leaves together to secure itself from birds, etc., like the rest of this tribe. On the 5th of September it spun up in the leaves and became a chrysalis two days after. The butterfly was produced the 10th of April following. It is also a native of Virginia, but not very common.

The larval food plants are Locust (*Robinia*), Honey Locust (*Gladitsia*), and other leguminous plants, including *Lespedeza* and *Desmodium*.

COLOR PLATES

Color Plate 1
SWALLOWTAILS (Family Papilionidae)

1. *Graphium marcellus telamonides* ♂, Harris Trail, Fulton Co.;
   p. 171
2. *Graphium marcellus lecontei* ♂, Susina Plantation, Beachton,
   Grady Co.; p. 171
3. *Papilio polyxenes asterius* ♂, Folkston, Charlton Co.; p. 159
4. *Papilio polyxenes asterius* ♀, Wakulla Co., Fla.; p. 159
5. *Battus philenor* ♂, Birdsong Plantation, Beachton, Grady Co.;
   p. 157
6. *Battus philenor* ♀ (lower side), Cooper Creek, Fannin Co.;
   p. 157
7. *Battus polydamus lucayus* ♀, Winter Haven, Fla.; p. 159
8. *Battus polydamus lucayus* ♀ (lower side), Winter Haven, Fla.;
   p. 159

110

Color Plate 2

SWALLOWTAILS (Family Papilionidae)

1. *Papilio troilus* ♂, Roswell, Fulton Co.; p. 166
2. *Papilio troilus* ♀, La Prades Camp, Rabun Co.; p. 166
3. *Papilio palamedes* ♂, Macon, Bibb Co.; p. 168
4. *Papilio troilus ilioneus* ♀, Miami, Dade Co., Fla.; p. 166
5. *Papilio glaucus* ♂, Cooper Creek State Park, Fannin Co.; p. 163
6. *Papilio glaucus australis* ♀, Susina Plantation, Beachton, Grady Co.; p. 163
7. *Papilio glaucus* ♀ (dark form), Susina Plantation, Beachton, Grady Co.; p. 163
8. *Papilio cresphontes* ♀, Sherwood Plantation, Beachton, Grady Co.; p. 161

113

Color Plate 3

SULPHURS AND WHITES (Family Pieridae)

1. *Nathalis iole* ♂, Stone Mountain, DeKalb Co.; p. 191
2. *Nathalis iole* ♀, Stone Mountain, DeKalb Co.; p. 191
3. *Eurema daira daira* summer form *jucunda* ♂, Thomas Co.; p. 187
4. *Eurema daira daira* summer form *jucunda* ♀, Atlanta, Fulton Co.; p. 187
5. *Eurema daira daira* aberration *fusca* ♀, Atlanta, Fulton Co.; p. 187
6. *Eurema lisa* ♂, Susina Plantation, Beachton, Grady Co.; p. 189
7. *Eurema lisa* ♀, St. Simons Island, Glynn Co.; p. 189
8. *Eurema nicippe* ♂, Macon, Bibb Co.; p. 190
9. *Colias philodice* ♂, Atlanta, Fulton Co.; p. 181
10. *Colias eurytheme* spring form *ariadne* ♂, Cobb Co.; p. 179
11. *Colias eurytheme* spring form *ariadne* ♀, Sherwood Plantation, Grady Co.; p. 179
12. *Colias eurytheme* summer form *keewaydin* ♂, Beachton, Grady Co.; p. 179
13. *Colias eurytheme* summer form *keewaydin* ♀, Atlanta, Fulton Co.; p. 179
14. *Pieris protodice* ♂, Jenkinsburg, Butts Co.; p. 173
15. *Pieris protodice* ♀, Atlanta, Fulton Co.; p. 173
16. *Pieris rapae* ♂, Greenwood Plantation, Thomasville, Thomas Co.; p. 175
17. *Pieris rapae* ♀, Helen, White Co.; p. 175
18. *Pieris virginiensis* ♂, 3 miles east of Old Fort Mountain, Murray Co.; p. 174
19. *Ascia monuste* ♂, Savannah, Chatham Co.; p. 177
20. *Ascia monuste* ♀, Ft. Myers, Fla.; p. 177
21. *Phoebis sennae eubule* ♂, Susina Plantation, Beachton, Grady Co.; p. 184
22. *Phoebis sennae eubule* ♀, Susina Plantation, Beachton, Grady Co.; p. 184
23. *Phoebis statira* ♂, Miami, Fla.; p. 186
24. *Phoebis statira* ♀, Miami, Fla.; p. 186

114

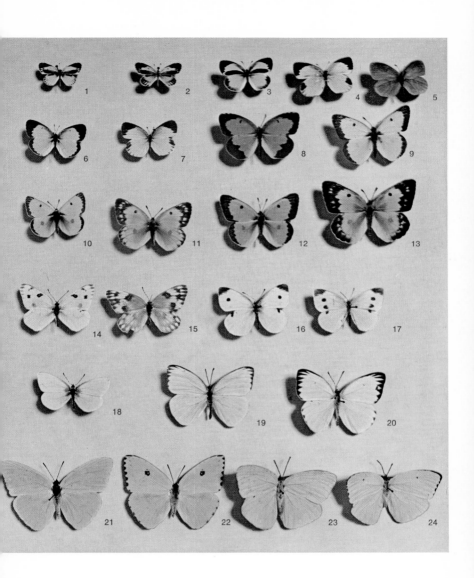

Color Plate 4
HAIRSTREAKS (Family Theclinae)

1. *Callophrys (Mitoura) gryneas* ♀, Stone Mountain, DeKalb Co.; p. 213
2. *Callophrys (Mitoura) gryneas* ♂ (lower side), Stone Mountain, DeKalb Co.; p. 213
3. *Chrysophanus titus mopsus* ♂ (lower side), Stone Mountain, DeKalb Co.; p. 196
4. *Chrysophanus titus mopsus* ♀ (lower side), Atlanta, Fulton Co.; p. 196
5. *Calycopis cecrops* ♂, Old Fort Mountain, Murray Co.; p. 207
6. *Calycopus cecrops* ♀ (lower side), Savannah, Chatham Co.; p. 207
7. *Strymon melinus* ♂, Cooper Creek, Union Co.; p. 222
8. *Strymon melinus* ♀ (lower side), Birdsong Plantation, Beachton, Grady Co.; p. 222
9. *Euristrymon favonius* ♀, Savannah, Chatham Co.; p. 216
10. *Euristrymon favonius* ♂ (lower side), Jekyll Island, Glynn Co.; p. 216
11. *Euristrymon ontario* ♀, Spring Creek, Decatur Co.; p. 218
12. *Euristrymon ontario* ♂ (lower side), Spring Creek, Decatur Co.; p. 218
13. *Satyrium edwardsii* ♂, Blackjack Mountain, Cobb Co.; p. 206
14. *Satyrium edwardsii* ♂ (lower side), Blackjack Mountain, Cobb Co.; p. 206
15. *Satyrium caryaevorus* ♂, Riverside, Connecticut; p. 204
16. *Satyrium caryaevorus* ♀ (lower side), Wolf Pen Gap, Union Co.; p. 204
17. *Satyrium calanus* ♂, Greenwood Plantation, Thomasville, Thomas Co.; p. 201
18. *Satyrium calanus* ♀ (lower side), Savannah, Chatham Co.; p. 201
19. *Satyrium calanus falacer* ♂, Kennesaw Mountain, Cobb Co.; p. 203
20. *Satyrium calanus falacer* ♀ (lower side), Atlanta, Fulton Co.; p. 203
21. *Satyrium kingi* ♂ (lower side), Indian Trail Road, Atlanta, Fulton Co.; p. 199
22. Satyrium kingi ♀ (lower side), Savannah (type locality, Chatham Co.; p. 199
23. *Satyrium liparops* ♂, Macon, Bibb Co.; p. 197
24. *Satyrium liparops* ♀ (lower side), Indian Trail Road, Atlanta, Fulton Co.; p. 197
25. *Panthiades m=album* ♂, Istachatta, Fla.; p. 221
26. *Panthiades m=album* ♀, Savannah, Chatham Co.; p. 221
27. *Atlides halesus* ♂, Savannah, Chatham Co.; p. 214
28. *Atlides halesus* ♀, Macon, Bibb Co.; p. 214

Color Plate 5

ELFINS, COPPERS, AND BLUES (Family Lycaenidae)

1. *Lephelisca virginiensis pumila* ♀, Roberta, Crawford Co.; p. 195
2. *Lephelisca virginiensis pumila* ♀ (lower side), Roberta, Crawford Co.; p. 195
3. *Lycaena phlaeas americana* ♂, Augusta, Maine; p. 226
4. *Lycaena phlaeas americana* ♀, Lamont, Illinois; p. 226
5. *Callophrys (Incisalia) augustinus* ♂, Old Fort Mountain, Murray Co.; p. 211
6. *Callophrys (Incisalia) augustinus* ♀ (lower side), Old Fort Mountain, Murray Co.; p. 211
7. *Callophrys (Incisalia) irus* ♀, Old Fort Mountain, Murray Co.; p. 208
8. *Callophrys (Incisalia) irus* ♀ (lower side), Old Fort Mountain, Murray Co.; p. 208
9. *Callophrys (Incisalia) henrici* ♂, Indian Trail Road, Atlanta, Fulton Co.; p. 209
10. *Callophrys (Incisalia) henrici* ♀ (lower side), Atlanta, Fulton Co.; p. 209
11. *Callophrys (Incisalia) niphon* ♂, Old Fort Mountain, Murray Co.; p. 212
12. *Callophrys (Incisalia) niphon* ♂ (lower side), Atlanta, Fulton Co.; p. 212
13. *Brephidium isophthalma pseudofea* ♂, St. Simons Island, Glynn Co.; p. 227
14. *Brephidium isophthalma pseudofea* ♀, Merritt Island, Fla.; p. 227
15. *Hemiargus ceraunus antibubastus* ♂, Folkston, Charlton Co.; p. 228
16. *Hemiargus ceraunus antibubastus* ♀ (lower side), Folkston, Charlton Co.; p. 228
17. *Everes comyntas comyntas* ♂, Helen, White Co.; p. 229
18. *Everes comyntas comyntas* ♀, Avondale Estates, DeKalb Co.; p. 229
19. *Glaucopsyche lygdamus nittanyensis* ♂, 3 miles east of Fort Mountain Park, Gilmer Co.; p. 231
20. *Glaucopsyche lygdamus nittanyensis* ♂ (lower side), Old Fort Mountain, Murray Co.; p. 231
21. *Celastrina argiolus pseudargiolus* ♂, Cooper Creek, Fannin Co.; p. 233
22. *Celastrina argiolus pseudargiolus* ♀, Indian Trail Road, Atlanta, Fulton Co.; p. 233

Color Plate 6

HACKBERRY BUTTERFLIES, ANGLE-WINGS AND SULPHURS (Families Nymphalidae and Pieridae)

1. *Asterocampa celtis* ♂, Macon, Bibb Co.; p. 239
2. *Asterocampa celtis* ♀, Macon, Bibb Co.; p. 239
3. *Asterocampa celtis alicia* ♂, Tall Timbers Research Station, Leon Co., Fla.; p. 239
4. *Asterocampa celtis alicia* ♀, Savannah, Chatham Co.; p. 239
5. *Asterocampa clyton* ♂, Macon, Bibb Co.; p. 241
6. *Asterocampa clyton* ♀, Macon, Bibb Co.; p. 241
7. *Asterocampa clyton flora* ♂, Lake Apopka, Fla.; p. 241
8. *Asterocampa clyton flora* ♀, Lake Apopka, Fla.; p. 241
9. *Polygonia comma* ♂, Blackjack Mountain, Cobb Co.; p. 257
10. *Polygonia comma* ♂ (lower side), Old Fort Mountain, Murray Co.; p. 257
11. *Polygonia faunus smythi* ♂, Fannin Co.; p. 258
12. *Polygonia faunus smythi* ♀ (lower side), Cooper Creek, Union Co.; p. 258
13. *Polygonia interrogationis fabricii* ♂, Albany, Dougherty Co.; p. 254
14. *Polygonia interrogationis* form *umbrosa* ♀, Birdsong Plantation, Beachton, Grady Co.; p. 254
15. *Anaea andria* ♂, near Margret, Fannin Co.; p. 238
16. *Anaea andria* ♀, Macon, Bibb Co.; p. 238
17. *Nymphalis antiopa* ♂, Avondale Estates, DeKalb Co.; p. 253
18. *Phoebis philea* ♂, Montezuma, Macon Co.; p. 185
19. *Phoebis philea* ♀, Sarasota, Fla.; p. 185

Color Plate 7

CHECKERSPOTS, HARVESTER, AND SNOUT BUTTERFLY
(Family Nymphalidae)

1. *Chlosyne nycteis* ♂, Atlanta, Fulton Co.; p. 260
2. *Chlosyne nycteis* ♂ (lower side), Atlanta, Fulton Co.; p. 260
3. *Chlosyne gorgone* ♂, Old Fort Mountain, Murray Co.; p. 261
4. *Chlosyne gorgone* ♀, Old Fort Mountain, Murray Co.; p. 261
5. *Chlosyne gorgone* ♂ (transition, near *"ismeria"*), Stone Mountain, DeKalb Co.; p. 261
6. *Chlosyne gorgone* ♂ (transition, near *"ismeria,"* lower side), Atlanta, Fulton Co.; p. 261
7. *Chlosyne gorgone* ♀ (transition, near *"ismeria"*), Old Fort Mountain, Murray Co.; p. 261
8. *Chlosyne gorgone* ♀ (lower side), Kennesaw Mountain, Cobb Co.; p. 261
9. *Phyciodes (Tritanassa) texana seminole* ♂, Savannah, Chatham Co.; p. 266
10. *Phyciodes (Tritanassa) texana seminole* ♀, Savannah, Chatham Co.; p. 266
11. *Phyciodes p. phaon* ♂, St. Simons Island (type locality), Glynn Co.; p. 270
12. *Phyciodes p. phaon* ♀ (lower side), St. Simons Island, Glynn Co.; p. 270
13. *Phyciodes t. tharos* spring form *marcia* ♂, Fannin Co.; p. 268
14. *Phyciodes t. tharos* spring form *marcia* ♀ (lower side), Screven Co.; p. 268
15. *Phyciodes t. tharos* summer form *morpheus* ♂, Grady Co.; p. 268
16. *Phyciodes t. tharos* summer form *morpheus* ♂ (lower side), Coleman River, Rabun Co.; p. 268
17. *Phyciodes batesii* ♂, Coleman River, Rabun Co.; p. 269
18. *Feniseca tarquinius* ♂, Atlanta, Fulton Co.; p. 225
19. *Libytheana bachmanii* ♂, Cobb Co.; p. 236

ZEBRA, FRITILLARIES AND MONARCHS
(Families Heliconiidae, Nymphalidae, and Danaidae)

1. *Heliconius charitonius tuckeri* ♂, Susina Plantation, Beachton, Grady Co.; p. 281
2. *Agraulis vanillae nigrior* ♀, Indian Trail Road, Atlanta, Fulton Co.; p. 282
3. *Agraulis vanillae nigrior abberation fumosus* ♀, Macon, Bibb Co.; p. 282
4. *Agraulis vanillae nigrior* (partial albino) ♂, Macon, Bibb Co., p. 282
5. *Speyeria idalia* ♂, Porter County, Indiana; p. 275
6. *Speyeria cybele* ♂, Old Fort Mountain, Murray Co.; p. 278
7. *Speyeria cybele* ♀ (lower side), Wolf Pen Gap, Union Co.; p. 278
8. *Danaus plexippus* ♀, Avondale Estates, DeKalb Co.; p. 284
9. *Speyeria aphrodite* ♀, Pittsburgh, Pa.; p. 279
10. *Speyeria aphrodite* ♂ (lower side), Wolf Pen Gap, Union Co.; p. 279
11. *Danaus g. berenice* ♀, Key Largo, Fla.; p. 291
12. *Speyeria diana* ♂, Cooper Creek, Fannin Co.; p. 276
13. *Speyeria diana* ♀, Cooper Creek, Fannin Co.; p. 276

Color Plate 9

ORANGE-TIP, DOG-FACE, AND
BRUSH-FOOTED BUTTERFLIES
(Families Pieridae and Nymphalidae)

1. *Anthocaris midea annickae* ♂, Marietta, Cobb Co.; p. 193
2. *Anthocaris midea annickae* ♀, Marietta, Cobb Co.; p. 193
3. *Colias (Zerene) cesonia* ♂, Susina Plantation, Beachton, Grady Co.; p. 182
4. *Colias (Zerene) cesonia* ♀, Susina Plantation, Beachton, Grady Co.; p. 182
5. *Junonia coenia* ♂, Milhaven, Screven Co.; p. 251
6. *Vanessa atalanta* ♂, New Smyrna Beach, Fla.; p. 246
7. *Anartia jatrophae guantanamo* ♀, Flamingo, Fla.; p. 246
8. *Euptoieta claudia* ♂, Macon, Bibb Co.; p. 280
9. *Euphydryas phaeton* ♀, Riverside Drive, Fulton Co.; p. 272
10. *Vanessa virginiensis* ♂, Avondale Estates, DeKalb Co.; p. 247
11. *Vanessa virginiensis* ♀ (lower side), Avondale Estates, DeKalb Co.; p. 247
12. *Vanessa cardui* ♂, Atlanta, Fulton Co.; p. 248
13. *Vanessa cardui* ♀ (lower side), Avondale Estates, DeKalb Co.; p. 248
14. *Limenitis archippus* ♂, Macon, Bibb Co.; p. 244
15. *Limenitis archippus abberation lanthanis* ♂, Macon, Bibb Co.; p. 244
16. *Limenitis astyanax* ♂, Brasstown Bald, Union Co.; p. 243
17. *Limenitis astyanax* ♂ (lower side), Stone Mountain, DeKalb Co.; p. 243

126

127

Color Plate 10

SKIPPERS AND GIANT SKIPPERS
(Families Hesperiidae and Megathymidae)

1. *Urbanus proteus* ♂, Susina Plantation, Beachton, Grady Co.; p. 105
2. *Poanes aaroni howardi* ♂, Augusta, Richmond Co.; p. 56
3. *Poanes aaroni howardi* ♂ (lower side), Yankeetown, Fla.; p. 56
4. *Poanes yehl* ♂, Milhaven, Screven Co.; p. 57
5. *Poanes yehl* ♀, Savannah, Chatham Co.; p. 57
6. *Euphyes arpa* ♂, Bunnell, Fla.; p. 48
7. *Euphyes arpa* ♀, Bunnell, Fla.; p. 48
8. *Euphyes palatka* ♂, Collier Co., Fla.; p. 48
9. *Euphyes palatka* ♀, Wakulla Co., Fla.; p. 48
10. *Epargyreus clarus* ♂, Thomasville, Thomas Co.; p. 106
11. *Epargyreus clarus* ♀ (lower side), Atlanta, Fulton Co.; p. 106
12. *Achalarus lyciades* ♂, Atlanta, Fulton Co.; p. 101
13. *Achalarus lyciades* ♀ (lower side), Thomasville, Thomas Co.; p. 101
14. *Megathymus yuccae yuccae* ♂, Atlanta, Fulton Co.; p. 25
15. *Megathymus yuccae yuccae* ♀, Atlanta, Fulton Co.; p. 25
16. *Autochton cellus* ♂, Atlanta, Fulton Co.; p. 102
17. *Calpodes ethlius* ♂, Rubonia, Fla.; p. 37
18. *Megathymus harrisi* ♂, Atlanta, Fulton Co.; p. 31
19. *Megathymus harrisi* ♀, near Roswell, Fulton Co.; p. 31
20. *Megathymus cofaqui* ♂, Sarasota, Fla.; p. 28
21. *Megathymus cofaqui* ♀, Sarasota, Fla.; p. 28

BLACK AND WHITE PLATES

Black and White Plate 1

Inside of Yucca tent lined with silk, with empty pupal case of *Megathymus yuccae*. (Photo by Carolyn Carter.)

Black and White Plate 2

Tent of *Megathymus harrisi* at base of Yucca plant.

Black and White Plate 3

On the left, tent of *Megathymus harrisi* from base of Yucca plant;
on the right, tent of *Megathymus yuccae*. (Photos by Carolyn
Carter.)

135

Black and White Plate 4

SKIPPERS (Family Hesperiidae)

1. *Panoquina panoquin* ♂, St. Simons Island, Glynn Co.; p. 35
2. *Panoquina panoquin* ♂ (lower side), St. Simons Island, Glynn Co.; p. 35
3. *Panoquina ocola* ♂, Stone Mountain, DeKalb Co.; p. 36
4. *Panoquina ocola* ♀ (lower side), Atlanta, Fulton Co.; p. 36
5. *Oligoria maculata* ♂, Folkston, Charlton Co.; p. 38
6. *Oligoria maculata* ♀ (lower side), Flamingo, near Homestead, Fla.; p. 38
7. *Lerodea eufala* ♂, Atlanta, Fulton Co.; p. 39
8. *Lerodea eufala* ♂ (lower side), Folkston, Charlton Co.; p. 39
9. *Amblyscirtes samoset* ♂, Stone Mountain, DeKalb Co.; p. 40
10. *Amblyscirtes samoset* ♀ (lower side), Atlanta, Fulton Co.; p. 40
11. *Amblyscirtes aesculapius* ♂, Atlanta, Fulton Co.; p. 40
12. *Amblyscirtes aesculapius* ♀ (lower side), Atlanta, Fulton Co.; p. 40
13. *Amblyscirtes carolina* form *reversa* ♂, Atlanta, Fulton Co.; p. 41
14. *Amblyscirtes carolina* form *reversa* ♂ (lower side), Atlanta, Fulton Co.; p. 41
15. *Amblyscirtes vialis* ♂, Old Fort Mountain, Murray Co.; p. 43
16. *Amblyscirtes vialis* ♂ (lower side), Old Fort Mountain, Murray Co.; p. 43

137

Black and White Plate 5

SKIPPERS (Family Hesperiidae)

1. *Amblyscirtes celia belli* ♂, Atlanta, Fulton Co.; p. 44
2. *Amblyscirtes celia belli* ♂ (lower side), Atlanta, Fulton Co.; p. 44
3. *Amblyscirtes alternata* ♂, Atlanta, Fulton Co.; p. 45
4. *Amblyscirtes alternata* ♀, Atlanta, Fulton Co.; p. 45
5. *Atrytonopsis hianna* ♂, Atlanta, Fulton Co.; p. 46
6. *Atrytonopsis hianna* ♀, Atlanta, Fulton Co.; p. 46
7. *Atrytonopsis loammi* ♂, Sarasota, Fla.; p. 47
8. *Atrytonopsis loammi* ♀ (lower side), Sarasota, Fla.; p. 47
9. *Euphyes bimacula* ♂, near Blichton, Bryan Co.; p. 51
10. *Euphyes bimacula* ♀, near Blichton, Bryan Co.; p. 51
11. *Euphyes vestris metacomet* ♂, Atlanta, Fulton Co.; p. 52
12. *Euphyes vestris metacomet* ♂ (lower side), Cooper Creek, Union Co.; p. 52

139

Black and White Plate 6

SKIPPERS (Family Hesperiidae)

1. *Euphyes berryi* ♂, Collier Co., Fla.; p. 50
2. *Euphyes berryi* ♀ (lower side), Screven Co.; p. 50
3. *Euphyes dion* ♂ (lower side), Blichton, Bryan Co.; p. 49
4. *Euphyes dion* ♀, Macon, Bibb Co.; p. 49
5. *Poanes zabulon* ♂, Stone Mountain, DeKalb Co.; p. 55
6. *Poanes zabulon* ♂ (lower side), Atlanta, Fulton Co.; p. 55
7. *Poanes zabulon* ♀, Atlanta, Fulton Co.; p. 55
8. *Poanes hobomok* ♂, Old Fort Mountain, Murray Co.; p. 54
9. *Poanes hobomok* ♂ (lower side), Atlanta, Fulton Co.; p. 54
10. *Poanes hobomok* ♀, Atlanta, Fulton Co.; p. 54

Black and White Plate 7

SKIPPERS (Family Hesperiidae)

1. *Poanes viator* ♂, Savannah, Chatham Co.; p. 58
2. *Poanes viator* ♀, Augusta, Richmond Co.; p. 58
3. *Problema byssus* ♂, Atlanta, Fulton Co.; p. 60
4. *Problema byssus* ♀, Madras, Coweta Co.; p. 60
5. *Problema bulenta* ♂, Jasper Co., S. C.; p. 61
6. *Problema bulenta* ♀, Jasper Co., S. C.; p. 61

7. *Atrytone arogos* ♂, Orange Co., Fla.; p. 63
8. *Atrytone arogos* ♀, Orange Co., Fla.; p. 63
9. *Atrytone delaware* ♂, Unicoi Gap, White Co.; p. 65
10. *Atrytone delaware* ♀, Stone Mountain, DeKalb Co.; p. 65
11. *Atalopedes campestris* ♂, Lake Burton, Rabun Co.; p. 66
12. *Atalopedes campestris* ♀, Lake Burton, Rabun Co.; p. 66

143

Black and White Plate 8

SKIPPERS (Family Hesperiidae)

1. *Polites themistocles* ♂, Stone Mountain, DeKalb Co.; p. 72
2. *Polites themistocles* ♀, Macon, Bibb Co.; p. 72
3. *Polites origines* ♂, Riverside Drive, Atlanta, Fulton Co.; p. 73
4. *Polites origines* ♀, Macon, Bibb Co.; p. 73
5. *Polites vibex* ♂, Milhaven, Screven Co.; p. 73
6. *Polites vibex* ♂ (lower side), Riverside Dr., Atlanta, Fulton Co.; p. 73
7. *Polites vibex* ♀, Milhaven, Screven Co.; p. 73
8. *Polites vibex* ♀ (lower side), Susina Plantation, Beachton, Grady Co.; p. 73
9. *Hesperia metea* ♂, Fort Mountain, Murray Co.; p. 74
10. *Hesperia metea* ♀ (lower side), Fort Mountain, Murray Co.; p. 74
11. *Hesperia sassacus* ♂, Roan Mountain, Mitchell Co.; N.C.; p. 76
12. *Hesperia sassacus* ♀, Roan Mountain, Mitchell Co.; N.C.; p. 76
13. *Hesperia meskei* ♂, Terrell Mill Road, Cobb Co.; p. 76
14. *Hesperia meskei* ♀, Forsyth, Monroe Co.; p. 76
15. *Hesperia attalus* ♂, near Weeki Wachee Springs, Fla.; p. 78
16. *Hylephila phyleus* ♂, Rabun Co.; p. 78
17. *Hylephila phyleus* ♀, Susina Plantation, Beachton, Grady Co.; p. 78

145

Black and White Plate 9

SKIPPERS (Family Hesperiidae)

1. *Copaeodes minima* ♂, Macon, Bibb Co.; p. 79
2. *Copaeodes minima* ♀, Macon, Bibb Co.; p. 79
3. *Ancyloxypha numitor* ♂, Cox Road, Cobb Co.; p. 80
4. *Ancyloxypha numitor* ♀, Roswell, Cobb Co.; p. 80
5. *Pholisora catullus* ♂, Birdsong Plantation, Beachton, Grady Co.; p. 83
6. *Pholisora catullus* ♀, Ellenwood, Clayton Co.; p. 83
7. *Staphylus hayhurstii* ♂, Atlanta, Fulton Co.; p. 96
8. *Staphylus hayhurstii* ♀, Harris Trail, Fulton Co.; p. 96
9. *Pompeius verna* ♂, Screven Co.; p. 67
10. *Pompeius verna* ♀, Macon, Bibb Co.; p. 67
11. *Wallengrenia otho* ♂, Harris Trail, Fulton Co.; p. 68
12. *Wallengrenia otho* ♀, Milhaven, Screven Co.; p. 68
13. *Wallangrenia egeremet* ♂, Atlanta, Fulton Co.; p. 70
14. *Polites coras* ♂, Coleman River, Rabun Co.; p. 71
15. *Polites coras* ♀, Coleman River, Rabun Co.; p. 71
16. *Polites baracoa* ♂, Istachatta, Fla.; p. 71
17. *Polites baracoa* ♀, Sarasota, Fla.; p. 71

Black and White Plate 10

SKIPPERS (Family Hesperiidae)

1. *Nastra lherminier* ♂, Stone Mountain, DeKalb Co.; p. 82
2. *Nastra lherminier* ♂ (lower side), Folkston, Charlton Co.; p. 82
3. *Lerema accius* ♂ (lower side), Atlanta, Fulton Co.; p. 81
4. *Lerema accius* ♀, Stone Mountain, DeKalb Co.; p. 81
5. *Pyrgus communis communis* ♂, Folkston, Charlton Co.; p. 85
6. *Pyrgus communis communis* ♀, Atlanta, Fulton Co.; p. 85
7. *Erynnis (Erynnis) icelus* ♂, Old Fort Mountain, Murray Co.; p. 88
8. *Erynnis (Erynnis) icelus* ♀, La Prades Camp, Rabun Co.; p. 88
9. *Erynnis (Erynnis) brizo* ♂, Old Fort Mountain, Murray Co.; p. 89
10. *Erynnis (Erynnis) brizo* ♀, Atlanta, Fulton Co.; p. 89
11. *Erynnis (Erynnides) baptisiae* ♂, Helen, White Co.; p. 90
12. *Erynnis (Erynnides) baptisiae* ♀, La Prades Camp, Rabun Co.; p. 90
13. *Erynnis (Erynnides) zarucco* ♂, Stone Mountain, DeKalb Co.; p. 91
14. *Erynnis (Erynnides) zarucco* ♀, Stone Mountain, DeKalb Co.; p. 91
15. *Erynnis (Erynnides) martialis* ♂, Stone Mountain, DeKalb Co.; p. 92
16. *Erynnis (Erynnides) martialis* ♀, Atlanta, Fulton Co.; p. 92

149

Black and White Plate 11

SKIPPERS (Family Hesperiidae)

1. *Erynnis (Erynnides) horatius* ♂, St. Simons Island, Glynn Co.; p. 93

2. *Erynnis (Erynnides) horatius* ♀, Decatur Co.; p. 93

3. *Erynnis (Erynnides) juvenalis* ♂, Blackjack Mountain, Cobb Co.; p. 95

4. *Erynnis (Erynnides) juvenalis* ♀, Old Fort Mountain, Murray Co.; p. 95

5. *Thorybes bathyllus* ♂, Stone Mountain, DeKalb Co.; p. 97

6. *Thorybes bathyllus* ♀, Thomasville, Thomas Co.; p. 97

7. *Thorybes pylades* ♂, Atlanta, Fulton Co.; p. 99

8. *Thorybes pylades* ♀, Atlanta, Fulton Co.; p. 99

9. *Thorybes confusis* ♂, Stone Mountain, DeKalb Co.; p. 100

10. *Thorybes confusis* ♀, Screven Co.; p. 100

151

SATYRS AND WOOD NYMPHS (Family Satyridae)

1. *Euptychia gemma* ♂, Atlanta, Fulton Co.; p. 296
2. *Euptychia gemma* ♀ (lower side), Atlanta, Fulton Co.; p. 296
3. *Euptychia areolata* ♂, Greenwood Plantation, Thomasville, Thomas Co.; p. 298
4. *Euptychia areolata* ♀ (lower side), Savannah, Chatham Co.; p. 298
5. *Euptychia hermes sosybius* ♂, Stone Mountain, DeKalb Co.; p. 299
6. *Euptychia hermes sosybius* ♀ (lower side), Sherwood Plantation, Beachton, Grady Co.; p. 299
7. *Euptychia cymela cymela* ♂, Atlanta, Fulton Co.; p. 300
8. *Euptychia cymela cymela* ♀ (lower side), Folkston, Charlton Co.; p. 300
9. *Lethe portlandia* ♂, Atlanta, Fulton Co.; p. 292
10. *Lethe portlandia* ♀, Atlanta, Fulton Co.; p. 292
11. *Lethe eurydice appalachia* ♂, Cooper Creek, Union Co.; p. 295
12. *Lethe eurydice appalachia* ♀ (lower side), Cleveland, White Co.; p. 295

153

SATYRS AND WOOD NYMPHS (Family Satyridae)

1. *Lethe creola* ♂, Atlanta, Fulton Co.; p. 293
2. *Lethe creola* ♀, Atlanta, Fulton Co.; p. 293
3. *Cercyonis pegala abbotti* ♂, Coleraine Plantation, Camden Co.; p. 301
4. *Cercyonis pegala abbotti* ♀, Coleraine Plantation, Camden Co.; p. 301
5. *Cercyonis pegala alope* ♂, Lithonia, DeKalb Co.; p. 301
6. *Cercyonis pegala alope* ♀ (lower side), Cox Road, Fulton Co.; p. 301
7. *Cercyonis pegala alope* form *carolina* ♂, Yonah Mountain, White Co.; p. 301
8. *Cercyonis pegala alope* form *carolina* ♀, Cooper Creek, Union Co.; p. 301

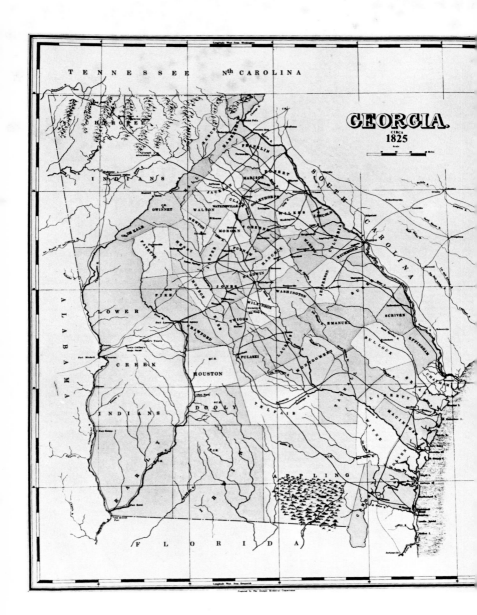

GEORGIA.
CIRCA
1825

SUPERFAMILY PAPILIONOIDEA

Family PAPILIONIDAE—Swallowtails

Genus *Battus*

Pipe-vine Swallowtail. *Battus philenor* Linnaeus
(Page 111)

Distribution and Records: *B. philenor* is common throughout the state.

Mountain Region—*Lumpkin Co.*: Auraria, five specimens 15 Apr 1967 BMR. *Fannin Co.*: near Margret, several specimens 16 Apr 1967 BMR and JCS. *Banks Co.* and *Habersham Co.*: 26 June–7 Sept 1930 RWM (see Montgomery, 1931). *Towns Co.*: Brasstown Bald, 12 Aug 1951 LHJ (TTRS).
Piedmont Region—*Monroe Co.*: Forsyth, 24 Feb 1957 FTN; Forsyth, 13 Mar 1955 FTN. *Coweta Co.*: Madras, 26 Mar 1950 MES; Madras, 1 Apr 1951 MES. *Fulton Co.*: Atlanta area, 18 Apr 1958 LHJ (TTRS); Atlanta area, 21 June 1940 LHJ (TTRS). *Cobb Co.*: Marietta area, 5 Sept 1949 LHT (TTRS).
Coastal Region—*Grady Co.*: Beachton, Susina Plantation, 2 Jan 1965 LHJ (TTRS). *Colquitt Co.*: Moultrie area, 11–16 Mar 1945 HVAV (UWO). *Grady Co.*: Beachton, Susina Plantation, 28 Mar 1964 LHJ (TTRS). *Houston Co.*: Warner Robins, 30 Mar 1957 FTN. *Screven Co.*: Millhaven, 25 May 1968 BMR. *Grady Co.*: Beachton, Susina Plantation, 5 July 1957 LHJ (TTRS). *Thomas Co.*: Boston, Bar-M Ranch, 18 July 1967 ESS (TTRS). *Baker Co.*: Newton area, 6 Oct 1964 LN.

157

There are several broods during the year. The individuals that emerge in early spring are usually much smaller than those that emerge later. They first appear in southern Georgia during warm periods in January and February. In central and northern Georgia, it is usually March before the Pipe-vine Swallowtail first appears. It increases in number as the season progresses, and can be found throughout the state until late fall. It visits flowers freely and frequents flower gardens, fields, orchards, and open woodlands.

The larva is a dark purplish brown, usually with three paired rows of fleshy tentacles, one anterior pair very long and three posterior pairs longer than the rest. The larval food plants are Snakeroot and Pipe-Vine (*Aristolochia*), Knotweed (*Polygonum*), and perhaps Wild-Ginger (*Asarum*).

In central Georgia, in the Bibb County area, James C. Brooks found *B. philenor* to be very common, but he noted that it seldom entered heavily populated areas. He reported that the caterpillars that he found were feeding only on Samson's Snakeroot and Black Snakeroot. He did not find it on *Asarum*. He observed also that *Aristolochia* is found in Bibb County only in cultivation.

In Baker County, in southwestern Georgia, an aberration was captured by Leon Neel on October 6, 1964. This specimen lacked the pale spots that normally are found on the upper surface of the hindwing.

The observations made by John Abbot were recorded (Smith, 1797) as follows:

One of these caterpillars was found feeding on the Black Snakeroot, *Aristolochia serpentaria*, and attached itself to the branch by its tail, the 24th of April, two days afterward it changed to a chrysalis, and the fly appeared May 4th. Another spun itself up on June 20th, changed 21st, and the fly came out on the 5th of July. This is one of the most common butterflies, frequently seen on the blossoms of the peach and other trees in the spring, and is no less plentiful in Virginia. The retractile horns of this caterpillar seem appropriate to the swallowtail tribe.

Smith (1797) commented on Abbot's drawing in a single sentence: "There is no difficulty in determining this species, though the female has much less of the green hue, except in some particular lights, than the male."

Tailless Swallowtail; Polydamus Swallowtail.
Battus polydamus lucayus Rothschild and Jordan
(Page 111)

Distribution and Records: *B. p. lucayus* is found in Georgia only as a rare stray or as an infrequent visitor from Florida.

Dr. James C. Brooks made the following observation for the Macon area, "Up until 1962 only three have been seen in Bibb County, all worn and flown. On June 12, 1962 a fresh female was taken in our yard in Macon. Perhaps a hold-over from a fall stray."

Its flight period in Florida has been given by Kimball (1965, p. 31) as April through November, inclusive, and occasionally in the winter. It may be fairly common at times, but it is locally distributed in Florida; its general range is south of a line from Cross City to Gainesville to Palatka.

Masters (1967, pp. 206–209) reported that it is apparently becoming established near Norfork in Baxter County, Arkansas, feeding on *Aristolochia*.

Genus *Papilio*

Black Swallowtail; Parsnip Swallowtail.
Papilio polyxenes asterius Stoll (Page 111)

Distribution and Records: *P. p. asterius* is fairly common throughout the state, but is often local in occurrence.

Mountain Region—*Union Co.*: Suches area, 15 Apr 1967 BMR. *Murray Co.*: Old Fort Mountain, 17 Apr 1953 LHJ (TTRS). *Banks Co.* and *Habersham Co.*: several specimens 12–20 Aug 1930 RWM (see Montgomery, 1931).
Piedmont Region—*Monroe Co.*: Forsyth, 24 Feb 1957 FTN.

Coweta Co.: Madras, 25 Mar 1951 MES. *DeKalb Co.*: Avondale Estates, 31 Mar 1955 LHJ (TTRS).
Coastal Region—*Charlton Co.*: Folkston, 9 Feb 1952 LHJ (TTRS). *Colquitt Co.*: Moultrie, 11 Mar 1945 HVAV (UWO). *Thomas Co.*: Thomasville, 17 Mar 1966 LN. *Grady Co.*: Beachton, Birdsong Plantation, 2 June 1954 EVK (TTRS). *Thomas Co.*: Boston, Bar-M Ranch, 13 July 1967 ESS (TTRS). *Grady Co.*: Beachton, Sherwood Plantation, 26 July 1965 LN; Beachton, Sherwood Plantation, 24 Aug 1964 LN; Beachton, Sherwood Plantation, 1 Sept 1964 LN.

First appearing in February in south Georgia, *P. p. asterius* appears later (usually in March) in the middle and northern portions of the state. There are two or more broods. It may be found from spring until late October in the northern part of the state, and through November in the southern part.

For some reason, John Abbot's excellent drawing of *P. p. asterius*, which depicted a male, a female, the food plant, three caterpillars and a pupa, was very puzzling to Smith: after much study and consultation, he concluded it was *Papilio troilus* (Smith, 1797, table 1). At one point, he commented: "We beg leave only to remark, that *P. asterius*, Fabr. p. 6, seems not to be different from this."

He finally decided, however, to call it *P. troilus*, and stated: "The black dot in the orange spot of the anal angle seems a mark of *troilus*."

Because none of us are immune to making errors, this one shows kinship to our own efforts at times with some species. It is interesting to note that, as a result of this misidentification, he gave the name *ilioneus* to a subspecies of *P. troilus* that is still recognized.

Mrs. Ellen Robertson-Miller (1931), in her delightful book, tells about Maggie, her friend and neighbor, who told her about caterpillars that looked like bits of rag carpet feeding in her garden on the leaves of parsley, turnip, and dill. When her friend brought her some caterpillars in a can, she at once recognized them as the "rag carpet" worms. There were about a dozen caterpillars of various sizes, ranging from one-eighth of an inch to two inches long. The smallest was black, with two rows of dull orange "warts" and "saddle-cloths" of pale yellow.

The middle-sized caterpillars retained the "saddle-cloths," but had bright yellow spots in place of the dull orange "warts." They also showed faint bands of white and yellow. In the largest of the caterpillars, the white became green; on the black portions between these bands, the yellow was evenly distributed in the form of small disks.

She touched one with a twig and it shot forth from its head an orange-red V-shaped prong, which emitted a sickening odor. She learned later that this pliable double horn is called an osmaterium, and that its use is for defense—ill-smelling, but harmless. Many years have passed since November 26, 1931, when Mrs. Harris and I called on Mrs. Robertson-Miller at her winter cottage at Coronada Beach, Florida (now New Smyrna Beach), and talked about caterpillars, moths, butterflies, and the relaxation and enjoyment that may be found in collecting and studying these interesting creatures.

John Abbot (in Smith, 1797) wrote: "The caterpillar of this species eats fennel and rue. It changed to a chrysalis July 12th, and the butterfly came forth on the 20th. It is more frequent in Virginia than in Georgia." The larval food plants include parsley, carrots, caraway, parsnips, and various wild species belonging to the family Umbelliferae.

Giant Swallowtail. *Papilio cresphontes cresphontes* Cramer
(Page 113)

Distribution and Records: *P. c. cresphontes* is rare to locally frequent in the Piedmont Region, where local colonies sometimes occur; it is sporadic and rare in the Bibb County area, and casual to locally frequent on the Coastal plain, especially along the coast and in extreme south Georgia.

Mountain Region—None.

Piedmont Region—*Cobb Co.*: Kennesaw Mountain, 28 July 1957 JCS. *DeKalb Co.*: Stone Mountain, 22 Aug 1950 LHT (TTRS). *Coweta Co.*: Madras, 16 Sept 1950 MES.

Coastal Region—*Colquitt Co.*: Moultrie, 12 Apr 1945 HVAV (UWO). *Grady Co.*: Beachton, Susina Plantation, sight record 26 Apr 1967 LNH; Beachton, Birdsong Plantation, 21 July 1967 ESS; Beachton, Sherwood Plantation, 15 Aug 1965 LN. *Glynn Co.*: St. Simons Island, 20 Aug 1951 JRH (TTRS). *Grady Co.*: Beachton, Sherwood Plantation, 3 Sept 1967 LNH (TTRS). *Baker Co.*: 14 Sept 1964 LN.

A colony was discovered several years ago near the summit of Kennesaw Mountain in Cobb County by Prof. P. W. Fattig. He observed female Giant Swallowtails ovipositing on Prickly-Ash (*Zanthoxylum*) and discovered caterpillars of various sizes on the leaves of the plants. The colony was still in existence in 1968 when I checked it.

A similar colony was found in the wooded area at the base of Stone Mountain by Lucien Harris III, in August, 1950, when we were collecting around the mountain. The females were ovipositing on Prickly-Ash growing in rather open deciduous woods.

On some of the coastal islands—such as St. Simons, Jekyll, and Tybee—and in south Georgia, the Giant Swallowtail becomes more in evidence in August and September, when it reaches its maximum buildup in numbers. It is never abundant, even in the southern part of the state.

The caterpillar—especially in Florida, where it is found on citrus trees—is known as the "orange dog." It is nearly 2½ inches long when fully grown. It is dark brown, with the posterior section yellow; in the middle of the body, there is a large yellow saddle-shaped spot formed by the union of two large, more or less triangular, lateral spots; a broad yellow stripe reaches from the head to above the last pair of true legs.

In Georgia, the larval food plants are Prickly-Ash (*Zanthoxylum americanium*) and Hercules Club (*Zanthoxylum clavahercules*). In September, 1960, J. C. Brooks saw females ovipositing on Prickly-Ash near Danville, Twiggs County.

Tiger Swallowtail. *Papilio glaucus* Linnaeus
(Page 113)

Distribution and Records: *P. glaucus* is common, but not abundant, throughout the state.

Mountain Region—*Murray Co.*: Old Fort Mountain, 28 Mar 1961 LHJ (TTRS). *Lumpkin Co.*: Auraria, 15 Apr 1967 BMR. *Banks Co.* and *Habersham Co.*: 30 June–1 Sept 1930 RWM (see Montgomery, 1931). *Fannin Co.*: Margret, 14 Aug 1963 LHJ (TTRS). *Rabun Co.*: LaPrades, 21 Sept 1967 LNH (TTRS).
Piedmont Region—*Monroe Co.*: Forsyth, 12 and 13 Mar 1955 FTN; Forsyth, 18 and 19 Mar 1957 FTN. *Fulton Co.*: Atlanta, 7 Apr 1961 LHJ (TTRS). *Bibb Co.*: Macon, 5 May 1966 FTN. *DeKalb Co.*: Avondale Estates, 17 June 1950 LHT (TTRS). *Fulton Co.*: Atlanta, Harris Trail, 22 Aug 1967 JMB; Atlanta, 31 Aug 1952 LHT (TTRS).
Coastal Region—*Grady Co.*: Beachton, Sherwood Plantation, 1 Jan 1965 LN; Beachton, Sherwood Plantation, 6 Jan 1965 LN. *Colquitt Co.*: Moultrie, 16 Mar 1945 HVAV (UWO); Moultrie, 9 Apr 1945 HVAV (UWO). *Grady Co.*: Beachton, Sherwood Plantation, 19 Apr 1965 LN. *Thomas Co.*: Boston, Bar-M Ranch, 2 Aug 1967 ESS (TTRS). *Grady Co.*: Beachton, Susina Plantation, 16 Sept 1965 LHJ (TTRS). *Charlton Co.*: Billy's Island, Okefenokee Swamp, sight record 21 Oct 1937 LHJ.

Although essentially a woodland species, this butterfly is quite a wanderer, and strays into fields, orchards, and gardens. It is attracted to flowers, damp spots, and wet areas along roads and paths. From spring until fall, this handsome butterfly is a frequent visitor to flower gardens and to flowering shrubs. It is very fond of the small, bell-shaped, pinkish flowers of *Abelia*, a genus of ornamental shrubs widely planted in the South. Many species of butterflies are attracted to *Abelia* flowers in the daytime, and moths, especially sphinx moths, visit the blossoms at night.

Early spring individuals of the Tiger Swallowtail are much smaller than the ones that emerge later. They first appear in quantity in south Georgia in March, although a few may appear earlier; in the Atlanta area and northward, the spring brood appears in April. A few individuals may appear much earlier during warm spells. As the season progresses, the emerging individuals are larger; in late summer, there are some specimens of very large size. In south Georgia, these individuals often are ochreous in color and represent the form *P. g. f. australis* Maynard, which occurs mainly in Florida.

The Tiger Swallowtail manifests a striking example of a type of dimorphism that is confined to one sex; in this species, the female is dimorphous, but only in part of the geographical area over which the butterfly is found. The species occurs from Canada to Florida; in the region north of lat. 40° N, roughly, the females are the yellow form; south of that latitude, a dark form replaces the yellow form to a large extent, but both forms occur. In the south, a female may lay several eggs, part of which will produce the yellow form and part the black form, both groups being of the same sex.

For the Bibb County area, Brooks estimated that, of the total number of females in the *P. glaucus* population that he observed, about 95% were the dark form, 3% the orange form *P. g. australis*, and 2% the yellow form. He further noted that *P. glaucus* was not usually common until about the 10th of August, but that it remained common through late September.

There are forms that appear to represent intergrades between the two commonest forms of the female, the yellow female and the dark female. Clark (1932) gave a detailed account of six of these forms. Each form was figured in the accompanying plates.

The same forms that he found in the District of Columbia

also occur in Georgia: specimens of these that I collected are now in the collection at Tall Timbers Research Station.

Clark (1932) also points out that there are three recognizable forms of the male, namely the usual clear light yellow males (which are the commonest), ochreous males (which are rather rare), and short-winged males (in which the outer and lower margins of the forewing are at right angles to each other, and the hindwings are usually broad).

Some very striking aberrations of *P. glaucus* have been taken. At least one example is known of a *P. glaucus* female that was a "split personality," being like the yellow form on the two wings on one side and like the dark form on the opposite two wings. This was first reported by Edwards (1868) who received it on September 1, 1868, from a young friend in Coalburgh, West Virginia (Brown, 1960).

The larva of the Tiger Swallowtail is about two inches long when fully grown. The body is a deep green. The rings of the body just back of the head are much swollen and, on top of the swollen part, there are two large circular marks that resemble eyes. When the caterpillar is at rest, it withdraws its head and holds up the front of the body in such a way that, when first seen, it gives the impression of being the head of a small snake. This may have some protective value in frightening enemies.

The larval food plants, according to L. P. Brower (1958), are a variety of trees and shrubs, including *Liriodendron* (Tulip Tree), *Populus* (Poplar), *Fraxinus* (Ash), and *Prunus* (Wild Cherry).

P. glaucus winters as a chrysalis, and the first butterflies emerge in March and April. They remain upon the wing for a few weeks. Eggs deposited by the females produce a summer brood; this brood, in turn, lays eggs that produce the generation that overwinters as chrysalids to emerge the following spring. There is some likelihood that there may be two summer broods in south Georgia.

The earliest known picture of an American butterfly is one of a Tiger Swallowtail. According to Dr. W. J. Holland, it is very likely that this picture was painted by John White, the commander of Sir Walter Raleigh's third expedition to "Virginia" in the year 1587. The original is in the collection of the British Museum (Holland, 1931, pp. 304–305).

Spice-Bush Swallowtail. *Papilio troilus* Linnaeus
(Page 113)

Distribution and Records: *P. troilus* is found throughout the state, and is one of our common swallowtails.

Mountain Region—*Lumpkin Co.*: Woody Gap, 16 Apr 1967 JCS and LHJ (TTRS). *Fannin Co.*: Margret, 16 Apr 1967 BMR. *Union Co.*: Blairsville, 27 June 1957 JCS (TTRS). *Banks Co.* and *Habersham Co.*: 13 July–7 Sept 1930 RWM (see Montgomery, 1931). *White Co.*: Unicoi Gap, 2 Aug 1957 LHJ (TTRS). *Fannin Co.*: Cooper Creek State Park (alt. 2947 ft), 14 Aug 1963 LHJ (TTRS).

Piedmont Region—*Monroe Co.*: Forsyth, 3 and 12 Mar 1955 FTN; Forsyth, 22 Mar 1956 FTN. *Bibb Co.*: Macon area, 5 May 1966 FTN. *Fulton Co.*: Atlanta area, 10 July 1965 LHJ.

Coastal Region—*Grady Co.*: Beachton, Sherwood Plantation, 4 Jan 1966 JN and LN. *Colquitt Co.*: Moultrie, 11–16 Feb 1945 HVAV (UWO). *Grady Co.*: Beachton, Susina Plantation, 2 Apr 1965 LHJ (TTRS). *Colquitt Co.*: Moultrie, 9 Apr 1945 HVAV (UWO). *Grady Co.*: Beachton, 6 June 1960 LHJ (TTRS); Beachton, Susina Plantation, 24 July 1965 LHJ. *Thomas Co.*: Boston, Bar-M Ranch, 24 July 1967 ESS (TTRS). *Glynn Co.*: St. Simons Island, 10 Aug 1955 JRH (TTRS)*; St. Simons Island, 10 Aug 1958 JRH (TTRS)*. *Grady Co.*: Beachton, Sherwood Plantation, 3 Sept 1967 LHJ (TTRS); Beachton, Sherwood Plantation, 26 Sept 1964 LN (TTRS); Beachton, Sherwood Plantation, 27 Sept 1964 LN (TTRS)*; Beachton, Sherwood Plantation, 15 Nov 1964 LN.

There are two broods, with a partial third brood. Further studies may show a full third brood on the Lower Coastal Plain.

Adults begin to appear as early as the latter part of January, in south Georgia, increasing in numbers in March and April. In middle Georgia, adults of the first brood emerge in March and April. In the Mountain Region, adults of the first brood appear in April and May.

The summer brood appears in July and August throughout the state, and adults may be seen as late as September in north Georgia and November in south Georgia.

The subspecies *P. t. ilioneus*, the type locality of which is Georgia, was named by J. E. Smith (1797) from a watercolor drawing by John Abbot that depicted the upper sides of two specimens of *P. troilus*. The one having enlarged, light, submarginal spots as one of its chief characteristics was *P. t. ilioneus*.

It should be borne in mind, however, that specimens of *P. t. ilioneus* represent only a small part of the *P. troilus* population in Georgia. They are usually found near the coast and in the southeastern part of the state, but they are infrequent to rare. In Florida, *P. t. ilioneus* is reported to be the dominant race (Kimball, 1965, p. 32).

In Georgia, the individuals of the spring brood of *P. t. troilus* are smaller than the individuals of the summer brood. There is very little variation among the spring brood adults, whereas a considerable amount of variation may be seen in a good series of specimens of the summer brood. For example, some males have black tails and some have green tails. On the latter, the green extends into the tail along one or both sides of the caudal vein. The green gives the appearance, in some specimens, of having been poured onto the tail like paint from the green crescent just above the tail. The amount of green in the tails varies.

Males of the closely related *P. palamedes* have a similar (but more pronounced) extension of yellow onto the tails from

* Records followed by an asterisk indicate specimens of *P. t. ilioneus*; all others are *P. t. troilus*.

the yellow crescent on the wings. Good examples are shown in the color plates of W. J. Holland (1931, pl. XLII) and A. B. Klots (1951, pl. 24). These variations were brought to my attention by Desmond Lanktree when he examined specimens from Georgia in the Hal and Ann Vogel collection at the University of Western Ontario.

Good examples of a male *P. palamedes* with black tails and a male *P. troilus* with green tails are shown by Clark and Clark (1951, pl. 22).

The larva of *P. troilus* is about two inches long when fully grown. It is dark green above and light green beneath. The body is enlarged at the third thoracic segment; the eyespots on this segment are light yellow with double "pupils," the upper one blue and the lower one black. Near the front edge of the first abdominal segment, there are a pair of pale yellow spots rimmed with black and with blue centers. The other abdominal segments each bear six blue oval dots edged with black.

The food plants are Spice-Bush (*Benzoin*), Sassafras (*Sassafras*), Sweet Bay (*Magnolia glauca*), Prickly-Ash (*Zanthoxylum*), Redbud (*Cercis canadensis*), and perhaps others.

Abbot (in Smith, 1797) wrote:

Its food is the sassafras, the caterpillar folding a leaf together for an habitation, and removing to a new one as the sustenance around is exhausted. The caterpillars exhale a remarkable scent whence they are sometimes called mellow-worms. Having changed in the beginning of October, they remained in the chrysalis state until the 10th of March. One of them in Virginia changed October 13th, and the fly did not come out until April 5th. This butterfly is frequent about blossoms in the spring, and as the weather grows hotter, resorts to wet places in court-yards, fords of rivulets, etc.

Palamedes Swallowtail. *Papilio palamedes* Drury
(Page 113)

Distribution and Records: *P. palamedes* is, for the most part, a

Coastal Region species, and is common at times along the coast and in the extreme southern portion of the state. It is infrequent to rare in central Georgia, and very rare in the upper Piedmont, being found there only as a stray.

Mountain Region—None.

Piedmont Region—*Fulton Co.*: Atlanta, Piedmont Road, sight record late Apr 1938 JCS; Atlanta, Northside Drive, sight record early May 1938 JCS. *Bibb Co.*: Macon area, 10 July 1956 FTN. *Monroe Co.*: Forsyth area, 13 July 1958 FTN; Forsyth area, 15 Aug 1957 FTN. *Bibb Co.*: Macon area, 3 Sept 1930 HFS (TTRS).

Coastal Region—*Charlton Co.*: Folkston area, 9 Feb 1952 LHJ (TTRS). *Colquitt Co.*: Moultrie, two males and one female 11–18 Mar 1945 HVAV (UWO). *Houston Co.*: Warner Robins, 29 Mar 1957 FTN. *Colquitt Co.*: Moultrie, three males 2–9 Apr 1945 HVAV (UWO). *Grady Co.*: Beachton, Susina Plantation, 12 Apr 1965 LHJ (TTRS). *Camden Co.*: Kingsland, Coleraine Plantation, 14 Apr 1952 LHJ (TTRS). *Glynn Co.*: St. Simons Island, 23 Apr 1959 LHJ (TTRS). *Grady Co.*: Beachton, Birdsong Plantation, 5 July 1957 LHJ (TTRS). *Glynn Co.*: Jekyll Island, 17–18 Aug 1960 JCS. *Lee Co.*: Leesburg, Leeland Farms, 25 Aug 1965 LN. *Grady Co.*: Beachton, Sherwood Plantation, 25 Sept 1964 LN. *Charlton Co.*: Okefenokee Swamp, sight record 21 Oct 1937 LHJ.

There are at least two broods. Adults may occasionally appear in February, but usually appear in March and April; they may be found as late as October and November in south Georgia. The individuals of the first brood to appear in spring are somewhat smaller in size than those of the later summer brood. *P. palamedes* is somewhat variable in its size and markings (see *P. troilus*, p. 166).

On April 14, 1952, I observed a small but noticeable flight of *P. palamedes* from southeast to northwest in Camden County. The location was a small elevation near the St. Mary's River on Coleraine Plantation, which, at that time, was owned by the Daniel V. Hebard family. Although it appeared to be a minor migration it was of special interest because, every other time I have sighted this butterfly, there have been only one or two individuals casually flying about.

An interesting observation was made by J. C. Brooks on the distribution of *P. palamedes* in Bibb County. He found that it occurred with greater frequency in the area of the county south of the fall line—in the northernmost part of the Coastal Region —than it did above the fall line—in the southernmost part of the Piedmont Region. Although such a distribution might be expected of a Coastal Region species, it is of interest, none-theless, that such a noticeable contrast between the two regions exists along the fall line in Bibb County.

The larva is pale velvety green with lighter green specks and markings. The last two thoracic and the first abdominal seg-ments are enlarged, giving a "humpbacked" appearance; the eyespots on the third segment are black, and have a glossy black "pupil" in a circle of orange.

The larval food plants are Red Bay (*Persea*), Sweet Bay (*Magnolia glauca*), and Sassafras (*Sassafras*). Brooks (1962, p. 198) states:

For several years I have been trying to rear *Papilio palamedes*. Klots (1951) stated the foods as *Persea borbonia*, *Magnolia glauca* (now *virginiana*), and *Sassafras albidum*. I tried *Sassafras* and *Magnolia* but without results—the females refused to oviposit After a visit to the Georgia coast where I found *palamedes* abundant, I decided to try again. This time I used *Persea* which was very fresh. About 5,000 eggs were secured. Since *Persea* is in poor condition when *palamedes* is common in central Georgia, I decided to try the larvae on fresh *Magnolia* and tender *Sassafras* and found the following to also be acceptable; avacado [*Persea americana*], *Glabraria aestivalis*, *Nectandra* sp. and *Misanteca* sp. It appears that *palamedes* feeds only on Lauraceae and that the females in a certain area are more addicted to one foodplant than the other; the larvae seem to be less sensitive. This is the opposite of [*P.*] *glaucus* which oviposits on peach but whose larvae will not accept it.

Genus *Graphium*

Kite Swallowtail; Zebra Swallowtail. *Graphium marcellus*
Cramer (Page 111)

Distribution and Records: *G. marcellus* is abundant over the entire state.

Mountain Region—*Lumpkin Co.*: Auraria, 15 Apr 1967 BMR; Auraria, 15 Apr 1967 LHJ (TTRS). *Murray Co.*: Old Fort Mountain, 16 May 1950 LHJ (TTRS).

Piedmont Region—*Bibb Co.*: Macon, 13 Feb 1961 FTN. *Monroe Co.*: Forsyth, 2 Mar 1957 FTN; Forsyth, 27 Mar 1963 FTN. *Fulton Co.*: Atlanta, 30 Mar 1957 LHJ (TTRS). *Monroe Co.*: Forsyth, 31 Mar 1957 FTN. *Fulton Co.*: Atlanta, 27 Apr 1957 LHJ (TTRS). *Bibb Co.*: Macon, 5 May 1966 FTN. *Coweta Co.*: Madras, 27 May 1950 MES. *Fulton Co.*: Atlanta, 30 May 1958 LHJ (TTRS).

Coastal Region—*Grady Co.*: Beachton, Sherwood Plantation, 28 Feb 1965 LN. *Colquitt Co.*: Moultrie, ten specimens 12–24 Mar 1945 HVAV (UWO). *Grady Co.*: Beachton, Birdsong Plantation, 19 Mar 1952 EVK (TTRS). *Thomas Co.*: Thomasville, Millpond Plantation, 16 and 19 Apr 1967 ESS. *Grady Co.*: Beachton, Susina Plantation, 20 July 1963 LHJ (TTRS). *Thomas Co.*: Boston, Bar-M Ranch, 8 and 10 Aug 1967 ESS. *Charlton Co.*: Billy's Island, Okefenokee Swamp, sight record 21 Oct 1937 LHJ.

There are three seasonal forms in Georgia. The early spring form, generally known as *G. marcellus* f. *marcellus*, often appears as early as February in extreme south Georgia; it appears progressively later in the middle and northern portions of the state. The early spring individuals are the smallest in size. The red spot at the anal angle of the hindwing is large. The tail is rather short and has a white tip.

The late spring form, *G. marcellus* f. *telamonides*, may appear in late April and May in south Georgia; in north Georgia, it flies in May and June. The individuals of this form are larger. The wings are somewhat longer and the black markings are slightly more extensive. The red spot on the hindwing is smaller. The tails are longer and the outer portion is bordered with white, which extends more than halfway to the base.

The summer form, *G. marcellus* f. *lecontei*, flies from early July to late October. The individuals are larger than those of the preceding forms. The tails are much longer and the white margin extends almost to the base. The red spot at the anal angle of the hindwing is small. The dark markings of the wings are extended and the outer half of the hind wings are mostly black.

The flight of the Zebra Swallowtail is swift—especially that of the early spring form, which flies through the woods when few flowers are in bloom. The flight of the summer form is less hurried; it is often difficult to catch perfect specimens, however, because the insect is wary and not easy to net. The long tails are fragile and will break in the net unless carefully handled.

J. C. Brooks reported from Macon that butterflies of the spring brood are much more common there, appearing about February 2, and that those of the fall brood are next in abundance. He captured an aberration of the spring form on April 13, 1957, at Warner Robins (near Macon) in which the black was replaced by rusty brown.

One of my very pleasant recollections is of a day spent afield with Fred Naumann, during which he showed me how to identify Papaw (*Asimina triloba*), the food plant of the Zebra Swallowtail, and how to find the eggs and caterpillars of the species. He also showed me the fruit of the Papaw, which resembles miniature bananas and has a fairly pleasant taste.

Abbot (in Smith, 1797) wrote: "The caterpillar feeds on the highland as well as the swamp pawpaw; and having tied itself up the 22nd of May, changed to a chrysalis on the 24th. The fly came out June 16th."

The larva is about two inches long before pupation. It is

largest at the third thoracic segment, which is made conspicuous by a wide, black, velvety band edged with yellow. The rest of the body is pea green, with narrow cross bands of yellow and black.

Family PIERIDAE—Whites and Sulphurs

Genus *Pieris*

Checkered White. *Pieris protodice protodice*
Boisduval and LeConte (Page 115)

Distribution and Records: Although somewhat rare and local, the Checkered White is found throughout the state.

Mountain Region—*Banks Co.* and *Habersham Co.*: 24–30 Aug 1930 RWM (see Montgomery, 1931).
Piedmont Region—*Bibb Co.*: Macon, 29 May 1926 HFS (TTRS). *Fulton Co.*: Atlanta, 23 June 1958 LHJ (TTRS). *Monroe Co.*: Forsyth, 23 and 30 June 1961 FTN. *Fulton Co.*: Roswell, Wayt's Farm, 25 July 1964 LHJ (TTRS). *Butts Co.*: Jenkinsburg, 25 July 1967 LHJ (TTRS).
Coastal Region—*Chatham Co.*: Savannah, several specimens (no dates) MHM (CU). *Sumter Co.*: Americus, 1 Aug 1965 JN. *Thomas Co.*: Thomasville, Greenwood Plantation, 28 Sept 1964 LN.

The spring form, *P. p. protodice* f. *vernalis* Edwards, appears in March and April. It is followed by the summer brood in late May, June, and July, which is followed in turn by a late summer or fall brood in August and September.

J. C. Brooks found it locally common in Bibb County in March and April and again in August. Fred Naumann found it in Monroe County in June. J. P. Knudsen (1954a) recorded it as "casual" in the vicinity of Oglethorpe College near Atlanta. He saw one flying along the edge of the campus at Peachtree Road.

Several were observed by John Symmes and me in a field on the John A. Wayt farm, near Roswell (Fulton County), and a

173

specimen was collected. In south Georgia, several specimens were collected by Mrs. Leon Neel on August 1, 1965. She discovered them in a field near Americus, in Sumter County.

Also in south Georgia, on Greenwood Plantation, near Thomasville (Thomas County), Leon Neel collected a specimen of the Checkered White on September 28, 1964. A number of specimens of this butterfly collected by M. H. Mead in Savannah (Chatham County) are now in the collection at Cornell University.

The larva is about one inch long and downy with alternate yellow and greenish purple stripes running lengthwise along the body. The larval food plants are various members of the family Cruciferae, including cabbage, mustard, turnips, and wild peppergrass (*Lepidium*).

Virginia White; West Virginia White. *Pieris virginiensis*
Edwards (Page 115)

Distribution and Records: *P. virginiensis* is rare and has eluded Georgia collectors until recent years. It inhabits the deciduous woods of the Transition Zone where its food plant, Toothwort (*Dentaria diphylla*), is found.

Mountain Region—*Murray Co.*: Old Fort Mountain, 26 Mar 1961 JCS; Old Fort Mountain, 9 Apr 1961 JCS (TTRS). *Rabun Co.*: Rabun Bald, 15 May 1962 JCBS; Bee Gum Gap, 15 May 1962 JCBS.
Piedmont Region—None.
Coastal Region—None.

I had the pleasure of being with John Symmes when he discovered and caught the first Georgia specimen of this species on March 26, 1961, on Old Fort Mountain, near Chatsworth. Symmes collected a few strays that seemed to be either seeking mates or in search of the food plant. We hoped to find a colony somewhere in the area but were unsuccessful in our search for it. We had been alerted to the possibility of its presence by Dr.

W. J. Reinthal of Knoxville; he had already taken *P. virginiensis* in the Great Smoky Mountains of Tennessee and North Carolina.

In the spring of 1962, James C. Brooks went on a field trip in Rabun County with a botany class. His most surprising find was not a plant but a butterfly: he collected a series of butterflies that he first thought were *P. napi*; later, they proved to be *P. virginiensis*. He found most of them in Rabun County near Rabun Bald along a wet mountain road in fairly dense woods. The butterflies were alighting or resting on the leaves of *Kalmia latifolia* as moving clouds alternately revealed and obscured the sun. None were on flowers—in fact, very few flowers were in bloom. Luckily, he had found a well-established colony, as the butterflies were common in this particular area.

In another location, near Bee Gum Gap (near or just over the Georgia–North Carolina boundary), he collected a few additional specimens of *P. virginiensis*.

Mather (1964) reviewed the published data on the southern limits of the range of *P. napi* and *P. virginiensis*, and concluded (p. 47) that the "southern limit of the range of *virginiensis* appears to be reached in the Appalachian Mountains of West Tennessee and eastern North Carolina." Thus, its discovery in Georgia at three localities is a major extension of the known range.

The larva of this butterfly has been described as dark yellowish green with a narrow dorsal stripe and a pair of lateral green stripes.

European Cabbage Butterfly. *Pieris rapae* Linnaeus
(Page 115)

Distribution and Records: *P. rapae* is a common species that is found throughout the state. It was introduced into North America about 1860 in Quebec and by 1868 it had spread into the state of New York. It has spread over most of the continent since that time.

Mountain Region—*Lumpkin Co.*: Auraria, 15 Apr 1967 JCS. *White Co.*: Helen, 25 July 1951 JRH (TTRS). *Rabun Co.*: LaPrades, Lake Burton, 25 Aug 1949 LHJ (TTRS). *Banks Co.* and *Habersham Co.*: 26 May–30 Aug 1930 RWM (See Montgomery, 1931).

Piedmont Region—*Fulton Co.*: Atlanta, 9 Mar 1937 LHJ (TTRS). *Monroe Co.*: Forsyth, 23 Mar 1956 FTN. *DeKalb Co.*: Avondale Estates, 24 Mar 1950 LHJ (TTRS). *Clarke Co.*: Athens, Mar and May 1967 LRT; Athens, July 1966 LRT. *DeKalb Co.*: Avondale Estates, 21 July 1960 LHJ (TTRS).

Coastal Region—*Grady Co.*: Melton Place, 6 Jan 1965 LN. *Screven Co.*: Sylvania, Mar–Sept 1946 OB (AMNH). *Baker Co.*: Newton, Blue Springs Plantation, 14 Aug 1964 LN. *Grady Co.*: Beachton, Sherwood Plantation, 19 and 25 Sept 1964 LN (TTRS). *Thomas Co.*: Thomasville, Greenwood Plantation, 28 Sept 1964 LN (TTRS). *Grady Co.*: Beachton, Sherwood Plantation, 11 Nov 1964 LN. *Chatham Co.*: Savannah, no dates MHM (CU).

There are several broods each year. The butterflies of the early spring brood, which are from overwintering chrysalids, are smaller and of a duller white than the butterflies of the summer broods. Occasionally, individuals may be found with the black spots and other dark markings greatly reduced.

A detailed study of the effect of certain environmental factors and chemicals on the markings of *P. rapae* has been made by John M. Kolyer (1966). His studies of the factors that produce brown pupae instead of green ones show that larvae reared in darkness produce only brown pupae. He found that a reduced temperature, in conjunction with darkness, caused reduced intensity of markings in about one of every four butterflies. This suggests that the lighter markings of the spring brood are the result of similar conditions in a natural situation. He found that darkness alone, at normal summer temperatures, had no effect on the markings.

The larva, about one inch long when mature, are green in color, with a yellowish stripe down the back and on each side. The larval food plants are members of the family Cruciferae, including cabbage, collards, mustard greens, and a variety of related plants. The larvae may, at times, become a pest on these plants in gardens and on farms.

Genus *Ascia*

Great Southern White. *Ascia monuste phileta* Fabricius
(Page 115)

Distribution and Records: *A. m. phileta* is found in the Coastal Region of Georgia. Although it is fairly common at times, especially near or on the coast and coastal islands, it is very sporadic in occurrence. Further inland, it becomes infrequent to very rare; it is of sporadic occurrence in the area near Macon, being found mainly in the fall as a stray.

Mountain Region—None.
Piedmont Region—*Bibb Co.*: Macon area, fall strays reported by JCBS.
Coastal Region—*Screven Co.*: several specimens Mar–Sept 1946 OB (AMNH). *Glynn Co.*: St. Simons Island, migration observed Apr 1936 LHJ. *Chatham Co.*: Savannah, 28 May 1960 LHJ (TTRS); Savannah, dark female (no date) MHM (CU).

John Abbot's drawing, figured by Boisduval and LeConte (1829–1833, pl. 16) as *A. m. cleomes*, delineates the upper and lower sides of a male, the upper side of a female, a larva, and a pupa. The slightly wider and continuous black border on the forewings of the male and female are the principal features of this illustration that differ from *A. m. phileta*.

The Great Southern White is variable, and it is possible that Abbot may have figured a heavily marked individual; or, as Klots (1951, p. 203) has pointed out, *A. m. cleomes* may possibly have been "a now extinct or diluted subspecies of the coastal plain from Georgia northward. The variability and migratory habits make definite subspecific divisions very difficult."

The Great Southern White has two female forms, the

"normal" form (white), and the melanic form (dark). The dark female was thought to be the "migratory" form. Now, through studies and experiments made by Roger W. Pease, Jr. (1962), it has been learned that the capacity to produce melanic females is conferred by a gene or genes, and that exposure to light for a sufficient length of time is one factor that stimulates dimorphism.

Pease conducted a carefully controlled experiment on a group of individuals for the duration of the full life cycle in which he found that exposure to sixteen hours of light and eight hours of dark resulted in all females being melanic (nine were black, five were gray, and three were light gray) and all males being white. In a group that received eight hours of light and sixteen hours of dark, all of the females (sixteen individuals) were white, as were all of the males.

Pease reported that white females are the only type found in Florida from November through February. A sample of ninety-nine females taken by Thomas Pliske at Jupiter Island, Florida, on July 30, 1961, included fifty-six melanics, thirty-three intermediates, and ten whites. It would be interesting to make a similar count of a sizable Georgia catch and compare the results.

In April, 1936, I saw a small migration in progress on St. Simons Island. The butterflies were flying low in a northwesterly direction across a golf course. Although they were widely spaced, there were always several individuals in sight at a time.

Years ago, a large migration was witnessed by Dr. Mellichamp at Bluffton, South Carolina. His account was recorded by Comstock and Comstock (1920, pp. 72–73). He saw thousands of these butterflies passing over Bluffton from west to east, apparently against the wind, for two days. Being white, they could be easily seen flying along in twos, threes, and fours—sometimes in greater numbers—seldom stopping, flying steadily fifteen or twenty feet above the earth.

In 1952, Mr. and Mrs. Bryant Mather witnessed a migration along the gulf coast of Mississippi. Mather (1953) related that a few specimens were observed flying from west to east on June 13 and 14. Then, on Sunday morning, June 15, from 10 A.M. to 11 A.M., the Mathers watched them passing in a more or less steady stream. The direction of movement was strikingly constant and precisely parallel to the highway, US 90. They passed at an average of one per minute and travelled at an estimated speed of 8 to 10 miles per hour.

The larva is about 1.5 inches long. The general color varies from lemon yellow, through true yellow, to straw color; there are several lateral stripes or bands ranging from purplish green to dark gray. The larval food plants are various members of the families Cruciferae and Capparidaceae, including native and cultivated species both. Among the cultivated crucifers that are eaten by the larvae are cabbage, kale, turnips, and broccoli.

Genus *Colias*

Orange Clover Butterfly; Orange Alfalfa Butterfly.
Colias (Colias) eurytheme Boisduval (Page 115)

Distribution and Records: *C. eurytheme* is common over most of the state; in the southernmost areas it becomes very local. It prefers open areas, especially fields and roadsides with growths of its food plants, clover, vetch, and alfalfa.

Mountain Region—*Lumpkin Co.*: Auraria, 15 Apr 1967 LHJ. *Union Co.*: Suches, 15 Apr 1967 BMR. *Towns Co.*: Brasstown Bald (alt. 4500 ft), 8 June 1967 LNH. *White Co.*: Helen, 15 June 1952 JRH (TTRS). *Banks Co.*: 21 June 1930 RWM (see Montgomery, 1931). *Habersham Co.*: 7 Sept 1930 RWM (see Montgomery, 1931).
Piedmont Region—*Coweta Co.*: Madras, 26 Jan 1950 MES; Madras, 25 Feb 1951 MES. *Clarke Co.*: Athens, Apr 1967 LRT. *Fulton Co.*: Atlanta, 6 June 1957 LHJ (TTRS). *Clarke Co.*: Athens, July 1966 LRT. *Fulton Co.*: Atlanta, 23 Sept

1949 LHT (TTRS). *Coweta Co.*: Madras, 13 Oct 1950 MES. *Clarke Co.*: Athens, Nov 1966 LRT.

Coastal Region—*Grady Co.*: Beachton, Susina Plantation, 7 Jan 1965 LHJ (TTRS). *Colquitt Co.*: Moultrie, 1, 2, and 10 Apr 1945 HVAV (UWO). *Glynn Co.*: St. Simons Island, 23 Apr 1954 LNH (TTRS). *Grady Co.*: Beachton, Sherwood Plantation, 21 May 1951 LHJ (TTRS); Beachton, Birdsong Plantation 6 June 1960 LHJ (TTRS); Beachton, Sherwood Plantation, 24 Oct 1964 LN. *Baker Co.*: Newton, Blue Springs Plantation, 10 Nov 1964 LN.

This is a variable species and a number of seasonal and varietal names have been given to it.

The spring form usually flies in March and April, but may appear earlier in the year on warm days. There are two female forms, the typical orange-yellow one and the white form *C. eurytheme* female form *alba* Strecker.

The summer form is much larger in size and with a deeper orange coloration. It, also, has two female forms, the normal orange one and the white form. The summer form appears in south Georgia in the latter half of June and in the remainder of the state from the end of June through the summer.

A number of studies have been made to determine some of the factors that produce variations. For example, the width of the black borders on the wings of male *C. eurytheme* were studied by S. Albert Ae (1957), who found that those of male butterflies reared in a ten-hour period of daily light were much narrower than those of males reared in a fourteen-hour period of daily light. The females, similarly exposed, did not show such a difference.

Klots (1951) gave a brief but excellent account of *C. eurytheme* and its close relationship to *C. philodice.*

In south Georgia, Leon Neel found *C. eurytheme* in some numbers on Sherwood Plantation (Grady County) between October 24 and November 10, 1964. His specimens included some with variations that seemed to indicate some previous hybridization with *C. philodice*, which he also collected in the same general area on Sherwood Plantation.

On Susina Plantation, which is about three miles from Sherwood Plantation, Mrs. Harris and I observed a fresh hatching of hundreds of *C. eurytheme* concentrated in a large field near the plantation's Alligator Pond. In a few days, most of these had disappeared. Very few were observed elsewhere in the vicinity of the field or in other fields on the plantation.

In the Macon area of middle Georgia, J. C. Brooks found it common in March and April and fairly common in July and August. At Oglethorpe College in the Atlanta area, J. P. Knudsen (1954a) recorded it as "common, March–November. Spring broods are yellow flushed with orange. Summer broods are orange. Albino females are fairly common especially in summer."

In the mountain valleys of north Georgia, the flight periods begin two or three weeks later than in south Georgia and continue into September.

The larva is about one and one-fourth inches long. It is grass green in color, with an indistinct line down the back, and a white stripe, edged with black below, along each side.

Yellow Clover Butterfly; Clouded Sulphur.
Colias (Colias) philodice Godart (Page 115)

Distribution and Records: *C. philodice* is usually infrequent to rare over most of the state, but a few active, local colonies have been found with sizable populations. More collecting is needed to fill in the gaps in our present records so that its local distribution and the months in which it flies may be more definitely ascertained.

Mountain Region—None.
Piedmont Region—*Bibb Co.*: Macon, 1 Mar 1959 JCBS; Macon, 12 Mar 1962 JCBS; Macon, 12 Apr 1961 JCBS. *Clarke Co.*:

181

Athens, May 1967 LRT. *Fulton Co.*: Atlanta, 23 Sept 1949 LHT (TTRS).

Coastal Region—*Grady Co.*: Beachton, Sherwood Plantation, 26 Oct 1964 LN (TTRS); Beachton, Sherwood Plantation, 1 Nov 1964 LN. *Baker Co.*: Newton, Blue Springs Plantation, 10 Nov 1964 LN (TTRS).

In the Macon area, J. C. Brooks collected specimens in March and April. He collected a white female on March 12, 1962.

In Grady county, which borders on Florida, Leon Neel found an active colony of this butterfly on Sherwood Plantation. He also collected it in Baker County which is about forty miles northwest of Grady County.

It is worth noting that *C. philodice* has not been recorded from Coweta County, Monroe County, or the Oglethorpe College campus by the three excellent collectors in those areas.

The larva is green with faint stripe down the back and a pale whitish or pinkish stripe along the side. In some individuals, the body may be pale yellowish along the sides. The larval food plants are clover, vetch, alfalfa, lupine, and other legumes.

Dog-Face. *Colias* (*Zerene*) *cesonia* Stoll (Page 127)

Distribution and Records: *C. cesonia*, the type locality of which is Georgia, is found throughout the state. It is a common species in south Georgia; in the Piedmont and Mountain regions it is local and rare.

Mountain Region—*Murray Co.*: Old Fort Mountain, 25 Aug 1953 JPK.

Piedmont Region—*Bibb Co.*: Macon, 4 Mar 1961 FTN; Macon, 24 Mar 1957 FTN. *Coweta Co.*: Madras, 1 Apr 1951 MES. *DeKalb Co.*: Stone Mountain, 19 Apr 1955 LHJ (TTRS). *Coweta Co.*: Madras, 22 Apr 1950 MES. *Fulton Co.*: Oglethorpe College, Sept 1953 JPK (see Knudsen, 1954a).

Coastal Region—*Thomas Co.*: Thomasville, Millpond Plantation, 22 Feb 1967 ESS. *Colquitt Co.*: Moultrie, eleven specimens 3 Mar–14 Apr 1945 HVAV (UWO). *Grady Co.*: Beachton,

Susina Plantation, 10 Mar 1964 LHJ (TTRS). *Screven Co.*: Sylvania area, 1, 5, and 12 Apr 1946 OB (AMNH)*. *Thomas Co.*: Thomasville, Greenwood Plantation, 2 June 1954 EVK (TTRS). *Screven Co.*: Millhaven, 25 May 1968 BMR and WB. *Grady Co.*: Beachton, Sherwood Plantation, 10 July 1944 LHJ (TTRS). *Thomas Co.*: Boston, Bar-M Ranch, 15 July 1967 ESS (TTRS). *Grady Co.*: Beachton, Susina Plantation, 20 July 1963 LNH (TTRS); Beachton, Birdsong Plantation, 15 Aug 1949 LHJ (TTRS).

This butterfly prefers the open woodlands, and I have observed that it may be locally common in one area and very rare in an adjacent area. On a plantation in Grady County, it is common on a section containing nearly one thousand acres between two paved highways, but is rare in similar areas beyond the highways. An abundance of the food plant in the first area seems to be the reason for this type of distribution.

There are three broods. Adults sometimes emerge during warm days in winter in the southernmost parts of the state. The form "rosa," with pink shading on the underside, is the cold-weather form.

In the Macon area, in 1962, the Dog-Face began to emerge in late February and continued through March, becoming locally common. The form *C. cesonia* f. *rosa* M'Neill was prevalent in this brood. The following September, there was another brood flying, which was the normal form of the species. J. C. Brooks observed that the Dog-Face occurs in hot, dry, scrub-oak groves in sandy areas in the southern portions of Bibb and Crawford counties.

In the Oglethorpe College area, near Atlanta, it was reported by J. P. Knudsen (1954a) as infrequent. He captured one specimen and saw another in September of 1953.

Knudsen found a number of specimens on Old Fort Mountain, near Chatsworth (Murray County), on August 25, 1953.

* Buchholz reported that he collected three specimens of *C. cesonia* f. *rosa*, one on each of the dates listed.

There was a very large and rather dark female of the form *C. cesonia* f. *rosa* in the group of specimens he collected.

The larva is green and thickly covered with small, black, hair-bearing tubercles; its markings are variable, according to Klots (1951, p. 189). The larval food plants are False Indigo (*Amorpha fruticosa*) and Clover (*Trifolium*).

Genus *Phoebis*

Cloudless Sulphur. *Phoebis sennae eubule* Linnaeus
(Page 115)

Distribution and Records: *P. s. eubule* is found throughout the state.

Mountain Region—*Banks Co.* and *Habersham Co.*: 25 Aug and 1 Sept 1930 RWM (see Montgomery, 1931).
Piedmont Region—*Monroe Co.*: Forsyth, 19 Mar 1957 FTN; Forsyth, 2 Apr 1956 FTN. *Fulton Co.*: Atlanta, Harris Trail, 22 Aug 1967 LHJ.
Coastal Region—*Grady Co.*: Beachton, Susina Plantation, 2 Jan 1965 LHJ (TTRS); Beachton, Susina Plantation, 19 Jan 1968 LHJ (TTRS). *Charlton Co.*: Folkston, 9 Feb 1952 LHJ (TTRS). *Colquitt Co.*: Moultrie, eight specimens 12–24 Mar 1945 HVAV (UWO). *Grady Co.*: Beachton, Birdsong Plantation, 19 Mar 1952 LHJ (TTRS). *Colquitt Co.*: Moultrie, 9 Apr 1945 HVAV (UWO). *Thomas Co.*: Boston, Bar-M Ranch, 22, 28, and 30 July 1967 ESS; Boston, Bar-M Ranch, 4 and 10 Aug 1967 ESS (TTRS). *Grady Co.*: Beachton, Susina Plantation, 7 Sept 1963 LNH (TTRS). *Charlton Co.*: Billy's Island, Okefenokee Swamp, 21 Oct 1937 LHJ. *Baker Co.*: Newton, Blue Springs Plantation, 13 Nov 1964 LN.

The Cloudless Sulphur is a common butterfly and is easily distinguished by its large size, yellow color, and rapid flight. It usually becomes abundant in August, continuing into the fall months, at which time it becomes migratory, with individuals flying steadily on a course generally southeast toward Florida. The bright yellow wings of this strong flier make it easy to see and to follow its flight.

The annual fall migration of he Cloudless Sulphur in Georgia coincides with that of the Monarch. Whether or not there is a spring migration of the Cloudless Sulphur is not known.

The larva is pale yellowish green, with a yellowish stripe along each side. The segments are dotted with black in crosswise rows.

The larval food plant is Senna (*Cassia*), of which there are several species; Clover has also been reported as a food plant. Smith's (1797) observations about the colors of the flowers of *Cassia* and those of *P. s. eubule* are of interest:

It is curious to observe the conformity of colours between the flowers of this plant and the fly bred upon it. We shall have occasion to note other instances of the same kind, and there are many of them throughout nature. In some cases those resemblances seem to answer the purpose of protection; as when a chrysalis resembles the back to which it is fixed; or a caterpillar the flower or leaf it feeds upon; but that purpose seems not to be answered here.

Do such similarities of appearance, in serving to exercise the attention of discrimination of animals destined to devour the fly, or of others that feed upon the flower, thus increase the general sum of happiness in consequence of the employment of intellect and the success of its exertion?

Orange-barred Sulphur; Red-barred Sulphur. *Phoebis philea* Johansson (Page 121)

Distribution and Records: *P. philea* is a casual visitor in the Coastal Region. Sometimes a female will pause in an area long enough to establish a temporary local colony.

Mountain Region—None.
Piedmont Region—*Bibb Co.*: Macon, Sept 1957 JCBS. *Monroe Co.*: Forsyth, 28 Oct 1957 FTN; Forsyth, 14 Nov 1957 FTN.
Coastal Region—*Houston Co.*: Perry, 30 Sept 1930 HFS (TTRS). *Macon Co.*: Montezuma, 30 Sept 1930 HFS (EUM); Montezuma, 1 and 6 Oct 1930 LHJ (EUM). *Decatur Co.*: Bainbridge, 15 Nov 1930 LHJ (EUM).

I first found a colony of this beautiful sulphur on September 30, 1930, in the city of Montezuma, about fifty miles south of Macon. Females were ovipositing on a species of *Cassia* that had been planted as an ornamental shrub. An examination of the plant revealed caterpillars in all stages of development and a number of chrysalids. *P. philea* continued to be fairly common in Montezuma through November of that year.

Colonies were also found in several other places, including Thomasville, Bainbridge, and Augusta—adults were seen flying around *Cassia* plants in these cities—but none of these colonies became permanently established.

In the Macon area, J. C. Brooks found that, although *P. philea* is not common, a few can usually be observed during the fall months, mainly in November. In September, 1957, he found a number of them in an old corn field near Warner Robins, Houston County. The females were laying their eggs on *Cassia* growing in the field among the fallen corn stalks.

The larva is yellowish green (darker dorsally), transversely wrinkled, and strongly tapered at each end. There are numerous fine, black granulations bearing small, shiny, black spines. Each side of the larva has a narrow blackish or reddish black band with a wider yellow band below it that contains reddish black spots, each ringed with a whitish area.

Statira Sulphur. *Phoebis statira floridensis* Neumoegen
(Page 115)

Distribution and Records: The type locality of *P. s. floridensis* is the Upper Indian River in Florida. There is but a single record of this species in Georgia: James C. Brooks captured a specimen in Waycross, Ware County, on August 12, 1960.

At times, Brooks has found it locally common in Florida, in late summer, as far north as Jacksonville. Kimball (1965) noted that it seems to be spreading northward and cites evidence to this effect.

This rare sulphur is about the same size as the common Cloudless Sulphur, and the two are difficult to distinguish in flight. The males of *P. s. floridensis* have a wide, satiny border that is lighter than the yellow of the inner portion of the wings.

The larval food plants are *Dalbergia ecastophyllum* and *Calliandra* (Kimball, 1965, p. 35).

Genus *Eurema*

Barred Sulphur; Fairy Yellow. *Eurema daira daira* Godart
(Page 115)

Distribution and Records: *E. d. daira* is common on the Coastal Plain, locally common in mid-Georgia in the Macon area, infrequent and very local in the Atlanta area of the Piedmont Region, and rare or absent in the northern portion of the state.

Mountain Region—*Rabun Co.*: Lake Rabun, July 1927 AGR (see Richards, 1931, p. 232).

Piedmont Region—*Coweta Co.*: Madras, 8 Apr 1950 MES; Madras, 15 Apr 1949 MES. *Fulton Co.*: Atlanta, Oglethorpe College, June–Oct JPK (see Knudsen, 1954a). *Clarke Co.*: Athens, Aug 1966 LRT. *Monroe Co.*: Forsyth, 27 Aug 1956 FTN. *Bibb Co.*: Macon, 3 Sept 1953 LHJ (TTRS). *Fulton Co.*: Atlanta, Buckhead area, 20 Sept 1949 LHT (TTRS); Atlanta, Morningside area, 19 Oct 1926 FTN (TTRS)*.

Coastal Region—*Charlton Co.*: Folkston, 9 Feb 1952 LHJ (TTRS). *Grady Co.*: Beachton, Susina Plantation, 10 Mar 1964 LHJ (TTRS). *Colquitt Co.*: Moultrie, 11 Mar 1945 HVAV (UWO); Moultrie, 21 Apr 1945 HVAV (UWO). *Thomas Co.*: Thomasville, Greenwood Plantation, 16 May 1953 LHJ (TTRS). *Grady Co.*: Beachton, Susina Plantation, 10 June 1964 LHJ (TTRS). *Thomas Co.*: Thomasville, Greenwood Plantation, 8 July 1957 LHJ (TTRS). *Grady Co.*: Beachton, Susina Plantation, 8 Aug 1963 LNH (TTRS); Beachton, Susina Plantation, 27 Aug 1967 LNH (TTRS); Beachton, Birdsong Plantation, 2 Sept 1956 LHJ (TTRS); Beachton, Birdsong Plantation, 3 Dec 1952 EVK (TTRS).

* This is the type specimen of *E. d. daira* ab. *fusca*.

E. d. daira has distinct seasonal forms which are as follows: (1) the winter form, *E. d. daira* f. *daira*, with the under side of hindwings dark, tan, or pinkish, and the upper side of the hindwing with a partial black border; (2) the summer form, *E. d. daira* f. *jucunda*, with the underside of hindwings white or whitish and the upper side of the hindwing with extensive black borders; and (3) the spring and fall form, *E. d. daira* f. *delioides*, intermediate between the winter and summer forms. Although these forms were once thought to be more than one species, there now seems to be little doubt that they are simply distinct forms of the same subspecies.

The aberration *E. d. daira* ab. *fusca* was described (Harris, 1931) from a melanic female of the summer form collected by Fred T. Naumann in Atlanta on October 19, 1926. The original description, with a photograph of the type specimen, stated:

The photograph has intensified and brought out almost microscopically tiny black markings that do not appear (so clearly) on the butterfly. The butterfly itself has no markings and is an almost uniform mouse brown on both the upper and lower surfaces of the wings. For this aberrant form I propose the name "fusca."

The type is now in the collection at the Tall Timbers Research Station.

The albino female form, *E. d. daira* female form *pallidula*, was described by Klots. A female was taken in the Oconee Hill Cemetery at Athens by A. G. Richards (1931). He wrote:

A very light female very close to form female *pallidula* Klots taken in the Cemetery 9-VIII-26 (this form was described from Guatemala and Mexico, and has not yet been reported from the U.S. to my knowledge), and several slightly washed females of scattered dates are intermediate.

In south Georgia, the winter form can be found sparingly throughout the winter months, as the seasonal temperature there is milder than that of north Georgia. The population gradually increases through the spring months and the spring and summer forms become successively common.

Mather (1956) has made a detailed study of the relationships of the various forms of *E. d. daira* to the changes in the seasonal temperatures in Mississippi.

In the Macon area J. C. Brooks found *E. d. daira* locally common around such grassy areas as golf courses and cemeteries but keeping more to the woods bordering those areas, while the summer form, during its period of flight, was more often found in the open areas.

The body of the larva is light green above and semitransparent green below, with a pale stripe along the sides separating the two green shades. The body is cross-corrugated and dotted with minute white spots. There is an indistinct, darker mid-dorsal line. The larval food plants are Joint Vetch (*Aeschynomene viscidula*), Pencil Flower (*Stylosanthes biflora*), and perhaps other leguminous plants.

The life history has been described by J. R. Haskin (1933, pp. 153–156). Abbot's drawing of the larva, pupa, and adults was reproduced by Boisduval and LeConte (1829–1833, pl. 19).

Little Sulphur. *Eurema lisa* Boisduval and LeConte
(Page 115)

Distribution and Records: *E. lisa* is one of our very abundant butterflies and is found throughout the state.

Mountain Region—*Banks Co.* and *Habersham Co.*: common 21 July–7 Sept 1930 (see Montgomery, 1931). *Towns Co.*: Brasstown Bald, 29 July 1954 LHJ (TTRS).
Piedmont Region—*Coweta Co.*: Madras, 11 June 1951 MES. *Fulton Co.*: Atlanta, Buckhead area, 5 Sept 1949 LHT (TTRS).
Coastal Region—*Grady Co.*: Beachton, Sherwood Plantation, 2 Jan 1965 LHJ (TTRS). *Charlton Co.*: Folkston, 9 Feb 1952 LHJ (TTRS). *Colquitt Co.*: Moultrie, 1 Apr 1945 HVAV (UWO). *Thomas Co.*: Metcalf, 31 May 1954 EVK (TTRS); Boston, Bar-M Ranch, 13 July 1967 ESS (TTRS). *Camden Co.*: Kingsland area, Coleraine Plantation, 15 July LHJ (TTRS). *Glynn Co.*: St. Simons Island, 20 Aug 1951 LHJ (TTRS).

Grady Co.: Beachton, Susina Plantation, 27 Aug 1967 LNH (TTRS). *Thomas Co.*: Metcalf, 2 Oct 1964 LN (TTRS).

E. lisa appears in early spring. By midsummer it is common everywhere. It flies close to the ground and may be seen along roadsides, in fields and in open woods. During hot summer days, it can be found in numbers around small puddles of water or on moist patches of ground. There are several broods, and adults may be seen until late fall.

The Little Sulphur is well named. The ground color of the males is usually light clear yellow but individuals may be found having a deep yellow color or perhaps a dull orange tinge.

The females are usually slightly larger in size and the ground color of the upper surface of their wings is paler than that of the males. There is a creamy white or chalky white form of the female, *E. lisa* female form *alba* Strecker, which occurs with some frequency.

The larva is about three-fourths of an inch long when fully grown. The downy body is grass green with one or two white lines along each side. The larval food plants are *Cassia* and other legumes. Comstock and Comstock (1920) state that it seems to prefer those species with finely divided leaves.

Sleepy Orange. *Eurema nicippe* Cramer (Page 115)

Distribution and Records: *E. nicippe* occurs throughout the state and is common everywhere.

Mountain Region—*Union Co.*: Suches, 15 Apr 1967 JCS. *Banks Co.* and *Habersham Co.*: 24 Aug 1930 RWM (see Montgomery, 1931). *Rabun Co.*: LaPrades, Lake Burton, 21 Sept 1967 LNH (TTRS).

Piedmont Region—*Monroe Co.*: Forsyth, 9 Jan 1951 FTN; Forsyth, 19 Mar 1957 FTN; Forsyth, 23 Apr 1955 FTN. *Fulton Co.*: Atlanta, Buckhead area, 2 Apr 1950 LHT (TTRS). *Clarke Co.*: Athens, Aug 1966 LRT. *Bibb Co.*: Macon, 11 Sept 1942 LHJ (TTRS). *DeKalb Co.*: Avondale Estates, 20 Sept 1948 LHJ (TTRS). *Fulton Co.*: Atlanta, Buckhead area, 15 Oct 1949 LHT (TTRS). *Clarke Co.*: Athens, Nov 1966 LRT.

Coastal Region—*Grady Co.*: Beachton, Susina Plantation, 2 Jan 1965 LHJ (TTRS). *Thomas Co.*: Boston, Bar-M Ranch, 15 Apr 1967 ESS (TTRS). *Colquitt Co.*: Moultrie, eleven specimens 17 Mar–27 Apr 1945 HVAV (UWO). *Grady Co.*: Beachton, Birdsong Plantation, 2 June 1954 EVK (TTRS). *Thomas Co.*: Boston, Bar-M Ranch, 13 July 1967 ESS (TTRS); Boston, Bar-M Ranch, 4 Aug 1967 ESS. *Grady Co.*: Beachton, Sherwood Plantation, 16 Sept 1964 LN. *Thomas Co.*: Metcalf, 2 Oct 1964 LN (TTRS). *Grady Co.*: Beachton, Sherwood Plantation, 1 Nov 1964 LN.

This is an attractive species. The males are a deep orange with black borders. The females are a yellow orange, with borders that are wider on the upper part of the forewing but narrow abruptly below the second branch of the cubital vein.

A yellow form, *E. nicippe* f. *flava*, is very rare in Georgia. Dr. A. Glenn Richards captured a male of this form in Athens, and a male and a female were taken in Macon by H. F. Strohecker. I collected a male and a female of the yellow form on Sherwood Plantation in Grady County in August, 1949. They met with an accident while still on the spreading boards, and none have been collected since!

Even rarer than the yellow form are such melanic forms as *E. nicippe* f. *dammersi* Gunder.

The larva is an inch long, slender, and downy; its body is green, with a white stripe along the side marked with yellow and bordered below with blackish. The larval food plants are various species of Senna (*Cassia* spp.), Clover (*Triticum* spp.) and other leguminous plants.

Genus *Nathalis*

Dainty Sulphur. *Nathalis iole* Boisduval (Page 115)

Distribution and Records: *N. iole* is found in the Coastal and Piedmont regions. It is very local, but when a colony is found, it usually contains a number of adults, often flying actively about over a rather limited area. The habitats of the Dainty

Sulphur have been extremely interesting, for it seemed to be equally at home in a colony on the southeast slope of Stone Mountain as it is in grassy areas on the coastal islands of Georgia. More collecting is needed in the Coastal Region for additional records.

Mountain Region—None.

Piedmont Region—*Bibb Co.*: Macon, 6 May 1958 JCBS. *DeKalb Co.*: Stone Mountain, 2 Aug 1952 LHJ (TTRS). *Clarke Co.*: Athens, Aug 1966 LRT. *Monroe Co.*: Forsyth, 20 Aug 1958 FTN. *DeKalb Co.*: Avondale Estates, 9 Sept 1959 LHJ (TTRS). *Fulton Co.*: Atlanta, Harris Trail, 8 Oct 1955 JCS. *DeKalb Co.*: Stone Mountain, 28 Oct 1955 KR (TTRS). *Fulton Co.*: Atlanta, J. A. White Golf Course, 29 Nov LHJ (EUM); Atlanta, J. A. White Golf Course, 13 Dec 1931 LHJ (EUM).

Coastal Region—*Chatham Co.*: Savannah, one male and one female MHM (CU)*.

In the Piedmont Region, *N. iole* seems to be active from early May through October. However, it has been taken in November and December in the Atlanta area.

In the Piedmont Region more information is needed about the spring and summer broods, the months they appear, and the flight period of each brood. The Dainty Sulphur is easily overlooked because of its small size and its habit of flying close to the ground. It seems to prefer open grassy areas. I was very much surprised to find specimens of *N. iole* on November 29 and December 13, 1931, on the John A. White golf course in Atlanta, during a period of mild weather.

J. P. Knudsen captured one female on the athletic field at Oglethorpe College in August (Knudsen, 1954a), and John Symmes collected a specimen near his home in Atlanta on October 8, 1955.

The colony on Stone Mountain in DeKalb County was discovered by chance in August, 1952, when I was examining Yucca plants in the area for signs of *Megathymus* larva. The

* The female specimen is the orange form *N. iole* f. *irene* Fitch.

colony was still active several years ago when I last visited the area. Since then, the area has become a state park.

In the Macon area (Bibb County) J. C. Brooks observed that *N. iole* was locally abundant, often occurring near streams and rivers in hot weather. His earliest spring record is May 6, 1958. He found it common to abundant in August, September, and October, but practically absent in spring.

The larva is one-half inch long. The body is dark green with a purple stripe down the back and a double stripe of yellow and black along each side, and covered with stiff hairs. The segment next to the head has a pair of reddish tubercles that project forward. The food plants are Fetid Marigold (*Dyssodia*), Garden Marigold (*Tagetes*), Chickweed (*Stellaria media*), and Sneezeweed (*Helenium*).

Genus *Anthocaris*

Falcate Orange-Tip. *Anthocharis midea* Hübner
(Page 127)

Distribution and Records: *A. midea*, the type locality of which is Georgia, is very local and usually rare but is widely distributed throughout the state. The northern race *A. m. annickae* dos Passos and Klots occurs in the Mountain and Piedmont regions. The southern race *A. m. midea* Hübner occurs on the Lower Coastal Plain and on the coastal islands.

Mountain Region—*Murray Co.*: Old Fort Mountain, 26 and 29 Mar 1961 LHJ (TTRS); Old Fort Mountain, 9 Apr 1961 JCS. *Gilmer Co.*: four miles east of Old Fort Mountain, 21 Apr 1964 JCS.

Piedmont Region—*Cobb Co.*: Kennesaw Mountain, 24 Mar 1955 LHJ (TTRS). *Fulton Co.*: Atlanta, West Garmon Road, 26 Mar 1961 LHJ (TTRS). *Cobb Co.*: Kennesaw Mountain, 29 Mar 1953 JPK; Kennesaw Mountain, 4 Apr 1953 JPK; Kennesaw Mountain, 7 Apr 1950 LHJ (TTRS); Kennesaw Mountain, 18 Apr 1957 JCS. *Monroe Co.*: Juliette, 18, 20, and 25 Apr 1959 FTN. *Fulton Co.*: Atlanta, Indian Trail Road, 18 and 19

Apr 1958 JCS; Atlanta, Indian Trail Road, 20 Apr 1960 JCS.
Coastal Region—*Glynn Co.*: Jekyll Island, 17 Mar 1956 LHJ
(TTRS). *Chatham Co.*: Savannah, MHM (CU); Fort Pulaski,
6 Apr 1960 LHJ (TTRS); Fort Pulaski, 6 and 7 Apr 1960 JCS.

One of the differences between the two races is found in the
width of the orange patch on the forewings of the males. On
A. m. annickae, the orange patch does not include the black
dot on the forewing, whereas on *A. m. midea*, it touches or
includes the black dot. The orange color of the latter tends to
be a deeper shade of orange than that of the former.

Studies have been made by dos Passos and Klots that resolve
the nomenclatural problems and establish the general areas
occupied by the two races (dos Passos and Klots, 1969).

The Falcate Orange-Tip received its name from the falcate
(or hooked) shape of the apex of the forewing, and from the
orange patch near the tip of the forewing. The females lack the
orange patch, but an occasional female may have a faint trace
of yellow on the apex of the forewing. This form has been given
the name *A. midea* female form *flavida*.

J. P. Knudsen (1954) reported his observations on the
tendency of *A. m. annickae* for "hill-topping." He observed
that this butterfly, usually rare in the lowlands, could be found
in considerable numbers ascending the slopes of Kennesaw
Mountain and flying about at or near the summit. Knudsen
found it to be locally abundant near and at the top of the
mountain on March 29, 1953, with a ratio of about eighteen
males to one female. On April 4, 1953, the numbers had de-
creased noticeably.

The number of broods is usually given as one in the northern
states and two in the southern ones. Our present records do not
indicate that we have a second brood in Georgia. Adults fly
in March and April.

The larva is about four-fifths of an inch long when mature.
Its head has papillae on top; its body is bluish green—the color
is made up of many very fine stripes—with a light greenish

orange dorsal stripe down the back and whitish lateral stripes along each side. The larval food plants are various members of the family Cruciferae, usually the slender ones, such as Rock-Cress (*Arabis*), Bitter-Cress (*Cardamine*), Shepherd's Purse (*Capsella bursapastoris*), Winter-Cress (*Barbarea*), and Mouse-Ear-Cress (*Sisymbrium thaliana*).

Family RIODINIDAE—Metalmarks

Genus *Lephelisca*

Little Metalmark. *Lephelisca virginiensis pumila*
Boisduval and LeConte (Page 119)

Distribution and Records: Georgia is the type locality of *L. v. pumila*. It occurs chiefly in the Coastal Region, where it may be found in grassy areas, especially in or near pine woods or "pine flats" in the extreme eastern and southern parts of the state. It has also been found at the eastern edge of the Piedmont Region.

Mountain Region—None.
Piedmont Region—*Richmond Co.*: Augusta, 6 June 1945 HWE; Augusta, 27 Aug 1942 HWE.
Coastal Region—*Charlton Co.*: near Folkston, 17 Aug 1949 LHJ (TTRS). *Crawford Co.*: Roberta, 27 Sept 1956 JCS. *Charlton Co.*: Billy's Island, Okefenokee Swamp, 21 Oct 1937 LHJ.

Although *L. v. pumila* is very local in occurrence it is usually common where found. This butterfly is easily overlooked because of its very small size, and the rather dark, rusty color of its upper wings. Abbot's drawing (in Boisduval and Le-Conte, 1829–1833, pl. 37) is a very accurate depiction of this butterfly.

There are two broods. The Little Metalmark flies in April, May, and the first half of June, and again in August, September, and October. In Florida, Kimball (1965, p. 46) reported: "Not rare where found, mostly in April and May, and again from August to October, but appearing occasionally in other months."

In Virginia, Clark and Clark (1951, p. 69) reported, there are "three broods. The first flies in late April and in May, the second in July, and the third from early in September to early in October."

The larva and the life history are unknown.

Family LYCAENIDAE—Gossamer-Winged Butterflies

Subfamily THECLINAE

Genus *Chrysophanus*

Coral Hairstreak. *Chrysophanus titus mopsus* Hübner
(Page 117)

Distribution and Records: *C. t. mopsus*, the type locality of which is Georgia, occurs throughout the state, but is very local and somewhat rare.

Mountain Region—*White Co.*: Cleveland, 13 June 1967 LHT (TTRS).

Piedmont Region—*Richmond Co.*: Augusta, 26 and 29 May 1942 HWE. *Coweta Co.*: Madras, 28 May 1949 MES. *Richmond Co.*: Augusta, 30 May 1944 HWE. *Forsyth Co.*: Lake Lanier, near Cumming, 2 June 1962 JRH. *Monroe Co.*: Forsyth, 3 June 1959 FTN. *Fulton Co.*: Atlanta, Indian Trail Road, 6 June 1957 LHJ (TTRS). *DeKalb Co.*: Stone Mountain, 9 June 1954 LHJ (TTRS); Stone Mountain, six specimens, 11 June 1950 LHT. *Fulton Co.*: Atlanta, Indian Trail Road, 15 June 1957 LHJ (TTRS); Atlanta, Riverside Drive, 15 June 1961 LHJ (TTRS); Atlanta, Indian Trail Road, 20 June 1958 LHJ (TTRS). *Morgan Co.*: Madison, worn specimen 6 July 1968 JCS (TTRS).

Coastal Region—*Sumter Co.*: Americus, seven specimens 14 May 1967 LN; Americus, three specimens 16 May 1965 LN. *Screven Co.*: Sylvania, six specimens 20–30 May 1946 OB (AMNH).

C. t. mopsus may be distinguished from the typical *C. titus* by the conspicuous white rings about the black dots on the lower sides of the hindwings. The red is also less extensive than in *C. titus*.

This interesting butterfly is on the wing in May and June. It seems addicted to the flowers of the Orange Milkweed and may easily be captured while feeding on them.

Abbot's drawing (Boisduval and LeConte, 1829–1833, pl. 34) figures the life cycle with a pair of adults, a larva, and a pupa. The larva is small, about three-fourths of an inch long, and slug-shaped; its head is black, and its body is yellowish green and downy, with small rosy areas on the thorax and the posterior section of the back. The larval food plants are Wild Cherry and Plum (*Prunus* spp.).

Genus *Satyrium*

Striped Hairstreak. *Satyrium liparops* Boisduval and LeConte
(Page 117)

Distribution and Records: *S. l. liparops*, Boisduval and Le-Conte, type locality Screven County, Georgia, is the subspecies that occurs on the Lower Coastal Plain. *S. l. strigosa* T. W. Harris, type locality Massachusetts, is the subspecies that occurs on the Upper Coastal Plain of Georgia and northward. Intergrades occur in a fairly wide zone where the Upper and Lower coastal plains blend. John Symmes has taken intergrades as far above the blend zone as Dougherty County in an area between Albany and Radium Springs near the Flint River.

Mountain Region—*Union Co.*: Cooper Creek State Park, Wolf Pen Gap, 29 June 1960 LHJ (TTRS); Cooper Creek State Park, Wolf Pen Gap, 2 July 1958 LNH (TTRS); Cooper Creek State Park, Duncan Ridge Road, 9 and 16 July 1961 JCS. *Towns Co.*: Brasstown Bald, 29 July 1954 LHJ (TTRS).
Piedmont Region—*Fulton Co.*: Atlanta, Oglethorpe College, 15 and 16 May 1953 JPK. *Bibb Co.*: Macon, 24 May 1931 HFS. *Fulton Co.*: Atlanta, Riverside Drive, 28 May 1960 JCS; Atlanta, Riverside Drive, 1 June 1958 JCS; Atlanta, Indian Trail Road, 8 June 1962 JCS. *Cobb Co.*: Kennesaw Mountain, 8 June

1952 AT. *Bibb Co.*: Macon, 8 and 10 June 1960 FTN. *Fulton Co.*: Atlanta, Oglethorpe College, 9 June 1954 JPK; Atlanta, Indian Trail Road, 9 June 1959 LHJ (TTRS). *Bibb Co.*: Macon, eleven specimens 12 June 1961 JCBS and FTN. *Fulton Co.*: Atlanta, 20 June 1958 LHJ (TTRS); Atlanta, Indian Trail Road, 10 July 1961 JCS. *Bibb Co.*: Macon, 20 July 1962 JCBS. Coastal Region—*Grady Co.*: Beachton, Birdsong Plantation, 16 May 1953 LHJ (TTRS). *Baker Co.*: Newton, Pineland Plantation, 17 May 1966 LN. *Dougherty Co.*: south of Albany, near Radium Springs, 18 May 1964 JCS. *Lee Co.*: Leesburg, Leeland Farms, four specimens 13 May 1967 LN. *Echols Co.*: Statenville, ten specimens 18 May 1967 LN. *Dougherty Co.*: south of Albany, near Radium Springs, seven specimens 21 May 1961 JCS. *Grady Co.*: south of Beachton, near Hadley Ferry Bridge, 26, 27, and 28 May 1966 LN. *Chatham Co.*: Savannah, 26 May 1960 JCS.

S. l. liparops may be identified by the conspicuous orange-brown patches on the upper sides of the wings, frequently with one patch on each wing, but always with a patch on the forewings. A watercolor drawing by John Abbot of this species was reproduced by Boisduval and LeConte (1829–1833, pl. 31).

The subspecies *S. l. strigosa* occurs widely over the state north of the Lower Coastal Region. It usually lacks the orange-brown patches on the upper sides of the wings or has them greatly reduced in size.

Adults of both subspecies, *S. l. liparops* and *S. l. strigosa*, visit flowers of various shrubs and trees including Sourwood (*Oxydendron arboreum*), Chinquapin (*Castanea pumila*), Chinese Chestnut (*Castanea mollissima*), and Privet (*Ligustrum* spp.).

There is one brood, with adults in May, June, and July.

As figured by Abbot, the larva is small and slug-shaped; its body is light green, with a slightly darker green dorsal stripe and several oblique yellowish green stripes along each side. The larval food plants are Plum (*Prunus*), Apple (*Malus*), Willow (*Salix*), Blueberry (*Vaccinium*), Shadbush (*Amelanchier*), and Azalea (*Rhododendron calendulaceum*).

John P. Knudsen (1955) discovered that Azalea is a food plant for the larvae of this species on May 24, 1953, near Atlanta, Georgia, and wrote: ". . . two larvae were noted in a bouquet of wild Azalea . . . Both larvae were in their final instar, and they fed for only four or five days before beginning the pupation process."

Knudsen observed that the larvae appeared to feed only on the flowers and never on the leaves. When the larvae were ready to pupate, the process was a slow one that extended over a period of several days. In both observed cases, the duration of the pupal period was slightly more than two weeks, and emergence took place shortly before noon.

King's Hairstreak. *Satyrium kingi* Klots and Clench
(Page 117)

Distribution and Records: The type locality of *S. kingi* is Savannah, Georgia. It occurs locally throughout the state and is generally rare. It is most likely to be found in open hardwood forests, usually mixed hardwoods with some oak trees and low undergrowth. Typically, a small stream flows nearby.

Mountain Region—*Union Co.*: Duncan Ridge Road, 18 July 1960 JCS. *White Co.*: near Helen, 25 July 1951 JRH (TTRS).
Piedmont Region—*Bartow Co.*: Red Top Mountain State Park, 8 June 1955 JCS. *Fulton Co.*: Atlanta, Indian Trail Road, 8 June 1955 JCS; Atlanta area, ex larva 10 June 1957 JCS; Atlanta, Indian Trail Road, 10 June 1964 LHJ; Atlanta, Indian Trail Road, 10 June 1964 JCS (TTRS). *Bartow Co.*: Red Top Mountain State Park, 16 June 1964 LHJ (TTRS). *Fulton Co.*: Atlanta, Indian Trail Road, 30 June 1960 JCS; Atlanta, Indian Trail Road, 11 July 1961 JCS.
Coastal Region—*Chatham Co.*: Savannah, 11 and 12 May 1967 HLK; Savannah, 16 May 1949 HLK; Savannah, 27 May 1961 LHJ (TTRS); Savannah, 28 and 29 May 1960 JCS; Savannah, 30 and 31 May 1960 LHJ (TTRS); Savannah, 30 May 1964 LHJ (TTRS); Savannah, 1 June 1960 LHJ (TTRS).

S. kingi was described by A. B. Klots and H. K. Clench

(1952). In addition to giving an excellent description of the new species, the authors included photographs of *S. kingi* and other species that might be confused with it, thus making it easy to identify.

When Klots and Clench examined the material they had assembled before naming this species (Klots and Clench, 1952, p. 8), they found five specimens that they "excluded from the type series of the species *S. kingi* because of the danger of future subspecies confusion."

The five specimens were: three females, somewhat worn, from Helen, White County, Georgia, collected on July 25, 1951, by Robin Harris; one male, badly worn, from Conestee Falls, near Brevard, North Carolina, collected by W. R. Sweadner between August 8 and August 14, 19?? (Carnegie Museum Accession No. 12938); and one female, badly worn, from Sipsey, Walker County, Alabama, collected by R. L. Chermock on July 10, 1949.

Again we quote Klots and Clench (1952, p. 8):

The male is quite large (forewing, base of costa to apex, 17.0 mm.) and quite dark. The Alabama female is small (forewing, base of costa to apex, 14.4 mm.) and quite pale. The three Helen, Georgia, females are large (forewing, base of costa to apex, 15.8, 16.0, and 16.2 mm.) and have proportionately very short tails. The tails of the other specimens are too worn for accurate measurement. Since in related hairstreaks the tails of northern (and mountain) populations quite consistently average much shorter than those of more southern ones, there is the likelihood that at least the Helen, Georgia, specimens represent a more or less different, perhaps subspecifically distinct population.

Several years later, a number of north Georgia specimens were collected in different localities. These were similar to the specimens from Helen, Georgia, and I gave some thought to naming them for Robin Harris, who collected the three females that were recognizably different from individuals of the Coastal population; it seemed preferable, however, to leave this to the experts in this field.

Since 1952, the known range of *S. kingi* has been extended in the southeastern states, and now includes Alabama, Florida, Mississippi, North Carolina, South Carolina, and Virginia. A mature larva was found by John C. Symmes. It was slug-shaped and green, with darker green oblique stripes on the side. The larval food plant is Flame Azalea (*Rhododendron calendulaceum*) or a related species. When H. L. King, for whom the new species was named, collected *S. kingi* in the Savannah area, he saw the females ovipositing on a small plant not related to *Azalea*. No native *Azalea* plants were found by King in the hardwood, predominately oak hammock, where he collected his specimens. This suggests that *S. kingi* has two or more food plants, as John C. Symmes found and reared *S. kingi* larvae on Flame Azalea in the Atlanta area.

Florida Hairstreak. *Satyrium calanus* Hübner (Page 117)

Distribution and Records: *S. calanus*, type locality Georgia, is apparently found in a somewhat restricted area along the coast. In Florida, it occurs widely over the Florida peninsula, as shown by records listed by C. P. Kimball (1965, p. 48).

Mountain Region—None.
Piedmont Region—None.
Coastal Region—*Thomas Co.*: Thomasville, Greenwood Planta-
tion, 8 May 1954 EVK (TTRS). *Chatham Co.*: Savannah, 11
May 1967 HLK (TTRS); Savannah, 21 May 1959 JCS;
Savannah, 23 May 1960 JCS; Savannah, 27 May 1961 JCS;
Savannah, 29 May 1960 SSN (TTRS).

S. calanus is a large, dark hairstreak, somewhat variable in size and color. There is an orange spot on the upper side of the hindwing near the base of the tail. The row of spots on the lower side of the forewing is offset on some specimens in a manner similar to those of *S. kingi*; on others the row of spots form a continuous band similar to those of the subspecies *S. c. falacer*. The color of the lower sides of the wings may vary from a light beige to a dark grey.

For three consecutive years beginning in 1959, H. L. King, Col. S. S. Nicolay, John Symmes, and I met in Savannah each spring and collected hairstreaks. In the evening, we would meet in one of the rooms and look over the day's catch, comparing specimens and discussing the identities of the various hairstreaks before us. There were questions asked that we could not resolve to the satisfaction of all.

King sent some specimens to Dr. A. B. Klots and learned that Klots was already familiar with the problem. King had previously been puzzled by similar variations among some local Florida populations near Istachatta and elsewhere.

Leon Neel collected specimens in Thomas and Grady counties in southwest Georgia and in several locations in northwest Florida and found puzzling variations in each series. He sent a number of these to H. K. Clench for his expert opinion. Neel learned that his specimens show characters that in several ways were closest to *S. wittfeldii*, but they also show some traits of *S. calanus* and even of *S. c. falacer*.

With reference to the Savannah population, Klots (personal communication) suggested that it probably represents a population descending from some old ancestral stock when *S. calanus* and *S. c. falacer* were in contact after a glacial period. Several genitalia preparations that he examined showed that individuals of the Savannah population share some of the characteristics of the northern *S. c. falacer* and the peninsular Florida *S. calanus*.

Klots was in doubt about whether the Savannah population is worthy of a form or variety name or not. It was his opinion, for the present, that this population should be commented upon but not named. This was excellent advice, and I gladly leave the confusion to the experts.

The habitat of *S. calanus*, like that of *S. c. falacer*, is open, mixed deciduous woods, typically those bordering old fields or open areas.

Banded Hairstreak. *Satyrium calanus falacer* Godart
(Page 117)

Distribution and Records: *S. c. falacer* is widely distributed over the state.

Mountain Region—*White Co.*: near Helen, Unicoi Gap, 13 June 1957 LHT (TTRS); Helen, 15 June 1952 LHT (TTRS). *Union Co.*: Cooper Creek State Park, Wolf Pen Gap, 29 June 1960 LHJ (TTRS); Cooper Creek State Park, Wolf Pen Gap, 9 July 1960 LHJ (TTRS).

Piedmont Region—*Fulton Co.*: Atlanta, Indian Trail Road, 21 May 1957 FTN. *DeKalb Co.*: Stone Mountain, 22 May 1952 LHJ (TTRS). *Fulton Co.*: Atlanta, Indian Trail Road, 27 May 1957 LHJ (TTRS); Atlanta, Oglethorpe College, May–June JPK (see Knudsen, 1954a); Atlanta, Harris Trail, 2 June 1956 LHJ (TTRS). *Bibb Co.*: Macon, 3 June 1961 FTN. *Fulton Co.*: Atlanta, Davis Drive, 4 June 1958 LHJ (TTRS). *Monroe Co.*: Forsyth, 5 June 1961 FTN. *Cobb Co.*: Kennesaw Mountain, 6 June 1957 LHJ (TTRS). *Bibb Co.*: Macon, 8 June 1960 FTN. *Fulton Co.*: Atlanta, Indian Trail Road, 20 June 1958 LHJ (TTRS); Atlanta, Oglethorpe College, 1 June 1954 JPK; near Roswell, Wayte Farm, 10 June 1965 LHJ (TTRS).

Coastal Region—*Grady Co.*: Beachton, Sherwood Plantation, 3 and 21 May 1965 LN (TTRS). *Chatham Co.*: Savannah, 27 May 1961 LHJ (TTRS); Savannah, 28 May 1960 JCS; Savannah, 31 May 1964 LHJ (TTRS). *Grady Co.*: Beachton, Birdsong Plantation, 6 June 1960 LHJ (TTRS).

S. c. falacer lacks the orange spot on the upper side of the hindwing that is found on *S. calanus*. I have followed H. K. Clench (Ehrlich and Ehrlich, 1961, p. 194) in considering this butterfly a subspecies of *S. calanus*.

S. c. falacer may often be taken at flowers in or near open, mixed, deciduous woods. It is usually locally common where found. One of its habits, in keeping with those of other hairstreaks, is sitting on leaves of trees and shrubs when at rest. The collector should keep a watchful eye for them when walking along forest roads and paths.

One of my unforgettable experiences was the day when Mrs.

Harris and I visited Cooper Creek State Park in the mountains of north Georgia and saw hundreds of Banded Hairstreaks flitting about in the bright sunshine along a forest road. John Abbot's drawing in Boisduval and LeConte (1829–1833, pl. 29) illustrates the life history of *S. c. falacer* showing a pair of the butterflies, a larva, and a pupa. A species of *Crataegus* (Hawthorne) is shown as a food plant.

S. c. falacer is single-brooded, with adults appearing in May, June, and (rarely) July.

The larva is small and slug-shaped, and about one-half inch long. The body is light green, marked with several dark lines running lengthwise. Sometimes, the larvae are brown instead of green, but this does not affect the color of the adult butterflies.

The larval food plants are Oak (*Quercus*), Hickory (*Carya*), Butternut (*Juglans cinerea*)—which is rare in Georgia—and, according to Abbot, Hawthorne (*Crataegus*). It has been estimated by Wilbur H. Duncan (1941) that Georgia probably has about eighteen species of *Crataegus*.

Hickory Hairstreak. *Satyrium caryaevorus* McDunnough
(Page 117)

Distribution and Records: *S. caryaevorus* is known only from Union County in north Georgia, but it seems likely that it occurs locally but widely in the Mountain Region in suitable habitats where the larval food plant Hickory (*Carya*) occurs.

Mountain Region—*Union Co.*: Cooper Creek State Park, Duncan Ridge Road, 29 June 1960 JCS; Cooper Creek State Park, Duncan Ridge Road, 9 July 1960 JCS; Cooper Creek State Park, Wolf Pen Gap, 9 July 1961 LHJ (TTRS).
Piedmont Region—None.
Coastal Region—None.

S. caryaevorus is difficult to distinguish from *S. c. falacer* which is common throughout the state. An excellent study of the life history of *S. caryaevorus* has been made by Dr. A. B. Klots (1960). Klots's paper gives life-history details and other important information, including the similarity and differences between *S. caryaevorus* and *S. c. falacer*.

It was not until Gordon B. Small, Jr., recognized *S. caryaevorus* in a group of hairstreaks we had collected in the mountains of north Georgia that I learned it occurred in this state. Small was familiar with this species, because he had collected more than thirty specimens of it at Riverside, Connecticut, in June, 1959. His offer to take the specimen to Dr. Klots for his determination was accepted with thanks. A few weeks later, Small wrote:

I finally got the specimen which you caught at Wolf Pen Gap to Dr. Klots, who pronounced it *caryaevorus* after a check of the genitalia. This of course was not surprising as it had all of the superficial characteristics of *caryaevorus*. Thus you have a new species for Georgia, and the known range is now considerably south of what it was thought to be.

This was interesting news indeed! A new look was taken at north Georgia hairstreaks in local collections, and John Symmes discovered that he had specimens of *S. caryaevorus* that he had collected in 1960, a year earlier than my specimen, so his are actually the first records.

There is one brood, with adults in June and July.

The larva is slug-shaped; its body is green with a darker green, unbroken, middorsal stripe. In the larva of *S. c. falacer*, the middorsal stripe is broken into a series of dark triangles or isosceles trapezoids. On each side of the body of the *S. caryaevorus* larva, the diagonal lateral markings are more prominent than those of *S. c. falacer*, particularly the diagonal dark green lines about midway between the subdorsal line and the lateral edge.

Edwards' Hairstreak. *Satyrium edwardsii* Grote and Robinson
(Page 117)

Distribution and Records: *S. edwardsii* is rare and local but some colonies may exist for years. Although we have a number of records for the Piedmont Region, we have only one record, an old one, for the Mountain Region. This is somewhat surprising for *S. edwardsii* is essentially a northern species.

Mountain Region—*Rabun Co.*: no date JCBY (see Richards, 1931, p. 249).

Piedmont Region—*Bibb Co.*: Macon, 13 May 1933 HFS; Macon, 27 and 29 May 1962 JCBS. *Fulton Co.*: Atlanta, 28 May 1944 JCS. *Cobb Co.*: Marietta, Blackjack Mountain, 31 May 1958 LHJ (TTRS); Marietta, Blackjack Mountain, 1 June 1958 JCS. *Fulton Co.*: Atlanta, West End, 3 June 1945 JCS (TTRS). *Bibb Co.*: Macon, 4 and 19 June 1962 JCBS; Macon, 8 June 1960 FTN. *Fulton Co.*: Atlanta, 15 June 1957 LHJ (TTRS); Atlanta, West End, 24 June 1940 LHJ (TTRS). *Clarke Co.*: Athens, several specimens June and Aug (no year given) AGR (see Richards, 1931, p. 249). *Fulton Co.*: Atlanta, West End, 6 July 1928 LHJ.

Coastal Region—None.

On July 6, 1928, I found a colony of *S. edwardsii* in an open mixed hardwood forest adjacent to West View Cemetery in the southwestern section of Atlanta. The focal point of the colony was a small Scrub Oak of a type unfamiliar to me. This colony remained active for many years.

On May 31, 1951, a trip was made with Dr. Harry Sicher to Blackjack Mountain, near Marietta, in Cobb County. We found a stand of Scrub Oaks adjacent to an old field near the base of the mountain. A small colony of *S. edwardsii* was found among the oaks at the edge of the field. Individuals were also found sitting on leaves of oaks bordering an unpaved road that entered the woods.

In Bibb County, *S. edwardsii* was reported as rare by J. C. Brooks. He observed that it preferred open woods.

S. edwardsii has only one brood.

The larva is slug-shaped and brown with light brown markings. There are many small blackish tubercles with brown hairs on the body, and the head is black with a small white band. The larval food plants are Scrub Oak (*Quercus ilicifolia*) and other oaks.

Genus *Calycopis*

Red-banded Hairstreak; Cecrops. *Calycopis cecrops*
Fabricius (Page 117)

Distribution and Records: *C. cecrops* occurs throughout Georgia. It is usually common to abundant in most areas of the state.

Mountain Region—*Lumpkin Co.*: Auraria, 15 and 16 Apr 1967 BMR. *Murray Co.*: Old Fort Mountain, 5 May 1951 LHT (TTRS). *Banks Co.* and *Habersham Co.*: 24 Aug 1930 RWM (see Montgomery, 1931).

Piedmont Region—*Coweta Co.*: Madras, 26 Mar 1950 MES. *DeKalb Co.*: Stone Mountain, 11 Apr 1951 LHJ (TTRS). *Bibb Co.*: Macon, 3 June 1961 FTN; Macon, aberration 19 July 1962 JCBS. *Fulton Co.*: Atlanta, Harris Trail, 22 Aug 1967 LHJ (TTRS). *Clarke Co.*: Athens, July, Aug, and Oct 1966 LRT.

Coastal Region—*Thomas Co.*: Mill Pond Plantation, 23 Feb 1967 ESS. *Grady Co.*: Beachton, Susina Plantation, 3 Mar 1965 LHJ (TTRS). *Houston Co.*: Warner Robins, 29 Mar 1957 FTN. *Screven Co.*: Sylvania, Mar–Sept 1946 OB (AMNH). *Colquitt Co.*: Moultrie, 3 Apr 1945 HVAV (UWO). *Grady Co.*: Beachton, Birdsong Plantation, 12 Apr 1953 EVK (TTRS). *Chatham Co.*: Savannah, 27 May 1961 LHJ (TTRS). *Grady Co.*: Beachton, Susina Plantation, sight record 15 June 1968 LHJ. *Thomas Co.*: Thomasville, 10 July 1944 LHJ (TTRS); Boston, Bar-M Ranch, 13 July 1967 ESS (TTRS). *Grady Co.*: Beachton, Susina Plantation, 27 Aug 1967 LNH. *Charlton Co.*: Billy's Island, Okefenokee Swamp, 21 Oct 1937 LHJ.

At times, this butterfly may be abundant enough to be distracting to a collector who is intent on finding rarer species.

Sometimes a collector is rewarded, however, by finding and collecting an unusual specimen of *C. cecrops*, such as the aberration with extensive white below taken in July, 1962, by J. C. Brooks.

There are two broods; the spring and the summer broods each extend over a period of approximately three months.

Very little was known about the early stages of *C. cecrops* until George W. Rawson and Sidney A. Hessel (1951, pp. 79–84) made a thorough study of the life history. Their careful observation determined the food plant to be the Mountain Sumac or Dwarf Sumac (*Rhus copallina*).

Although Rawson and Hessel often found the butterflies on flowers of the food plant, they were more often hidden among the foliage until startled by a collector's close approach or by light tapping of the bush. Captured females were confined and lived from twelve to twenty-three days and laid an average of twenty-five eggs. After the caterpillars were hatched, the duration of the larval stage was approximately thirty-eight to forty-two days.

Rawson and Hessel described the larva:

Fifth instar; heavy pilous coat, dark brown with hoary tinge caused by generous interspersion of new type of finer and longer hairs wavy at tips. Bluish-green dorsal stripe on all except first thoracic and anal segments. Setae now cover entire dorsum. Head black, spiracles black. Cervical shield even more conspicuous, bisected longitudinally more or less prominently by a faint line or suture. First thoracic segment now developed into prominent hood. Length 11–13 mm. Duration of instar to pupa 10–13 days.

Genus *Callophrys*

Frosted Elfin. *Callophrys* (*Incisalia*) *irus* Godart
(Page 119)

Distribution and Records: Although *C. irus* is widely distributed over the state, it is rare and local.

Mountain Region—*Murray Co.*: Old Fort Mountain, 19 and 21 Apr 1964 LHJ (TTRS). *White Co.*: Tray Mountain, 4 May 1955 JCS. *Murray Co.*: Old Fort Mountain, 16 May 1950 LHJ (TTRS); Old Fort Mountain, 17 May 1950 JRH and LHT.

Piedmont Region—*Coweta Co.*: Madras, 26 Mar 1950 MES. *Bibb Co.*: Macon, 27 Mar 1961 JCBS. *Richmond Co.*: Augusta, 27 Mar 1948 HWE; Augusta, 6 Apr 1942 HWE. *Coweta Co.*: Madras, 10 Apr 1949 MES. *Richmond Co.*: Augusta, 15 Apr 1941 HWE.

Coastal Region—*Thomas Co.*: Thomasville, Greenwood Plantation, 14 Mar 1967 LN.

Abbot's two drawings of *C. irus* in Boisduval and LeConte (1829–1833, pls. 31 and 32) are of special interest: the figures on plate 31 were correctly identified as *C. irus*, but the figures on plate 32, which depict heavily marked specimens of *C. irus*, were assumed by Boisduval and LeConte to represent a different but closely related species, which they named *Incisalia arsace*.

C. irus is single-brooded. Adults appear in March and April in the Piedmont and Coastal regions, and in April and May in the mountains. My two sons and I collected seven specimens and saw several others near the summit of Old Fort Mountain in north Georgia on May 17, 1950.

The slug-shaped larva is yellowish green, becoming brownish red just before pupation. The larval food plants are False Indigo (*Baptisia*) and Lupine (*Lupinus*). Abbot's records of *Vaccinium* need to be verified: larvae should be looked for on the flowers of Huckleberry and related plants of the genera *Gaylussacia* and *Vaccinium*.

Henry's Elfin. *Callophrys* (*Incisalia*) *henrici*
Grote and Robinson (Page 119)

Distribution and Records: *C. henrici* occurs throughout the state, but it is very local; is usually rare but may be locally common when a colony is found where there is an abundant supply of the larval food plant, Huckleberry (*Gaylussacia*), in open woods. Adults may be found on the blossoms of Wild Plum (*Prunus*), Redbud (*Cercis*), Huckleberry, and other spring flowers.

Mountain Region—*Lumpkin Co.*: Auraria, 15 Apr 1967 BMR.
Piedmont Region—*Bibb Co.*: Macon, 15 Mar 1961 JCBS (TTRS); Macon, 15 and 16 Mar 1961 FTN; Macon, 27 Mar 1961 JCBS. *Cobb Co.*: Marietta, Blackjack Mountain, 8 Apr 1951 LHJ (TTRS). *Fulton Co.*: Atlanta, Indian Trail Road, 17 Apr 1955 LHJ (TTRS); Atlanta, Indian Trail Road, 18 and 19 Apr 1958 LHJ (TTRS); Atlanta, Indian Trail Road, 20 Apr 1955 JCS. *DeKalb Co.*: Stone Mountain, 1 May 1952 LHJ (TTRS).
Coastal Region—*Screven Co.*: Old Jacksboro, 6 Apr 1960 LHJ (TTRS). *Glynn Co.*: Jekyll Island, 16 Mar 1965 AT; St. Simons Island, 17 Mar 1965 AT.

C. Henrici is on the wing from late February to early April in south Georgia, and from late March to early May in north Georgia.

In the Bibb County area, J. C. Brooks found *C. henrici* to be uncommon, flying in the pine barrens and feeding on Wild Plum blossoms in late February and early March. He observed that *C. henrici* slightly precedes the peak of *C. n. niphon*.

In 1943, C. F. dos Passos described the subspecies *C. h. margaretae* from De Land, Florida. This subspecies is now known to occur in Georgia on the Lower Coastal Plain: In 1965, Abner Towers collected two specimens on Jekyll Island and one specimen on St. Simons Island in Glynn County. Mr. Towers and I compared these specimens with specimens of *C. h. margaretae* collected by H. L. King at Gold Head State Park, Clay County, Florida. Towers' specimens proved to be *C. h. margaretae*, a new state record.

The larva, which is slug-shaped, is a little less than one-half inch long. The body is light green with a paler dorsal stripe and oblique stripes on sides. Some larvae may be reddish brown with lighter brown stripes. In addition to Huckleberry (*Gay-*

lussacia), Wild Plum (*Prunus*) and Blueberry (*Vaccinium*) are eaten by the larvae.

Brown Elfin. *Callophrys* (*Incisalia*) *augustinus croesioides* Scudder (Page 119)

Distribution and Records: *C. a. croesioides* is the subspecies found in Georgia. It appears to be confined to the Piedmont and Mountain regions; although it is of local occurrence, it is often common where found.

Mountain Region—*Murray Co.*: Old Fort Mountain, 21 and 26 Mar 1962 JCS; Old Fort Mountain, 26 and 29 Mar 1961 LHJ (TTRS); Old Fort Mountain, 28 Mar 1963 LHJ (TTRS); Old Fort Mountain, 28 Mar 1963 JCS; Old Fort Mountain, 4 Apr 1953 LHJ and JPK; Old Fort Mountain, 17 Apr 1953 LHJ. *Gilmer Co.*: four miles east of Old Fort Mountain, 19 Apr 1964 JCS.
Piedmont Region—*Bibb Co.*: Macon area, 27 Mar 1961 JCBS. *Cobb Co.*: Marietta, Kennesaw Mountain, 29 Mar 1953 JPK; Marietta, Blackjack Mountain, 29 Mar 1953 LHJ.
Coastal Region—None.

The most likely places to find this little butterfly are in or near areas where Huckleberry plants abound in rather open woods. The population of *C. a. croesioides* reaches its peak in the latter half of March. The adults may be found on Wild Plum blossoms and other early spring flowers. On Old Fort Mountain, adults were observed alighting on the ground along an unpaved forest road that passed by an extensive stand of low Huckleberry bushes. There is one brood, with adults in March and April. *C. a. croesioides* hibernates as a pupa.

The larva is slug-shaped and about one-half inch long. The body is bright green with a thin middorsal stripe and wider oblique stripes and dashes on each side. The larval food plants are Huckleberry (*Gaylussacia*), Blueberry (*Vaccinium*), and Sheep Laurel (*Kalmia angustifolia*).

Pine Elfin; Banded Elfin. *Callophrys (Incisalia) niphon niphon*
Hübner (Page 119)

Distribution and Records: *C. n. niphon* is found locally
throughout the state, usually in the vicinity of the larval food
plants, which are pines.

Mountain Region—*Murray Co.*: Old Fort Mountain, 26 Mar
1961 LHJ (TTRS). *Gilmer Co.*: three miles east of Old Fort
Mountain, 28 Mar 1963 JCS. *Murray Co.*: Old Fort Mountain,
4, 5, and 17 Apr 1953 LHJ. *Fannin Co.*: Cooper Creek, 12 June
1959 JCS. *Union Co.*: Suches, 29 June 1958 JCS.

Piedmont Region—*Bibb Co.*: Stone Creek, 4 Mar 1961 FTN
(TTRS); Macon area, 7 Mar 1961 FTN; Stone Creek, 16 and
20 Mar 1966 FTN. *Richmond Co.*: Augusta, 17 and 20 Mar
1942 HWE. *Coweta Co.*: Madras, 24 Mar 1949 MES. *Fulton
Co.*: Atlanta, West Garmon Road, 25 Mar 1959 JCS. *Bibb Co.*:
Macon area, 27 Mar 1961 JCBS. *Fulton Co.*: Atlanta, 2 Apr
1950 LHT; Atlanta, Indian Trail Road, 7 Apr 1955 LHJ
(TTRS); Atlanta, 18 Apr 1958 JCS. *DeKalb Co.*: Stone Moun-
tain, 19 Apr 1952 GH. *Clarke Co.*: Athens, May 1967 LRT.
Clayton Co.: Lake Mirror, 8 May 1945 JCS.

Coastal Region—*Grady Co.*: Beachton, Susina Plantation, 3 Mar
1965 LN; Beachton, Susina Plantation, 6 Mar 1964 LHJ
(TTRS); Beachton, Sherwood Plantation, 9 and 17 Mar 1965
LN.

Adults emerge in March and April in south Georgia, in
March, April, and May in the Piedmont Region, and in late
March, April, May, and June in the mountains.

In the southern part of Bibb County, J. C. Brooks found
this butterfly to be common during March and April; in Crawford County, the adult population peaks in late March. Brooks
collected two specimens in northern Bibb County on May 5.

The Pine Elfin should be sought along the borders of young
pines in open pine woods. I have found them on pines along
the edge of roads in the woods. The adults visit Wild Plum
blossoms and other spring flowers.

The larva is slug-shaped and slightly more than one-half

inch long. The body is light green with two lengthwise whitish stripes on each side. The leaves of fairly young pine trees are the preferred food.

Olive Hairstreak. *Callophrys (Mitoura) gryneus gryneus* Hübner (Page 117)

Distribution and Records: *C. g. gryneus* occurs widely over the state but is very local. It is most often found in association with Red Cedar (*Juniperus virginiana*), which is the larval food plant. Prof. Wilbur H. Duncan (1941) states that Red Cedar is found "throughout the state. Common in the Piedmont and southward; uncommon in the mountains especially at high elevations."

Mountain Region—None.
Piedmont Region—*Bibb Co.*: Macon area, 27 Mar 1961 JCBS. *Monroe Co.*: Forsyth, 6 Apr 1958 FTN. *DeKalb Co.*: Stone Mountain, 11 Apr 1951 LHJ (TTRS). *Clarke Co.*: Athens, 19 Apr 1929 AGR. *DeKalb Co.*: Stone Mountain, 19 Apr 1955 LHJ (TTRS); Stone Mountain, 3 May 1952 LHJ (TTRS). *Clarke Co.*: Athens, May 1967 LRT. *Monroe Co.*: Forsyth, 3 June 1958 FTN. *Richmond Co.*: Augusta, 16 June 1942 HWE. *DeKalb Co.*: Stone Mountain, 17 July 1929 PWF (TTRS); Stone Mountain, 6 Aug 1955 PK. *Monroe Co.*: Forsyth, 26 Aug 1956 FTN. *DeKalb Co.*: Stone Mountain, 30 Sept 1955 PK (TTRS).
Coastal Region—None.

C. g. gryneus is double-brooded. The spring brood appears in April and May in the Piedmont Region. Adults of the summer brood are darker in color than those of the spring brood and appear in July and August with worn specimens being found as late as September. The dark summer form is *C. g. gryneus* f. *smilacis*. Boisduval and LeConte (1829–1833, pl. 33) described this form from a drawing by John Abbot, which illustrates a larva, a pupa, and a dark adult of the summer form.

213

The months of April, May, July, and August are best for collecting the Olive Hairstreak. Although colonies are very local, they may be found by carefully inspecting Red Cedars. First, look the trees over carefully for specimens; if none are seen, then try tapping or shaking each tree. If the butterfly is present, it will fly off; if it is not too frightened, it will usually return to the same tree.

The larva, when mature, is deep green in color with a slightly yellowish tint, so that it closely matches the color of its food plant. The body is slug-shaped, with subdorsal whitish bars on each side.

Genus *Atlides*

Great Blue Hairstreak. *Atlides halesus* Cramer (Page 117)

Distribution and Records: *A. halesus* is found locally in the Piedmont and Coastal regions. It occurs with greater frequency in the Coastal Region than it does in the Piedmont Region.

Mountain Region—None.

Piedmont Region—*Bibb Co.*: ten miles south of Macon, 4 Mar 1961 FTN; ten miles south of Macon, 11 Mar 1966 FTN. *Fulton Co.*: Atlanta area, 18 Mar 1957 JCS. *Bibb Co.*: Macon area, 27 Mar 1961 JCBS. *Fulton Co.*: Atlanta area, 4 Apr 1947 JPK; Atlanta, Oglethorpe College 1 July 1954 JPK. *Bibb Co.*: Macon area, 13 Sept 1930 HFS (TTRS). *Monroe Co.*: Forsyth, 19 Oct 1956 FTN. *Fulton Co.*: Atlanta area, 18 Nov 1942 JPK.

Coastal Region—*Grady Co.*: Melton Place, 6 Jan 1965 LN. *Glynn Co.*: Jekyll Island, 11 May 1958 JCS. *Chatham Co.*: Savannah, 16 May 1949 HLK; Savannah, 30 May 1960 LHJ (TTRS); Savannah, ex ova 28 June 1962 JCS. *Screven Co.*: Sylvania, two females 14 Aug 1946 OB (AMNH). *Grady Co.*: Beachton, Sherwood Plantation, 26 and 27 Sept 1964 LN; Beachton, Sherwood Plantation, 9 Oct 1964 LN. *Baker Co.*: Newton, Blue Springs Plantation, 13 Nov 1964 LN (TTRS).

Some authors have used, as a common name for *A. halesus*, "The Great Purple Hairstreak," which is a misnomer, *A.*

halesus being blue. I follow the usage of Brown, Eff, and Rotger (1957, p. 124) in calling it the "Great Blue Hairstreak," for the reasons they have set forth.

When a collector finds a colony located near plum trees, it is usually possible to collect a few specimens feeding at the plum blossoms each spring. The dark underside of this handsome hairstreak is easy to see against the white blossoms. The summer brood may be found on other flowers, including goldenrod, in late summer and early fall.

On March 27, 1961, J. C. Brooks had excellent collecting several miles south of Macon, taking, in addition to several other good specimens of various species, a rare aberrant of *A. halesus*. He wrote to me:

One of the *halesus* has the blue replaced entirely with green as in the Mexican *Thecla regalis*. It was a male and seemed normal otherwise but is outstanding in this respect. This reminds me of your *diana* aberrations.

Later, Brooks wrote:

Atlides halesus—very common in certain areas in late February and March, i.e., when wild plum is in bloom. Common in *Quercus* (oak) groves infested with mistletoe in dry sandy areas of Coastal Plain. From eggs secured March 3, pupae formed April 6, adults emerged April 27 through August 10! Spring brood much the commoner. Probably four or five broods.

John Symmes obtained eggs from a female *A. halesus* that he collected near Savannah in the spring of 1962. He reared a number of larva, which pupated, and the butterflies emerged in June. In the Atlanta area, Symmes found *A. halesus* on Wild Plum blossoms on Riverside Drive, north of the city limits, on March 18, 1957.

Other Atlanta captures were made by J. P. Knudsen at 2890 North Hills Drive, N.E., on April 4, 1947, and November 18, 1942. He noted that both specimens were fairly fresh and could not have been on the wing for more than a few days. He also collected a female on the Oglethorpe College campus on July 1, 1954. This specimen was feeding on White Clover blossoms.

The earliest date for south Georgia is for a specimen collected by Leon Neel in Grady County on January 6, 1965, and the latest is for one that he collected in Baker County on November 13, 1964.

In the Piedmont Region, the earliest date is for a specimen collected by Fred T. Naumann in Bibb County on March 4, 1961, and the latest is for one collected in Fulton County on November 18, 1942, by J. P. Knudsen.

Abbot's drawing of *A. halesus* in Boisduval and LeConte (1829–1833, pl. 25) illustrates the mature larva, pupa, the upper sides of male and female adults, and the lower side of a male.

The larva is slug-shaped and slightly downy. It is green with a slightly darker green stripe lengthwise along the middle of the back and nine oblique darker green bands on the sides; below the bands, there is a lateral yellowish stripe, which runs along the lower edge of the body.

The larval food plants are Mistletoe (*Phoradendron flavescens*), and, according to Abbot (in Boisduval and LeConte, 1829–1833, p. 85), *Quercus*—probably Live Oak (*Q. virginiana*), as Abbot's larva is figured on a partially eaten leaf of this tree.

Genus *Eurystrymon*

Southern Hairstreak. *Eurystrymon favonius* J. E. Smith
(Page 117)

Distribution and Records: *E. favonius* is a coastal species that is sometimes locally common. Its range includes the wooded, coastal islands, and extends inland from the coast to Screven County and southward, chiefly in the tier of counties bordering on the coast. Further inland, *E. favonius* appears to be replaced by *E. ontario*. Intermediates are occasionally taken, which may indicate that *E. favonius* is an extreme subspecies of *E. ontario*, as suggested by Harry K. Clench (in Ehrlich and Ehrlich, 1961, p. 213). W. T. M. Forbes (1960, p. 137) mentions a block of specimens from North Carolina in the National Museum as "apparently transitional from *ontario* to *favonius*."

Mountain Region—None.
Piedmont Region—None.
Coastal Region—*Chatham Co.*: Savannah, 11 and 12 May 1967 HLK. *Glynn Co.*: Jekyll Island, 11 May 1958 JCS (TTRS); Jekyll Island, 17 May 1960 JCS; St. Simons Island, 19 May 1965 LNH (TTRS). *Chatham Co.*: Savannah, 28 May 1960 JCS; Savannah, 29 May 1960 LHJ (TTRS); Savannah, 31 May 1964 LHJ (TTRS); Savannah, very worn specimens 6 June 1962 HLK.

E. favonius was described by Smith (1797, p. 27, pl. 14) from an Abbot drawing, which delineated the upper sides of a male and a female, the under side of a female, or pupa, and a larva feeding on a leaf of an Oak (*Quercus*). Smith identified the leaves as those of *Quercus rubra*, which is common in Georgia.

E. favonius is easily taken at flowers, but it is difficult to net when flying about in the dappled light of oak hammocks.

Among my most memorable collecting experiences was the visit to Savannah and the surrounding area with John Symmes, H. L. King, and Col. S. S. Nicolay, which resulted in our getting a number of rare and desirable species of hairstreaks, including *E. favonius, Satyrium kingi, S. l. liparops, S. calanus,* and *S. c. falacer*. These expert collectors carefully examined the trees that were in bloom, especially Chinese Chestnut (*Castanea mollissima*), which has been planted in some of the suburbs of Savannah and is in full bloom in late May, and such native trees as Chinquapin (*Castanea pumila*). A couple of

Chinese Chestnut trees in full bloom in a churchyard, quite some distance from the usual habitat of the various hairstreaks, attracted some choice specimens.

Another unforgettable experience with *E. favonius* began as a special trip with Mrs. Harris to St. Simons Island, near Brunswick, to find and collect some *Phyciodes phaon* for F. Martin Brown, who needed *P. phaon* specimens from the type locality for a special research project that he was working on at that time. Mrs. Harris not only found *P. phaon* flying in a grassy area, and collected a series for Brown, but she also found a strong colony of *E. favonius* in another area under a spreading canopy of great oaks. We took only a few of the freshest-looking specimens, and hoped that the colony, with similar treatment by other collectors, would continue to thrive through the years.

John and Jane Symmes had a similar experience on Jekyll Island, and it is hoped that their colony will also be preserved by judicious collectors.

Abbot's figure shows the larva to be slug-shaped, with a small head; the body is light green, with a narrow dark green stripe running lengthwise down the back; there are nine green oblique stripes on each side of the body, and a yellowish lateral stripe above the bases of the legs. The larval food plants are various Oaks (*Quercus*). Abbot stated (in Smith, 1797, p. 27): "Feeds on the forked leaved blackjack, and other oaks. Changed April 28, came out in the perfect state the 13th of May. It is not a very common species."

Ontario; Northern Hairstreak. *Euristrymon ontario ontario*
Edwards (Page 117)

Distribution and Records: In the Mountain and Piedmont regions *E. o. ontario* is very rare and local. In south Georgia, this hairstreak is locally common at times.

Mountain Region—None.

LYCAENIDAE—GOSSAMER-WINGED

Piedmont Region—*Richmond Co.*: Augusta, 26 Apr 1945 HWE; Augusta, 9 May 1942 HWE. *Fulton Co.*: Oglethorpe College, May 1950 JPK (see Knudsen, 1954a, p. 4)
Coastal Region—*Grady Co.*: Beachton, Susina Plantation, 29 and 30 Apr 1965 LN; Beachton, Birdsong Plantation, 30 Apr 1967 LN; Beachton, Sherwood Plantation, 5 May 1967 LN. *Decatur Co.*: Spring Creek, 7 May 1953 EVK and LHJ. *Thomas Co.*: Metcalf, 5 and 7 May 1960 HLK. *Decatur Co.*: US 84, 8 May 1963 HLK. *Grady Co.*: Beachton, Sherwood Plantation, 8 May 1966 LN. *Thomas Co.*: Metcalf, 11 May 1954 EVK (TTRS); Boston, Mitchell Place, 13 May 1953 EVK (TTRS). *Dougherty Co.*: Albany, 13 May 1967 LN. *Decatur Co.*: Brinson, 14 May 1960 JCS. *Grady Co.*: US 84, 14 May 1960 JCS. *Baker Co.*: Newton, Pineland Plantation, 17 May 1966 LN. *Echols Co.*: Statenville, 18 May 1967 LN. *Thomas Co.*: Metcalf, 18 May 1954 EVK (TTRS). *Grady Co.*: Beachton, Susina Plantation, 21 May 1964 JCS. *Thomas Co.*: Metcalf, 25 May 1960 EVK (TTRS). *Grady Co.*: Hadley Ferry Bridge, 27 May 1966 LN.

The specimens of *E. o. ontario* from the Mountain and Piedmont regions are similar in appearance to others in the northeastern states, and have very little, if any, indication of orange spots on the upper surfaces of the wings. J. P. Knudsen made an extensive collection of butterflies from the campus of Oglethorpe College on the outskirts of Atlanta. In his list, (1954, p. 4) he states: *"Ontario* is rare everywhere. One specimen taken on campus in May 1950 by another collector." Knudsen examined the specimen and observed that it had some slight indication of small areas of orange on the upper surfaces of its wings. In Augusta, specimens of *E. o. ontario* were collected by Henry W. Eustis, one on May 9, 1942, and the other on April 26, 1945.

Specimens of *E. o. ontario* from the Coastal Region appear to have some affinity with the western subspecies *E. o. autolycus*, which has prominent orange areas on the upper surfaces of its wings. Along the Georgia coast, *E. o. ontario* seems to be replaced by *E. favonius*, a closely related species. Ehrlich and Ehrlich (1961, p. 213) state that *E. favonius* is "possibly an extreme subspecies of *ontario* as intermediates are occasionally taken in Georgia."

A few intermediate specimens were taken by H. L. King, Col. S. S. Nicolay, J. C. Symmes, and myself on several of the annual trips we made jointly to Savannah.

Specimens of *E. ontario* from south Georgia may represent an extreme eastern form of the subspecies *E. o. autolycus* Edwards—the type specimen of which is from Dallas, Texas— or it may be an undescribed subspecies.

On May 7, 1954, accompanied by E. V. Komarek, we were searching for *Phyciodes* (*Tritanassa*) *texana seminole* near the type locality along Spring Creek, which forms the boundary between Seminole and Decatur counties, when Komarek found a number of hairstreaks on the small white flowers of some spurges (*Euphorbia sebastiana*) growing near a creek. We collected eighteen specimens, which we later sent to H. A. Freeman at Garland, Texas. Freeman studied them for some time, and compared them with Texas specimens and with specimens in the National Museum. It was his opinion that our specimens might represent the subspecies *E. o. autolycus*, and that the south Georgia specimens of *E. ontario* should not be given a new subspecific name for the present. Until further studies are made, I gladly leave this to the experts.

The place where the specimens were collected was just south of the point where the bridge on US 84 crosses Spring Creek. There are several other places along US 84 where *E. ontario* can be collected on other flowers that bloom in May, which is during the flight period of this hairstreak.

E. ontario has only one brood, with adults appearing in April and May.

The life history is not completely known. The larval food plants are Hawthorne (*Crataegus*) and Oak (*Quercus autolycus*), according to Klots (1951, p. 135).

Genus *Panthiades*

White M Hairstreak. *Panthiades m-album*
Boisduval and LeConte (Page 117)

Distribution and Records: Georgia is the type locality of *Panthiades m-album*. It is found locally throughout the state: it is very rare in the mountains, not so rare southward in the Piedmont Region, and locally common at times in the southern part of the Coastal Region.

Mountain Region—*Murray Co.*: Old Fort Mountain, 21 Apr 1964 LHJ (TTRS).
Piedmont Region—*Monroe Co.*: Forsyth, 10 Feb 1957 FTN. *Richmond Co.*: Augusta, 3 Mar 1945 HWE. *Bibb Co.*: Macon, 4 and 15 Mar 1961 FTN. *Fulton Co.*: Hapeville, 17 Mar 1961 JCS; Atlanta, 23 Mar 1959 JCS; Atlanta, 26 Mar 1957 JCS; Atlanta, Riverside Drive, 30 Mar 1957 LHJ (TTRS); Oglethorpe College, 20 Apr 1950 JPK. *Clarke Co.*: Athens, two specimens late spring AGR (see Richards, 1931, p. 249). *Richmond Co.*: Augusta, 30 Apr 1945 HWE. *Fulton Co.*: Atlanta, Riverside Drive, 10 June 1960 JCS; Atlanta, Indian Trail Road, 18 June 1961 JCS; Atlanta, Harris Trail, 22 Aug 1967 JCS. *Cobb Co.*: near Marietta, 27 Sept 1960 JCS. *Richmond Co.*: Augusta, 2 Oct 1940 HWE.
Coastal Region—*Baker Co.*: Newton, Blue Springs Plantation, 19 Feb 1965 LN. *Grady Co.*: Beachton, Susina Plantation, 7 Mar 1964 LHJ (TTRS). *Lee Co.*: Leeland Farms, 15 May 1965 LN. *Chatham Co.*: Savannah, 16 May 1949 HLK (TTRS). *Thomas Co.*: Metcalf, 18 May 1954 LHJ (TTRS). *Chatham Co.*: Bloomingdale, ex ova 27 June 1963 JCS. *Screven Co.*: Sylvania area, 8 July 1946 OB (AMNH). *Grady Co.*: Beachton, 18 Sept 1964 LN.

There are two broods in the northern part of the state and three in the southern. The earliest recorded date is for a specimen taken by Fred T. Naumann during a brief spell of warm weather at Forsyth (Monroe County) on February 10, 1957. In March, spring emergence is reaching its peak, and adults may be easily seen and captured on Wild Plum blossoms in localities where *P. m-album* occurs.

In the Bibb County area, according to J. C. Brooks, *P. m-album is* "rare. May be expected with [*Atlides*] *halesus* in March, June, July, August and September. More common in spring. Usually taken as an accident."

A most unusual accidental catch was made by John Symmes when collecting near his home with Dr. John M. Burns and me on August 22, 1967. A robber fly (*Asilus* sp.) was flying rapidly by with a small butterfly impaled on its beak. Symmes made a quick sweep with his net: to our surprise, the victim of the robber fly was a *P. m-album!*

The common name of this attractive little butterfly, White M Hairstreak, refers to the white M (or W, depending on how one looks at it) formed by the postmedian line on the lower sides of the hindwings. The real beauty of this hairstreak is displayed on the upper sides of its wings, which are resplendant with iridescent blue bordered with black.

Abbot's drawings of the adults, larva, and pupa were published by Boisduval and LeConte (1829–1833, pls. 26 and 27). Harry K. Clench, an expert on the family Lycaenidae, has given an excellent account of the early stages of *P. m-album* (1966, pp. 226–238).

The larva is about three-quarters of an inch long when mature. Its head is black, and its body green and downy. The back is marked by one dark green middorsal stripe; there are seven oblique dark green stripes on each side of the body. The larval food plants are various oaks (*Quercus*).

Genus *Strymon*

Gray Hairstreak. *Strymon melinus melinus* Hübner
(Page 117)

Distribution and Records: *S. m. melinus*, the type locality of which is Georgia, is found throughout the state.

Mountain Region—*Banks Co.* and *Habersham Co.*: 27 July 1930 RWM (see Montgomery, 1931). *Union Co.*: Cooper Creek State Park, 20 Aug 1951 PWF (TTRS).
Piedmont Region—*Coweta Co.*: Madras, 2 Mar 1951 MES. *Monroe Co.*: Forsyth, 11 Mar 1961 FTN; Forsyth, 16 and 20 Mar 1966 FTN. *Bibb Co.*: Macon, 21 Mar 1966 FTN. *Forsyth Co.*: Lake Lanier, near Cumming, 2 June 1962 JRH (TTRS).
Coastal Region—*Grady Co.*: Beachton, Sherwood Plantation, 1 Jan 1965 LN; Beachton, Susina Plantation, 2 Jan 1965 LHJ (TTRS). *Baker Co.*: Newton, Wildfair Plantation, 11 Feb 1965 LN. *Grady Co.*: Beachton, Birdsong Plantation, ex larva 12 Apr 1955 LHJ (TTRS). *Colquitt Co.*: Moultrie, 21 Apr 1945 HVAV (UWO). *Thomas Co.*: Metcalf, 18 May 1954 LHJ (TTRS); Thomasville, 2 June 1954 EVK (TTRS); Boston, Bar-M Ranch, 8, 13, and 15 July 1967 ESS (TTRS); six miles southeast of Metcalf, one normal and one aberration, 11 Aug 1965 LN. *Screven Co.*: Sylvania area, Mar–Sept 1946 OB (AMNH).

This is one of our most common hairstreaks. I have listed only a few representative records in the list above, as a long list seems unwarranted for so common a species. There are several broods, and the adults may be met with frequently during the spring, summer, and fall months. In the Bibb County area, J. C. Brooks found it common in March, May, July, and September. In Clarke County, at Athens, Leslie R. Tanner found *S. m. melinus* to be common in August and September of 1966 and in April of 1967.

S. m. melinus is easily identified by its clear blue-gray upper side and its light lower side. There is a prominent orange spot on both the upper and the lower surfaces of the hindwing near the tail.

An unusual aberration was collected by Leon Neel in Thomas County on August 11, 1965. Neel also collected a normal specimen at the same time and place.

On March 20, 1955, I made a visit to Grady County, where I found three small, slug-shaped caterpillars, pale green in color with oblique yellow stripes on each side, feeding on

Flame Azalea blossoms (*Rhododendron calendulaceum*). They were concealed inside the trumpet of the flower and were facing outward, eating the outer edge of the trumpet. They moved on to fresh flowers when they had eaten the original ones to the point where they were unable to conceal themselves.

The caterpillars and plants were collected and brought home to Avondale Estates on March 21. On the morning of March 27, one of the caterpillars became restless, and crawled down the plant to the floor of the container. It was placed on a fresh flower, but instead of feeding, it immediately began to crawl again and descended to the floor of the box, on which soil had been placed with some dead leaves and twigs from the woods.

It was noted that, during the several hours of continuous crawling on March 27, the caterpillar gradually changed from pale green with oblique yellow stripes to a very light or reddish brown with the stripes scarcely discernible. A few minutes after it was placed on the leaves and forest soil, it crawled underneath a brown leaf and became quiescent. When examined on March 28, no change was noted. On March 29, the color had changed from light brown to pale cream.

The caterpillar made a small silken mat on a leaf lying on the surface of the soil but hidden by another leaf above it. It changed to a pupa on March 30. At first, the color of the pupa was a pale cream, but by April 11, it had become brown in the area where the head, thorax, and wings were located. The abdomen remained pale cream in noticeable contrast to the dark anterior area. The butterfly emerged on April 12, 1955, and was a fine specimen of *S. m. melinus*, the Gray Hairstreak.

In addition to Flame Azalea, the larval food plants include Mallow (*Malva*), Globe-Mallow (*Sphaeralcea*), Knotweed (*Polygonum*), Hops (*Humulus*), Hounds-Tongue (*Cynoglossum*), Hawthorne (*Crataegus*), St. Johnswart (*Hypericum*), and cultivated beans of the genus *Phaseolus*.

Subfamily GERYDINAE

Genus *Feniseca*

The Harvester. *Feniseca tarquinius tarquinius* Fabricius
(Page 123)

Distribution and Records: *F. t. tarquinius* is widely distributed over the state but is very local.

Mountain Region—None.
Piedmont Region—*Monroe Co.*: Forsyth, 13 Feb 1961 FTN. *Fulton Co.*: Oglethorpe College, Mar 1954 JPK (see Knudsen, 1954a). *Coweta Co.*: Madras, 26 Mar 1951 MES. *Richmond Co.*: Augusta, 6 Apr 1941 HWE. *Clarke Co.*: Athens, early April AGR (see Richards, 1931). *Bibb Co.*: Stone Creek, 11 Apr 1960 JCBS and FTN. *Cobb Co.*: Marietta area, 21 Apr 1960 JCS. *DeKalb Co.*: Avondale Estates, 4 June 1949 LNH (TTRS); Avondale Estates, 6 June 1949 LHJ (TTRS). *Bibb Co.*: Macon, 11 June 1924 HFS (TTRS). *DeKalb Co.*: Avondale Estates, 1 July 1949 LHJ. *Fulton Co.*: Atlanta, 10 July 1957 JCS; Atlanta, 6 Aug 1958 JCS. *Richmond Co.*: Augusta, 31 Aug 1945 HWE. *Clarke Co.*: Athens, early Sept AGR (see Richards, 1931). *Fulton Co.*: Oglethorpe College, Sept JPK (see Knudsen, 1954a).
Coastal Region—*Screven Co.*: Sylvania, 8 July 1946 OB (AMNH). *Baker Co.*: Flint River, near Newton, 15 Sept 1968 LN.

The Harvester is most often found singly or in groups of two or three. Therefore, Fred T. Naumann and J. C. Brooks were understandably amazed as they stood in one spot in a small clearing near Stone Creek in Bibb County on April 11, 1960, and collected eight specimens from practically the same twig.

Brooks had already found that *F. t. tarquinius* was locally common in the Bibb County area, and noted that it was triple-brooded, with broods appearing in April, early July, and from late August through early September. He observed that the adults of the later broods were paler in color than adults of the April brood.

225

J. P. Knudsen (1954) found *F. t. tarquinius* to be infrequent on the Oglethorpe College campus. He stated that the larva "is carnivorus and feeds upon the woolly alder aphis. It is found only along streams or in swamps."

The larva is slug-shaped, and about one-half inch long when mature. Its body is brown with brownish stripes. The larval foods are mainly woolly aphids, especially the kind found on alders, and the cottony beechtree aphid.

Subfamily LYCAENINAE

Genus *Lycaena*

American Copper. *Lycaena phlaeas americana* T. W. Harris
(Page 119)

Distribution and Records: *L. p. americana*, a small, brightly colored species, reaches the southern limit of its range in the extreme eastern part of Georgia. Although it is a common species in the northeastern states, it becomes rare in the south; in Georgia, it is very local and rare.

Mountain Region—*Rabun Co.*: Lake Rabun, June and July AGR (see Richards, 1931). *Banks Co.* and *Habersham Co.*: 24 Aug 1930 RWM (see Montgomery, 1931).

Piedmont Region—*Richmond Co.*: Augusta, 3 Apr 1941 HWE. *Clarke Co.*: Athens, late Mar and Aug–Sept AGR (see Richards, 1931).

Coastal Region—None.

L. p. americana can easily be overlooked, like other small butterflies that fly close to the ground.

There are interesting accounts of the aggressive and pugnacious disposition of this little butterfly, which will establish a territory for itself and will fearlessly attack larger butterflies and animals in its efforts to drive them away.

There are three broods in the south.

The larva is slug-shaped and rosy red or sorrel with lateral stripes. It feeds on several species of Sorrel (*Rumex*).

Subfamily PLEBEIINAE

Genus *Brephidium*

Eastern Pygmy Blue. *Brephidium isophthalma pseudofea*
Morrison (Page 119)

Distribution and Records: The type locality of *B. i. pseudofea* is Florida. In Georgia, this little butterfly is found in salt marsh areas in the Coastal Region. It is locally common on some of Georgia's coastal islands, and at favorable localities at the edge of inland salt marshes which extend along rivers and inlets affected by the tidal flow near the coast.

Mountain Region—None.
Piedmont Region—None.
Coastal Region—*Glynn Co.*: St. Simons Island, 19 May 1965 LNH and LHJ; St. Simons Island, 5 June 1929 LHJ (TTRS). *Chatham Co.*: Savannah, Oglethorpe Cemetery, 30 July 1958 GBS; Oglethorpe Cemetery, 15 Aug 1958 GBS.

I found my first colony of the Eastern Pygmy Blue on St. Simons Island, near the monument that marks the historic battle of Bloody Marsh, on June 5, 1929; the colony was still in existence when I visited it again on May 19, 1965. Another colony was found in the low grass at the edge of the Frederica River adjacent to the ruins of Fort Frederica on St. Simons Island. Fort Frederica is now a national monument.

In Chatham County, Gordon B. Small, Jr., found the Eastern Pygmy Blue very abundant at the edge of the salt marsh at Oglethorpe Cemetery near Thunderbolt, a suburb of Savannah. He collected specimens there on July 30 and August 15, 1958.

The Eastern Pygmy Blue is so small that it is easily overlooked.

My experience with this species coincides with H. L. King's report (in Kimball, 1965, p. 49) that its presence is very spasmodic. It may seem to be absent for several years and then suddenly become plentiful.

The early stages of *B. i. pseudofea* have been described by George W. Rawson (1961, pp. 88–91). He reared the larvae on Glasswort (*Salicornia bigelovi*). He believes (Kimball, 1965, p. 49) that it also feeds on Saltwort (*Batis maritima*).

Genus *Hemiargus*

Ceraunus Blue. *Hemiargus ceraunus antibubastus* Hübner
(Page 119)

Distribution and Records: *H. c. antibubastus*, the type locality of which is Georgia, inhabits the Coastal Region. It is common along the coast and on the coastal islands. It is locally common inland on the Lower Coastal Plain; it is rare and local on the Upper Coastal Plain.

Mountain Region—None.
Piedmont Region—*Bibb Co.*: Macon, 8 Sept 1933 HFS.
Coastal Region—*Grady Co.*: Melton Place, 6 Jan 1965 LN. *Thomas Co.*: Metcalf, 11 Aug 1965 LN. *Camden Co.*: near junction of State Roads 40 and 110, 17 Aug 1949 LHJ (TTRS). *Glynn Co.*: St. Simons Island, 19 Aug 1951 LHJ (TTRS). *Grady Co.*: Beachton, Susina Plantation, 7 Sept 1963 LHJ (TTRS). *Chatham Co.*: Tybee Island, 25 Sept 1946 OB (AMNH). *Dougherty Co.*: Albany, Prehistoric Sand Dunes, 13 Oct 1966 LN. *Grady Co.*: Beachton, Sherwood Plantation, 25 Oct 1965 JN.

Otto Buchholz found *H. c. antibubastus* to be common on Tybee Island not far from Savannah, and I found a colony in the southwest corner of Camden County near the junction of State Roads 40 and 110. A number of new locations in southwest Georgia have been recorded in recent years by Leon and Julia Neel. Many years ago, on September 8, 1933, Fred Strohecker found an active colony in the Macon area in the Piedmont Region and collected several specimens.

A Georgia specimen from Tybee Island is figured by Klots, (1951, pl. 19, fig. 3).

There are at least two broods, perhaps three. The earliest date recorded for this butterfly in Georgia is January 6, 1965, and the latest is October 25, 1965; the specimens were collected by Leon Neel and Julia Neel, respectively.

The larva is dimorphic. In one form, the body is green with a reddish dorsal stripe; in the other the body is reddish with a greenish shading. The larval food plants are Partridge Pea (*Cassia brachiata*), Hairy Partridge Pea (*C. aspera*), and Crabs-Eye Vine or Rosary Pea (*Abrus precatorius*).

Subfamily PLEBEIINAE

Genus *Lycaeides*

Scudder's Blue. *Lycaeides argyrognomon scudderii*
Edwards

Distribution and Records: *L. a. scudderii* is not found in Georgia. This butterfly was included in *The Butterflies of Georgia, Revised* on the basis of an old, unconfirmed, 1905 record and a report that I received in 1950 that a butterfly closely related to "*scudderii*" had been recorded from Blantyre, North Carolina, and would be described "in the near future." This proved to be inaccurate information, for it developed later that the material was not from the south. It had been mislabeled through an understandable but regrettable error.

Genus *Everes*

Eastern Tailed Blue. *Everes comyntas comyntas* Godart
(Page 119)

Distribution and Records: *E. c. comyntas* is abundant and is found throughout the state from spring until fall. Because *E. c. comyntas* is very common, only a few representative records are listed.

Mountain Region—*Lumpkin Co.*: Auraria, 15 Apr 1967 LHJ

(TTRS); Woody Gap, 16 Apr 1967 BMR. *White Co.*: Helen, 15 June 1952 LHJ (TTRS). *Towns Co.*: Brasstown Bald, 16 June 1954 LHT. *Banks Co.* and *Habersham Co.*: 17 June–17 Sept 1930 RWM (see Montgomery, 1931).
Piedmont Region—*Clarke Co.*: Athens, abundant Mar 1967 LRT. *Monroe Co.*: Forsyth, 12 and 13 Mar 1955 FTN. *Coweta Co.*: Madras, 24 Mar 1950 MES. *DeKalb Co.*: Avondale Estates, 1 Apr 1945 LHJ (TTRS); Stone Mountain, 3 May 1952 LHJ (TTRS). *Fulton Co.*: Atlanta, Harris Trail, 22 Aug 1967 LHJ (TTRS). *Clarke Co.*: Athens, abundant Aug 1966 LRT; Athens, abundant Sept 1966 LRT.
Coastal Region—*Grady Co.*: Beachton, Sherwood Plantation, 19 Jan 1965 LN; Beachton, Sherwood Plantation, 10 Feb 1965 JN. *Colquitt Co.*: Moultrie, 12 and 17 Mar 1945 HVAV (UWO). *Screven Co.*: Millhaven, 15 Mar 1952 LHJ (TTRS). *Thomas Co.*: Mill Pond Plantation, 17 Apr 1967 ESS. *Grady Co.*: Beachton, Sherwood Plantation, 25 Apr 1965 LN; Birdsong Plantation, 16 May 1954 EVK (TTRS). *Baker Co.*: Newton, Blue Springs Plantation, 14 Aug 1964 LN. *Dougherty Co.*: Gillionville, 7 Sept 1964 LN. *Charlton Co.*: Billy's Island, Okefenokee Swamp, 21 Oct 1937 LHJ. *Baker Co.*: Newton, Blue Springs Plantation, 10 Nov 1964 LN.

This attractive and spritely little butterfly usually flies close to the ground. It seems to prefer open grassy areas, meadows, fields of clover, weedy pastures, and similar areas. It visits flowers freely, and is very fond of Sweet Clover blossoms.

Abbot's drawing (in Boisduval and LeConte, 1829–1833, pl. 36) delineates the larva, the pupa, and the upper and lower sides of the adults.

An excellent, detailed, illustrated account of the early stages is given by Lawrence and Downey (1966, pp. 61–96). The larva is small and slug-shaped with a brown stripe extending along the back of its green body. There are several brownish, oblique, lateral stripes along each side of the body, which is covered with very short downy hair.

The larvae are known to feed on a variety of leguminous plants. These include clovers, wild peas, False Indigo, and a number of other legumes. Lawrence and Downey (1966) found eggs and larvae on White Clover (*Trifolium repens*), Red Clover (*T. pratense*), and Bush Clover (*Lespedeza stipulaceae*).

Genus *Glaucopsyche*

Silvery Blue; Appalachian Blue. *Glaucopsyche lygdamus*
Doubleday (Page 119)

Distribution and Records: *G. l. lygdamus*, the type locality of which is Screven County, Georgia, is the Coastal Region subspecies; *G. l. nittanyensis* Chermock, the type locality of which is State College, Pennsylvania, is the subspecies found in the Mountain Region. Specimens have been taken at two widely separated locations. No specimens are known from the Piedmont Region of Georgia as yet.

Mountain Region—*Murray Co.*: Old Fort Mountain, 26 Mar 1961 LHJ (TTRS). *Lumpkin Co.*: Auraria, 15 Apr 1967 BMR. *Murray Co.*: Old Fort Mountain, 19 Apr 1964 JCS.
Piedmont Region—None.
Coastal Region—"Georgia" (no other data), (SI).

The only specimen of *G. l. lygdamus* from Georgia that I know of is one that has been in the Smithsonian Institution for many years. The label carries no data except the word "Georgia." The lower side of this specimen, a female, is figured by Clark and Clark (1951, pl. 15, fig. B). Also figured (pl. 15, fig. C) is the lower side of *G. l. nittanyensis*. The two photographs clearly show some of the chief features by which these two butterflies may be distinguished. *G. l. nittanyensis* is smaller, the white-edged black bar at the end of the cell on the lower side of the forewing is smaller, and the spots in the discal area of the lower side of the hindwing are much smaller, or nearly absent.

A. H. Clark (1948) states:

Edward Doubleday in 1842 ("The Entomologist," No. 14, p. 209,

231

December 1841) described *Polyommatus lygdamus* from a few specimens that had been collected by John Abbot presumably in the vicinity of his home at Jacksonboro, Screven County, Georgia. Jacksonboro has disappeared but it was about 10 miles north of the present county seat of Sylvania. Doubleday wrote, quoting Abbot, that *lygdamus* " 'inhabits the pine forests of North America, especially Georgia,' " adding that " 'it is very rare. It flies very swiftly.' "

Doubleday's specimens no longer exist, and since his time very few have been collected, though numerous attempts have been made to get additional material. The form that has passed as typical *lygdamus* is in reality quite distinct. True *lygdamus*, so far as we know, occurs on the coastal plain, whereas the form that passes as typical *lygdamus* seems to be confined to the Appalachians and the Ozarks.

Clark (1948) then described *Polyommatus boydi*, but learned afterward (1951, pp. 72–73) that *P. boydi* was a synonym of *G. l. nittanyensis*, which had been described by F. H. Chermock at an earlier date.

It seems likely that *G. l. nittanyensis* occurs rather widely but locally in the Mountain Region of north Georgia. Mrs. Harris and I first learned of its presence when we were collecting with Mr. and Mrs. J. C. Symmes on Old Fort Mountain in Murray County on March 26, 1961. Mrs. Harris called our attention to a swiftly flying blue, which, when captured, proved to be the first Georgia record of *G. l. nittanyensis*. On April 19, 1964, John Symmes collected two specimens on the same mountain road about one-fourth of a mile from the first locality.

On April 15, 1967, Bryant Mather, John Symmes, and I drove to Lumpkin County. We stopped near Auraria, and as we were getting out of the car Symmes spotted a specimen of *G. l. nittanyensis*. Mather grabbed a net and caught it on the first swing. This was a new record for this area of the state, which lies about seventy miles east-southeast of Old Fort Mountain. It was the only specimen of *G. l. nittanyensis* that we saw in two days of intensive collecting in a wide area around Dahlonega, but it was proof that this butterfly is established widely in north Georgia. It should be sought in March, April, and May in the mountainous parts of the state, especially in damp wooded valleys and on wooded hillsides and mountains where there are growths of its food plant, Carolina Vetch (*Vicia caroliniana*).

In November, 1950, in a personal communication, Otto Buchholz stated:

I have before me eleven *G. lygdamus*. These were taken by M. E. Smith only 30 miles west of Georgia at his former home, Anniston, Alabama, from March 31 to April 19, 1941. The general flora around there looks to me very much like western central Georgia.

The Buchholz collection is now located in the American Museum of Natural History.

Dr. Walfried J. Reinthal has collected *G. l. nittanyensis* in east Tennessee. He wrote to me:

So far found in the Knoxville area in two places. No doubt, however, if one would watch more closely its foodplant, Carolina Vetch (*Vicia caroliniana*) I am sure the distribution will be better known here. Its occurrence here in both cases is in rocky moist woods where it flies around its foodplant and along the wooded path. I visited the place in Oak Ridge on April 21 and 22, 1962. Both males and females were flying in company with *Everes comyntas*, and not always easily distinguishable in flight from each other. Watch for the foodplant on Old Fort Mountain slopes and you certainly will find more of *lygdamus*.

The larva of *G. lygdamus* is slug-shaped. The body is light green with flecks of white, the dorsal stripes are dark green bordered with yellowish green, and the head is black.

Genus *Celastrina*

Spring Azure. *Celastrina argiolus pseudargiolus*
Boisduval and LeConte (Page 119)

Distribution and Records: *C. a. pseudargiolus* is found

throughout the state. It is local in its occurrence and becomes locally common at times.

Mountain Region—*Murray Co.*: Old Fort Mountain, 21 Mar 1962 JCS; Old Fort Mountain, 26 and 29 Mar 1961 LHJ (TTRS); Old Fort Mountain, 28 Mar 1963 LHJ (TTRS). *Lumpkin Co.*: Auraria, 15 Apr 1967 LHJ. *Fannin Co.*: Margret, 16 Apr 1967 BMR. *White Co.*: Unicoi Gap (alt. 2900 ft), 15 June 1954 LHT (TTRS). *Fannin Co.*: Cooper Creek State Park, 7 Aug 1965 LNH (TTRS). *Rabun Co.*: LaPrades, Lake Burton, 18 Aug 1965 LHT. *Banks Co.* and *Habersham Co.*: 24 Aug 1930 RWM (see Montgomery, 1931).

Piedmont Region—*Monroe Co.*: Forsyth, 4 Mar 1961 FTN; Forsyth, 18 Mar 1957 FTN. *Fulton Co.*: Atlanta area, 28 Mar 1956 LHJ (TTRS). *Clarke Co.*: Athens, Mar, Apr, and May 1967 LRT. *Fulton Co.*: Atlanta area, 10 May 1956 JCS. *Coweta Co.*: Madras, 11 May 1950 MES. *Fulton Co.*: Atlanta, Riverside Drive, 12 May 1956 LHJ (TTRS); Atlanta, Indian Trail Road, 20 June 1958 LHJ (TTRS); Atlanta, Harris Trail (Symmes Field), 22 Aug 1967 LHJ (TTRS); Roswell, Ox Road, 26 Aug 1961 LHJ. *Clarke Co.*: Athens, July, Aug, and Sept 1966 LRT.

Coastal Region—*Thomas Co.*: Mill Pond Plantation, 10 Feb 1965 LN; Mill Pond Plantation, 16, 17, and 19 Apr 1967 ESS. *Grady Co.*: Beachton, Sherwood Plantation, 24 Apr 1965 LN; Beachton, Sherwood Plantation, 9 May 1965 LN; Beachton, Susina Plantation, 17 May 1967 LNH and LHJ. *Screven Co.*: Sylvania area, summer 1946 OB (AMNH). *Thomas Co.*: Thomasville, 10 July 1944 LHJ; Boston, Bar-M Ranch, 14 July 1967 ESS (TTRS). *Grady Co.*: Beachton, Sherwood Plantation, 29 July 1965 LN. *Thomas Co.*: Mill Pond Plantation, 29 July 1965 LN. *Charlton Co.*: Folkston, 17 Aug 1949 LHJ.

John Abbot was well acquainted with this beautiful blue butterfly, and his drawings of it were used by J. E. Smith (1797, pl. 15) and Boisduval and LeConte (1829–1833, pl. 36). Each drawing represented a different seasonal form.

There are three seasonal forms in Georgia. The spring form, *C. a. pseudargiolus* f. *violacea*, appears in March and is present through April into the first half of May. The butterfly visits the blossoms of Plum and Peach (*Prunus* spp.) and various other flowers. The summer form, *C. a. pseudargiolus* f. *neglecta*, appears in July and is present until September. It may often be found on moist patches of ground. Sometimes several individuals may be found in a single place. The third form, *C. a. pseudargiolus* f. *neglecta-major*, is a rare form that is larger in size than the others. It may appear between the spring and summer broods, usually in June. It is very local in occurrence and generally rare.

Professor P. W. Fattig found *C. a. pseudargiolus* f. *neglecta-major* in the mountains at Unicoi Gap in White County on State Highway 75. The butterflies were resting on leaves of blackberry bushes that were growing in an area about a hundred feet below the Unicoi Gap historic marker. Several years later, on June 15, 1954, my son Lucien and I collected some specimens in the same area. John Symmes has collected a number of beautiful specimens of the same form in an area near his home in Atlanta.

Mrs. Harris and I once found a cool, shady area by a rippling mountain brook where we paused to behold dozens of Spring Azures sitting on a moist patch of ground at the edge of the stream. They were eagerly partaking of some treat that nature had provided. Many such pleasant memories of beauty in quiet places are stored away in the minds and hearts of lepidopterists.

The larva is only two-fifths of an inch long when fully grown. The mature larva is slug-shaped, with a small, dark brown head. The body is pale, turning a rosy hue when the larva is nearing pupation. A dark stripe runs along the back lengthwise, and there are several oblique, dark green stripes on each side of the body. Klots (1951, p. 170) states that the larvae are much attended by ants. Ellen Robertson-Miller (1931, pp. 196–203) gives a delightful detailed account of finding and rearing larvae of the Spring Azure.

Abbot (in Smith, 1797, p. 29) wrote:

235

The caterpillar was taken feeding on the plant here represented [Scarlet-flowered Trumpet or Coral-honeysuckle, *Lonicera sempervirens*]; it also eats the red root or red shank [*Ceonanthus*], but is rarely met with, though the butterfly is often seen both in Georgia and Virginia. Its first [*sic*; last?] change took place on the 16th of June, and the fly appeared nine days afterwards.

The larval food plants are Black Snake-root or Black Cohash (*Cimicifuga racemosa*), New Jersey Tea (*Ceonanthus americana*), Dogwood (*Cornus florida*), Sumac (*Rhus* spp.), and a number of other plants.

Family LIBYTHEIDAE—Snout Butterflies

Genus *Libytheana*

Snout Butterfly. *Libytheana bachmanii bachmanii* Kirtland
(Page 123)

Distribution and Records: *L. b. bachmanii* is found throughout the state, but is somewhat local. It is rare in some areas, but it is locally common at times in other areas, especially in the vicinity of its food plant, Hackberry (*Celtis*).

Mountain Region—None [but, according to Richards (1931, p. 248), it is found "throughout the upper Austral Zone, but greatly restricted to the immediate vicinity of its food plant *Celtis*. April–October."].

Piedmont Region—*Morgan Co.*: Madison, 7 Jan 1967 JCS and LHJ. *Coweta Co.*: Madras, 18 Mar 1950 MES. *Cobb Co.*: Windy Hill Farm, near Marietta, 18–19 Mar 1950 LHT (TTRS). *Fulton Co.*: Atlanta, Riverside Drive, 25 Mar 1959 LHJ (TTRS). *Bibb Co.*: Macon, 24 June 1961 FTN. *Fulton Co.*: near Roswell, 10 July 1965 LHJ (TTRS). *Clarke Co.*: Athens, Sept 1966 LRT. *Bibb Co.*: Macon, 13 Sept 1953 LHJ (TTRS).

Coastal Region—*Baker Co.*: Newton, 9 Feb 1965 LN. *Grady Co.*: Beachton, Susina Plantation, 7 and 10 Mar 1964 LHJ (TTRS). *Decatur Co.*: near Bainbridge, 17 May 1953 EVK (TTRS). *Chatham Co.*: Savannah, 28 May 1960 LHJ (TTRS).

Screven Co.: May and June 1946 OB (AMNH). *Baker Co.*: Newton, Blue Springs Plantation, 4 and 14 Aug 1964 LN.

In March, it may be found on the blossoms of Plum and Peach (*Prunus* spp.), Dogwood (*Cornus* spp.), and other trees and shrubs. At times, several individuals may be seen flying around the blossoms of a single tree.

In July and August, *L. b. bachmannii* may be found sipping moisture from a damp spot on the ground, sometimes in company with the various "yellows."

In the Bibb County area, Brooks found that it was one of the first butterflies to appear in February. He observed that it became abundant in June and again in August.

The Snout Butterfly can easily be identified by its front wings, which look as if the tips had been clipped off with curved fingernail scissors, and by its "snout," which is formed by the palpi projecting about one-fourth of an inch straight out in front of the head.

Comstock and Comstock (1920, p. 211) state that the males have only four legs, while the females have six. One wonders why!

The body of the larva is dark green with three yellow lengthwise stripes. The head is small, and the body is enlarged behind the head with a hump bearing two black tubercles ringed basally with yellow.

Cuban Snout Butterfly. *Libytheana motya* (?)

Distribution and Records: Early in 1970, Mr. Cyril F. dos Passos advised me that he had received a photograph of an authentic specimen of *L. motya* collected in Texas. This posed an important question: Did John Abbot collect in Georgia the specimens of *L. motya* shown in his drawing of this species figured by Boisduval and LeConte (1829–1833, pl. 64)? Abbot's drawing includes the larva, the pupa, two of the butterflies, and the food plant (*Celtis*). Unfortunately, no text accompanied the illustration. It is not known where the specimens were found, nor by whom, nor how Abbot obtained them. There is a possibility that Abbot may have collected a specimen of *L. motya* as a rare stray in coastal Georgia, or that he may have obtained it from a source outside of Georgia, but without this vital information, anything we might conclude about the occurrence of this butterfly in Georgia would be pure speculation.

In addition to *L. motya*, two other Abbot drawings of Cuban butterflies were included by Boisduval and LeConte, namely *Papilio sinon* (pl. 3) and *Papilio villiersii* (pl. 14). The texts for these plates list Florida and Cuba as the habitat of both species, with *P. sinon* also occurring in Jamaica. Both species were noted to be rare in Florida. *P. sinon* is a synonym of *P. celadon*, and *P. villiersii* is a synonym of *P. devilliers*. There are no current authentic records for these species in Florida, according to Charles P. Kimball (1965, pp. 31–33).

Family NYMPHALIDAE—Brush-Footed Butterflies

Subfamily LIMENITINAE

Genus *Anaea*

Goatweed Butterfly. *Anaea andria andria* Scudder
(Page 121)

Distribution and Records: *A. a. andria* is found throughout the state, but is generally rare and very local.

Mountain Region—*Fannin Co.*: Blue Ridge Wildlife Area, 16 Apr 1967 BMR; Blue Ridge Wildlife Area, 16 Apr 1967 JCS. *Gilmer Co.*: four miles east of Old Fort Mountain, 6 May 1964 JCS.
Piedmont Region—*Coweta Co.*: Madras, 24 Mar 1949 MES. *Bibb Co.*: sight records Feb, Mar, June, Aug, and Sept JCBS; Macon, 12 Apr 1930 HFS (TTRS).
Coastal Region—*Colquitt Co.*: Moultrie, two females 17 Mar

1945 HVAV (UWO); Moultrie, one male 3 Apr 1945 HVAV (UWO).

The Goatweed Butterfly has a rapid flight and is not easily captured. It is usually seen most often in early spring. In the Bibb County area, J. C. Brooks found it to be uncommon to rare, with adults on the wing in February and March, June, August, and September. He found them near a swamp and also in dry pine barrens.

On April 5, 1953, J. P. Knudsen and I observed two males on Old Fort Mountain in Murray County. They were extremely wary, and would fly up quickly when approached. On April 16, 1967, Bryant Mather and John Symmes collected specimens in the mountain area of Fannin County near Margret.

Three specimens collected by Hal and Ann Vogel in Colquitt County, in the Coastal Region, are now in the collection that they presented to the University of Western Ontario. They were brought to my attention through the kindness of Desmond Lanktree.

A. a. andria has two forms, the summer or "dry-season" form, and the winter or "wet-season" form. The latter is known to hibernate (Klots, 1951, p. 117).

The length of the mature larva is about one and one-half inches. Its body is grayish green and covered with many raised points. Its head is gray green with small tubercles; the tubercles on the crown are slightly larger than the others. The larval food plants are various species of Goatweed (*Croton*). Several species of Goatweed occur in Georgia.

Genus *Asterocampa*

Hackberry Butterfly. *Asterocampa celtis*
Boisduval and LeConte (Page 121)

Distribution and Records: *A. c. celtis*, the type locality of which is Georgia, occurs widely over the state. It is sometimes locally common, and is found in close association with the

foodplant, Hackberry (*Celtis*). *A. c. alicia* Edwards, the type
locality of which is New Orleans, Louisiana, is found in Georgia along the coast—including some of the coastal islands,
such as Jekyll Island, St. Simons Island, and Sea Island—and
on the lower Coastal Plain. Dr. W. J. Reinthal, an authority on
the genus *Asterocampa*, has informed me that specimens closely resembling *A. c. alicia* have been found as far north as
Macon, Georgia.

Mountain Region—None.

Piedmont Region—*Monroe Co.*: Forsyth, females at bait trap 16
May 1962 FTN; Forsyth, males at bait trap 28 and 29 May
1966 FTN. *Fulton Co.*: Atlanta, 1 June 1950 PWF (TTRS).
Clarke Co.: Athens, 6 June 1929 AGR (USNM). *Monroe Co.*:
Forsyth, 2 and 9 June 1966 FTN. *Rockdale Co.*: Panola Moun-
tain, 12 June 1969 JC. *Bibb Co.*: Macon, 12 June 1961 FTN.
Fulton Co.: Atlanta, 23 June 1960 JCS; Atlanta, 7–10 July
1960 JCS. *Clarke Co.*: Athens, 4 Aug 1926 AGR (see Richards,
1931). *Monroe Co.*: Forsyth, 17 Aug 1965 HAF. *Troup Co.*:
LaGrange, 1 Sept 1963 HAF. *Coweta Co.*: Madras, 11 Sept
1952 MES. *Bibb Co.*: Macon, 11 Sept 1952 LHJ (TTRS);
Macon, 13 Sept 1953 LHJ (TTRS). *Bartow Co.*: near Etowah
Indian Mounds, 22 Sept 1968 JC.

Coastal Region—*Chatham Co.*: Savannah, 27 May 1960 JCS*;
Savannah, 28 May 1960 LHJ (TTRS)*; Savannah, no dates
MHM (CU)*. *Baker Co.*: Newton, Blue Springs Plantation,
14 Aug 1964 LN; Newton, Blue Springs Plantation, 15 Sept
1964 LN; Newton, Flint River Bridge, 26 Sept 1968 LHJ; Newton, Blue Springs Plantation, 6 Oct 1964 LN.

John Abbot's drawing of *A. c. celtis* (in Boisduval and
LeConte, 1829–1833, pl. 57) delineates the butterfly, the
larva, the pupa, and the food plant, Hackberry.

In the Macon area of Bibb County, *A. c. celtis* has been
found by J. C. Brooks and W. J. Reinthal to be abundant in
May, June, August, and September.

Certain records included in *The Butterflies of Georgia, Re-*

* Records followed by an asterisk indicate specimens of *A. C. alicia*; all
others are *A. C. celtis*.

vised (Harris, 1950) need clarification: Two unconfirmed records of *A. c. alicia* were reported. The Atlanta record was made about 1900 and is questionable. The other record was made in 1912 and probably represents *A. c. celtis* and not *A. c. alicia*.

Dr. W. J. Reinthal tells me, on the basis of his exhaustive studies, that *A. c. celtis* and *A. c. alicia* are actually distinct species. He is preparing for publication a paper to report his findings.

The fully grown larva is largest in the middle of the body, tapering evenly toward both ends. The head bears two erect horns, each having branching spines that give a "stag-horn" effect. The body is striped in yellow and green. The caudal segment of the body is forked.

Tawny Emperor. *Asterocampa clyton* Boisduval and LeConte
(Page 121)

Distribution and Records: The subspecies *A. c. clyton* occurs over most of the state, but is generally rare. Although we do not have records for the Mountain Region, it almost certainly occurs there. Joe Carter has collected it in Bartow County near the Etowah Indian Mounds at the edge of the Mountain Region. The subspecies *A. c. flora* Edwards, the type locality of which is Palatka, Florida, is reported by Charles P. Kimball (1965, p. 45) as being common in Florida. In Georgia, it occurs in the Coastal Region. More study and additional records are needed to determine the distribution of *A. c. flora*, but it seems likely that it may be fairly common in extreme south Georgia and along the coast, and possibly infrequent to rare on the Upper Coastal Plain.

Mountain Region—None.
Piedmont Region—*Monroe Co.*: Forsyth, at bait trap 1 June 1965 FTN. *Bibb Co.*: Macon, 7 June 1930 HFS (TTRS); Macon, at bait trap 12 June 1961 FTN; Macon, 10 and 19 Aug 1929 HFS

(TTRS). *Troup Co.*: LaGrange, 1 Sept 1963 HAF. *Bibb Co.*:
Macon, 10 Sept 1931 HFS (TTRS); Macon, 21 Sept 1929 HFS
(TTRS). *Bartow Co.*: near Etowah Indian Mounds, one female
A.c. clyton f. *prosperpina* 22 Sept 1968 JC.
Coastal Region—*Chatham Co.*: Savannah, no dates MHM (CU).
Lee Co.: Leesburg, Hickory Grove Plantation, 1 July 1965 LN.

In *The Butterflies of Georgia, Revised* (Harris, 1950), it
was stated that a specimen of *A. c. flora* was collected in Macon
in the fall of 1925. Also it was stated that *A. c. clyton* and *A. c.
flora* were taken in Augusta by the late H. W. Eustis. While
this seemed questionable at that time, it now appears likely
that these butterflies may actually be distinct species. Dr. W. J.
Reinthal considers them to be two separate species, and if he is
correct, the occurrence of the two sympatrically is, of course,
possible. Despite his efforts, he has not been able to examine
and determine the specimens in the H. W. Eustis collection in
Augusta. Therefore, he says, the question of which of these
butterflies occurs in the Augusta area remains open, pending
further investigation.

H. W. Eustis found that ripe figs attracted Hackberry Butterflies, and that they could easily be caught on this fruit. Reinthal
reports that he has had similar experiences in many states
where *Asterocampa* species, along with other nymphalids, have
been observed in large numbers feeding upon rotten fruit, particularly peaches, pears, plums, and persimmons.

The following observations were made by J. C. Brooks in
Bibb County:

Asterocampa clyton—common, much more local than [*A.*] *celtis*.
Prefers same woodland areas but seldom enters city [Macon]. Apparently two broods, June and August. Much slower feeder than
celtis as larva. *Clyton* ranges in color from a form with hindwings
above completely darkened (form *prosperpina*) to bright brick-red
specimens with well defined markings.

John Abbot's excellent watercolor painting of *A. clyton*
(Boisduval and LeConte, 1829–1833, pl. 56) figures the

butterfly, larva, pupa, and the foodplant, Hackberry (*Celtis*). The fully grown larva is largest in the middle of the body, tapering evenly toward both ends. The caudal segment is forked. The head bears two erect horns, each having branched spines that give a "stag-horn" effect. The body is striped with white and yellow, and has a well-defined, dark green middorsal line.

Genus *Limenitis*

Red-Spotted Purple. *Limenitis astyanax astyanax* Fabricius
(Page 127)

Distribution and Records: *L. a. astyanax* is found locally throughout the state.

Mountain Region—*Towns Co.*: Brasstown Bald (alt. 4500 ft), 8 June 1967 LHJ (TTRS). *Rabun Co.*: LaPrades, Lake Burton, 24 June 1956 LHT (TTRS). *Union Co.*: Cooper Creek State Park, Duncan Ridge Road, 17 July 1965 JCS. *Banks Co.* and *Habersham Co.*: 27 July and 24 Aug 1930 RWM (see Montgomery, 1931).

Piedmont Region—*Monroe Co.*: Forsyth, 12 Apr 1956 FTN. *Coweta Co.*: Madras, 30 Apr 1950 MES. *Monroe Co.*: Forsyth, 2 and 3 May 1962 FTN. *Fulton Co.*: near Roswell, 10 July 1965 LHJ (TTRS); Atlanta, Buckhead area, 15 Aug 1949 LHT (TTRS). *DeKalb Co.*: Stone Mountain, 22 Aug 1950 LHT (TTRS); Stone Mountain, 10 Sept 1950 LHJ (TTRS).

Coastal Region—*Grady Co.*: Beachton, Sherwood Plantation, 10 Apr 1965 LN; Beachton, Birdsong Plantation, 30 May 1954 EVK and LHJ. *Thomas Co.*: Thomasville, Greenwood Plantation, 28 July 1967 ESS; Boston, Bar-M Ranch, 5 Aug 1967 ESS (TTRS); Metcalf, 11 Aug 1965 LN. *Grady Co.*: Beachton, Sherwood Plantation, 18 Aug 1964 JN and LN; Beachton, Sherwood Plantation, 24 Aug 1964 LN.

L. a. astyanax begins to emerge in April, and specimens may be found until the end of September. It is local in occurrence, but is fairly common in midsummer. It will frequent mud puddles and moist places. It is readily attracted to crushed-apple bait, according to J. P. Knudsen (1954, p. 4). I have sometimes found a specimen in the open woods sitting on a favorite tree leaf from which it would take off and to which it would return at intervals. A specimen from Savannah is figured by Klots (1951, pl. 15).

The larva is about one and one-half inches long at maturity; the body is naked and humpy, and bears a number of tubercles. The tubercles on the second thoracic segment are thorny, and dark in color. The color of the body is mottled, streaked, and blotched with brown, green, and buff.

Abbot reported (in Smith, 1797) that "it also eats the wild cherry and willow. On the 8th of June it suspended itself by the tail, and changed to a chrysalis on the 9th. The butterfly appeared on the 18th." The larval food plants are Wild Cherry and Plum (*Prunus* spp.), Willow (*Salix*), Apple (*Malus*), and a number of other plants. It is a general feeder.

Viceroy. *Limenitis archippus archippus* Cramer
(Page 127)

Distribution and Records: *L. a. archippus* primarily inhabits the Piedmont and Coastal regions, although it may, on rare occasions, occur at low elevations in the northern part of the state.

Mountain Region—None.
Piedmont Region—*Fulton Co.*: Oglethorpe College, May–Sept JPK (see Knudsen, 1954a). *Cherokee Co.*: Cox Road, 2 July 1960 JCS. *Coweta Co.*: Madras, 6 July 1951 MES. *Fulton Co.*: near Roswell, 10 July 1965 LHJ (TTRS). *Clarke Co.*: Athens, July 1966 LRT. *Bibb Co.*: Macon, 13 Sept 1953 LHJ (TTRS); Macon, 6 Oct 1928 HFS (TTRS).
Coastal Region—*Thomas Co.*: Thomasville, Mill Pond Plantation, 16 Apr 1967 ESS. *Seminole Co.*: Spring Creek, 20 Apr 1954 LHJ (TTRS). *Thomas Co.*: Ochlocknee, 3 May 1965 LN; Boston, 31 May 1951 EVK (TTRS). *Ware Co.*: Okefenokee Swamp, 11 June 1970 TRM. *Screven Co.*: Sylvania area, 18 June 1946 OB (AMNH). *Grady Co.*: Beachton, Birdsong

Plantation, 5 July 1957 LHJ (TTRS); Beachton, Birdsong Plantation, 5 July 1954 EVK (TTRS). *Thomas Co.*: Boston, Bar-M Ranch, 27 July 1967 ESS (TTRS). *Chatham Co.*: Savannah, 15 Aug 1947 HLK (TTRS). *Glynn Co.*: Jekyll Island, 18 Aug 1960 JCS. *Clinch Co.*: near Fargo, State Road 94, 24 Sept 1965 LNH. *Grady Co.*: Beachton, Sherwood Plantation, 8 Sept 1965 JN and LN; Beachton, Sherwood Plantation, 9 Oct 1964 LN.

Specimens in central Georgia are typical *L. archippus*, and show no hybridization with the Floridian subspecies *L. a. floridensis*. An overlap occurs in south Georgia.

Recent surveys of the distribution of *L. a. archippus* and the melanic subspecies *L. a. floridensis* have been made by Thomas R. Manley and Dr. Charles L. Remington, and their report is now in press. Their surveys show a zone of overlap extending from the northern central highlands of Florida along US Route 90 to, and including, the southern tier of counties in Georgia paralleling the Florida highlands and the Alabama border—roughly, the area south of US Route 82. The overlap zone extends north along the coast into South Carolina. In Georgia, US Route 82 extends from coastal Georgia near Savannah, southwestward to Waycross, and west via Tifton and Albany, to the Alabama state line at Eufaula. In Florida, US Route 90 extends from Jacksonville Beach westward, via Tallahassee, to the Alabama state line.

L. a. archippus is found about willows, especially those along streams and along the borders of ponds. It occurs with greater frequency in lowlands. Adults fly from June to early October in the northern half of the state, and from late April to mid-October in the southern half.

Sometimes, an aberrant specimen may be found. One of these, *L. archippus* ab. *lanthanis* Cook and Watson, which lacks the narrow postmedian line across the hindwings, was taken in Screven County on June 18, 1946, by Otto Buchholz; in Macon, Bibb County, one was collected by Dr. H. F. Strohecker on October 6, 1928.

The larva is about one inch long. Its body is humped and naked, and studded with many tubercles; the longest pair, on the second thoracic segment, are club-shaped. The color of the body is dark brownish or olive green, with a pale buff or whitish saddle on the middle segment of the body. The food plants are Willow (*Salix*) and Poplar (*Populus*).

Subfamily NYMPHALINAE

Genus *Anartia*

White Peacock. *Anartia jatrophae guantanamo* Munro
(Page 127)

Distribution and Records: *A. j. guantanamo*, which is common in south Florida, sometimes strays into Georgia.

H. L. King lived in Savannah for several years prior to moving to Sarasota. He saw the White Peacock a few times in the Savannah area.

Genus *Vanessa*

Red Admiral. *Vanessa atalanta* Linnaeus (Page 127)

Distribution and Records: *V. atalanta* is found throughout the state. It is local in occurrence, and is usually found singly rather than in groups. I have not witnessed any migrations or massed groups in Georgia.

Mountain Region—*Towns Co.*: summit of Brasstown Bald, 12 Aug 1951 LHJ.
Piedmont Region—*Cobb Co.*: Blackjack Mountain, 31 Mar 1952 LHT (TTRS). *Fulton Co.*: Atlanta, Indian Trail Road, 7 Apr 1961 LHJ (TTRS). *Clarke Co.*: Athens, Apr 1967 LRT. *Coweta Co.*: Madras, 2 Apr 1950 MES. *Monroe Co.*: Forsyth, 3 June 1961 FTN; Forsyth, 9 June 1966 FTN. *Coweta Co.*: Madras, 10 Aug 1951 MES. *Monroe Co.*: Forsyth, 19 Oct 1959 FTN.
Coastal Region—*Grady Co.*: Beachton, 6 Jan 1965 LN; Beach-

ton, Susina Plantation, 10 Apr 1965 LHJ; Beachton, Sherwood Plantation, 20 June 1965 LN; Beachton, Sherwood Plantation, 18 Sept 1964 LN. *Baker Co.*: Newton, Blue Springs Plantation, 27 and 29 Oct 1964 LN.

V. atalanta first appears in early spring. Some of these adults may have overwintered from the fall brood, while others, which are fresh, may have emerged from overwintering pupa. Eggs laid by the females in spring produce a brood that appears in June and July. This brood, in turn, is followed by a fall brood, some of which overwinter as adults and others of which remain in the pupa stage until spring. Sometimes, adults may be found on the trunks of trees where they have been attracted to fermenting sap oozing from a bruised area.

In the Bibb County area, J. C. Brooks found that it was not as common as other locally occurring Nymphalids, but appeared in fair numbers in June, August, and September. The April brood was smaller, both in size and in numbers.

The larva is about one and one-fourth inches long. It is blackish to light olive, with mottled blackish and yellowish stripes along the sides. The body bears branching spines. The larval food plants are Nettles (*Urtica,*) Hops (*Humulus*), False Nettle (*Bochmeria*), and Pellitory (*Parietaria*).

American Painted Lady; Hunter's Butterfly.
Vanessa virginiensis Drury (Page 127)

Distribution and Records: *V. virginiensis* is common throughout the state in open areas, but it may sometimes be found in open woodlands.

Mountain Region—*Banks Co.* and *Habersham Co.*: 12 Aug–1 Sept 1930 RWM (see Montgomery, 1931).
Piedmont Region—*Monroe Co.*: Forsyth, 13 Mar 1955 FTN. *Coweta Co.*: Madras, 22 Mar 1951 MES. *Monroe Co.*: Forsyth, 27 Apr 1955 FTN. *Clarke Co.*: Athens, Apr 1967 LRT. *Monroe Co.*: Forsyth, 18 June 1956 FTN; Forsyth, 30 and 31 Oct 1956 FTN; Forsyth, 18 Nov 1956 FTN.

247

Coastal Region—*Grady Co.*: Beachton, Susina Plantation, 2 Jan 1965 LHJ (TTRS); Beachton, Sherwood Plantation, 19 Mar 1952 LHJ (TTRS). *Colquitt Co.*: Moultrie, four specimens 11 and 12 Apr 1945 HVAV (UWO). *Thomas Co.*: Thomasville, Mill Pond Plantation, 17 Apr 1967 ESS; Boston, Bar-M Ranch, 13 July 1967 ESS; Boston Bar-M Ranch, 4 Aug 1967 ESS (TTRS). *Baker Co.*: Newton, Blue Springs Plantation, 18 Aug 1964 LN. *Grady Co.*: Beachton, Sherwood Plantation, 1 Sept 1964 LN; Beachton, Sherwood Plantation, 4 Nov 1964 LN.

There are two broods in the northern part of the state, and three or more in the southern part. Adults appear in March and April, and may also be found during the summer and early fall months. Occasionally, an individual may appear on warm days from November through February. Specimens may vary in size from "dwarfs" to others that are a good deal larger than average.

The larva is one and one-fourth inches long. Its body is a velvety black, with narrow cross bands of yellow; there is a row of white spots on each side of the abdominal segments, and the spines are blackish. The larval food plants are Everlasting (*Gnaphalium Obtusifolium*, locally called "Rabbit Tobacco") and other composites.

Painted Lady; Cosmopolite. *Vanessa cardui* Linnaeus
(Page 127)

Distribution and Records: *V. cardui* occurs widely over the state. It is usually local and rare except from late August through October.

Mountain Region—*Banks Co.* and *Habersham Co.*: 27 July 1930 RWM (see Montgomery, 1931). *Rabun Co.*: LaPrades, Lake Burton, 19 Aug 1952 LHT (TTRS); LaPrades, Lake Burton, 21 Aug 1966 LNH (TTRS).

Piedmont Region—*Monroe Co.*: Forsyth, 13 Mar 1955 FTN. *Coweta Co.*: Madras, 17 Mar 1950 MES. *Bibb Co.*: Macon, 13 June 1931 HFS (TTRS). *Fulton Co.*: Atlanta, Riverside

Drive, sight record 11 July 1965 JCS and LHJ. *Bartow Co.*: Cartersville, 13 Aug 1965 HAF. *DeKalb Co.*: Avondale Estates, 31 Aug 1965 LNH (TTRS). *Fulton Co.*: Atlanta, Buckhead area, 23 Sept 1949 LHT (TTRS). *Monroe Co.*: Forsyth, 30 Oct 1956 FTN; Forsyth, 18 Nov 1957 FTN.

Coastal Region—*Grady Co.*: Beachton, 6 Jan 1965 LN. *Screven Co.*: Sylvania, Mar–Sept 1946 OB (AMNH). *Grady Co.*: Beachton, Susina Plantation, sight record 15 July 1965 LHJ. *Mitchell Co.*: Camilla, 30 Aug 1965 LN. *Grady Co.*: Beachton, Sherwood Plantation, 1 Nov 1964 LN.

In September and October, *V. cardui* sometimes appears in good numbers locally. Its appearance in the fall usually coincides with the arrival of the Monarchs (*Danaus plexippus*) and Cloudless Sulphurs (*Phoebis sennae eubule*), which are migrating southward at this time. However, the number of individuals involved in the *V. cardui* migration are far less numerous than either of the other two. *V. cardui* may pass through almost unnoticed in the fall.

A number of lepidopterists have carried on excellent studies of mass movements and migrations of butterflies. Foremost among these is Dr. C. B. Williams of England. He is the author of many important articles on butterfly migrations. In his presidential address to the Fellows of the Royal Entomological Society in 1949, he stated:

In North America *V. cardui* is found as an irregular immigrant. It appears in some summers in great numbers over most of the U.S.A. and southern Canada, and as far to the northeast as Newfoundland; while in other years scarcely any are seen. The only evidence of movement into the U.S.A. in spring is into southern California, Arizona, and New Mexico, which latter area has an arid climate not unlike that of North Africa. There is no evidence of immigration into or from Florida, and indeed, there is no suitable climate or known area of breeding anywhere to the south of U.S.A. except in the extreme west. There is also no evidence of survival of the butterflies in any stage during the winter over the greater portion of the U.S.A.

If these conclusions are correct we are left with the surprising possibility that the butterflies which appear sometimes in numbers in Newfoundland must have come from western Mexico—a distance of about 3,000 miles; although it is possible that this might be done in two generations. There is in North America no evidence of a return flight to the south in autumn; but against this must be set the fact that no one has looked with any assiduity for any such evidence.

In 1965, Dr. Williams was still working on the problem of establishing the location of the winter home of *V. cardui*. He wrote to me on June 8, 1965, and stated that he had found no real evidence of its winter survival, except in northwest Mexico and, perhaps, in southern California.

Several important studies on *V. cardui* movements and migrations have been reported by a number of observers in some of the western states, including C. H. Abbot (1950, 1951, 1962), Emmel and Wabus (1966), Howe (1967), Tilden (1962), and Williams (1937, 1958).

A. G. Richards, Jr. (1931, p. 247), found *V. cardui* common in March and October in Clarke County, Georgia, from 1924 through 1927, but uncommon from 1928 through 1930. In Bibb County, J. C. Brooks found that *V. cardui* was not common, typically appearing only from late August through October. In some years, it appeared in good numbers during these months.

Of special interest is the specimen of *V. cardui* collected by Leon Neel in Grady County near Beachton on January 6, 1965. This is the only winter record for this species in Georgia, and it may indicate that a diligent search should be made for additional overwintering specimens in south Georgia and along the Gulf coast.

The larva is one and one-fourth inches long. Its head is dark, with hairs on the top. Its body is dull, greenish yellow mottled with black, and has a brighter yellow stripe along each side. The spines on the body are yellowish. The larval food plants are various members of the family Compositae—including thistles and everlastings—hollyhocks (*Althaea*), and nettles.

250

Genus *Junonia*

Buckeye. *Junonia coenia coenia* Hübner (Page 127)

Distribution and Records: *J. c. coenia* is common throughout the state.

Mountain Region—*Banks Co.* and *Habersham Co.*: 27 July and 1 Sept 1930 RWM (see Montgomery, 1931).
Piedmont Region—*DeKalb Co.*: Stone Mountain (temp. 65° F), 17 Jan 1952 PWF (TTRS); Avondale Estates, 22 Feb 1949 LHJ (TTRS). *Coweta Co.*: Madras, 24 Mar 1950 MES; Madras, 10 Apr 1951 MES. *Clarke Co.*: Athens, July 1966 LRT; Athens, Sept 1966 LRT. *Morgan Co.*: Madison, Oct 1967 JCS.
Coastal Region—*Grady Co.*: Beachton, Sherwood Plantation, 2 Jan 1965 LN (TTRS). *Charlton Co.*: Folkston, 9 Feb 1952 LHJ (TTRS). *Chatham Co.*: Savannah, 6 Apr 1960 LHJ (TTRS). *Colquitt Co.*: Moultrie, five males and one female 2–27 Apr 1945 HVAV (UWO). *Grady Co.*: Beachton, Sherwood Plantation, 20 May 1954 LHJ (TTRS); Birdsong Plantation, 6 June 1960 LHJ (TTRS). *Thomas Co.*: Boston, Bar-M Ranch, 18 July 1967 ESS (TTRS). *Sumter Co.*: Americus, 1 Aug 1965 LN. *Grady Co.*: Beachton, Sherwood Plantation, 1 Nov 1964 LN. *Thomas Co.*: Thomasville, 29 Dec 1964 LN.

J. c. coenia becomes very numerous at times, but then the cycle of abundance declines. One summer many years ago, the population reached a peak and *J. c. coenia* could be seen on the streets of downtown Atlanta. Outside of the city, there were numerous pupa hanging from the wire fences enclosing fields. During the same period, *Phyciodes tharos* was very common, as were certain moths of the genus *Catocala*, including *C. maestosa* and *C. cara carissima*.

J. c. coenia has two color forms, a light and a dark form, but with many individuals being intermediate between the two. Guesses have been made as to whether these forms were due to cold or warm weather or, perhaps, to wet or dry weather. Mather (1967) found that the ground color of the lower sides of the wings is definitely related to seasonal change. His studies

251

revealed that, in Mississippi, no specimens with light ground color below were among those taken in January, February, and March, and that none with dark ground color below were among those taken in May, June, July, and August. The major seasonal shift from dark to light appears to take place between March and April, and from light to dark between August and September; the former shift is somewhat more abrupt than the latter.

He found that the March-April shift in central Mississippi coincides with a change in the mean temperature from below 60°F to above 60°F (16°C), and the August-September shift with a change from above 80°F to below 80°F (27°C). The mean rainfall for the area is highest in March (5.9 inches), and is lowest in October (2.5 inches). The August-September shift does not accompany an increase in average monthly rainfall, the mean values for August, September, and October being 4.0, 3.1, and 2.5 inches, respectively. Mather did not observe any association between the depth of the ground color below and the moistness of the habitat in Mississippi.

Mather also made studies on the length of the forewing, the subapical spot on the upper side of the forewing, and the relative size of the spots on the upper side of the hindwing; each of these he reported on in detail in the same article, with excellent tables, graphs, and a photograph.

Sometimes, a local population explosion may occur. An infestation of the caterpillars of *J. c. coenia* was found by John Symmes in the summer of 1967 on the *Acuba* plants being grown at his nursery near Madison in Morgan County. So far as we know, *Acuba* is a previously unreported food plant for this butterfly. When ready to pupate, the caterpillars crawled from the beds of these plants to nearby areas, including the open-slatted shelter covering the plants. The butterflies and caterpillars became very numerous and finally had to be controlled with a spray to save the plants. Symmes observed the butterflies in the area throughout the summer and as late in the fall as October.

The larva is one and one-fourth inches long. The body is dark gray with yellow lengthwise stripes and orange-yellow spots. There are a number of short, branching spines on the body, and one pair on top of the head.

The larval food plants are Plantain, (*Plantago*), *Geradia*, Snapdragon (*Antirrhinum*), Toadflax (*Linaria*), False Loosestrife (*Ludvigia*), Stonecrop (*Sedum*), and *Acuba*.

Abbot (in Smith, 1797) wrote:

Its caterpillar eats the toad flax which grows plentifully in corn fields in the spring. One of them suspended itself April 16, changed the 18th, and became a butterfly May 4th. This species continues breeding till late in the autumn, and is very common, frequenting damp places.

Genus *Nymphalis*

Mourning Cloak. *Nymphalis antiopa antiopa* Linnaeus
(Page 121)

Distribution and Records: *N. a. antiopa* is generally rare and local in the Mountain and Piedmont regions, and very rare in the Coastal Region.

Mountain Region—*Union Co.*: Cooper Creek State Park, Duncan Ridge Road, 11 July 1960 JCS. *Rabun Co.*: Clayton, Black Rock State Park, sight record 8 Oct 1966 HAF.
Piedmont Region—*Bibb Co.*: Macon, 17 May 1930 HFS (TTRS). *DeKalb Co.*: Avondale Estates, 8 June 1956 LNH (TTRS). *Monroe Co.*: Forsyth, one specimen with very light borders 13 Oct 1956 FTN. *Clarke Co.*: Athens, 26 Oct 1929 AGR (see Richards, 1931).
Coastal Region—*Grady Co.*: Beachton, Birdsong Plantation, 16 May 1958 MEVK (TTRS); Beachton, Susina Plantation, 27 Apr 1967 LNH.

This splendid butterfly is a strong and rapid flyer. There are two broods in Georgia.

Although essentially a woodland species, *N. a. antiopa* is quite a wanderer, and may be met with in unexpected places. Mrs. Harris caught one in our yard in Avondale Estates on June 8, 1956. In the spring of 1967, we saw a Mourning Cloak in the yard of our cottage in south Georgia (Grady County), but we were unable to catch it. The next day, we found a beautiful specimen on the porch. It had emerged from a pupa Mrs. Harris had found attached to a bucket in the yard and had placed on the porch.

Dr. and Mrs. H. A. Flaschka visited Black Rock Mountain State Park in north Georgia on October 8, 1966. Near the summit of the mountain, they saw a Mourning Cloak sitting on a rock, opening and closing its wings in the warm sunlight. The butterfly was wary, and flew when Dr. Flaschka approached it with a net.

In middle Georgia (Monroe County), Fred T. Naumann collected a Mourning Cloak that had very light (almost white) borders on its wings instead of the usual yellow borders. It appeared to be a fresh specimen. The date of capture was October 13, 1956.

In the Macon area of Bibb County, J. C. Brooks has observed that the Mourning Cloak appears in February and March and that it alights on oak trees which are exuding sap at the nodes.

The larva is about two inches long and velvety black with small, raised, white dots. There is a row of red spots along the back. The spines on the body are long, but there are no spines on the head. The known larval food plants are Willow (*Salix*), Poplar (*Populus*), and Elm (*Ulmus*), but there may be others.

Genus *Polygonia*

Question Sign; Question Mark; Violet-tip.
Polygonia interrogationis Fabricius (Page 121)

Distribution and Records: *P. interrogationis* is found throughout the state. It may be found in a variety of habitats, including open woodlands, the borders of roads, damp or moist meadows and fields, and orchards. It is usually common, but it is local in occurrence.

Mountain Region—*Murray Co.*: Old Fort Mountain, 25 Mar 1961 LHJ (TTRS). *Union Co.*: Brasstown Bald (alt. 4700 ft), 12 Aug 1951 LHJ (TTRS).

Piedmont Region—*Coweta Co.*: Madras, 18 Mar 1950 MES. *Monroe Co.*: Forsyth, several in bait trap 20 May 1962 FTN. *Richmond Co.*: Augusta, 29 May 1961 LHJ (TTRS). *Fulton Co.*: Atlanta, 4 July 1937 LHJ. *Bibb Co.*: Macon, 11 Sept 1952 LHJ (TTRS). *Monroe Co.*: Forsyth, 26 Oct 1956 FTN.

Coastal Region—*Charlton Co.*: Folkston, 1 Apr 1955 LNH and LHJ. *Baker Co.*: Newton, 14 Apr 1965 LN. *Lowndes Co.*: Valdosta, 12 May 1967 HLK (TTRS). *Grady Co.*: Beachton, Birdsong Plantation, 22 May 1954 EVK (TTRS). *Chatham Co.*: Savannah, 29 May 1960 LHJ (TTRS); Savannah, 29 May 1961 HLK and LHJ. *Grady Co.*: Beachton, Sherwood Plantation, 20 June 1965 LN. *Dougherty Co.*: Albany, 1 Nov 1965 LHJ. *Baker Co.*: Newton, Blue Springs Plantation, 8, 27, and 29 Oct 1964 LN.

Adults may be found feeding on moist areas of trees that have been bruised, and on fermenting fruits in orchards. They will sometimes come to traps that have been baited with a fermented mixture.

There are three broods in Georgia. The adults of the fall brood hibernate during the winter and reappear in early spring. The eggs laid by the overwintering females produce a fresh brood, which emerges from mid-May to early June. This late spring brood, in turn, produces a summer brood, which emerges in July. The July brood produces the fall generation, which emerges in September and October.

P. interrogationis is dimorphous. In the light form, *P. interrogationis* f. *fabricii*, the upper surface of the hindwings are almost as light in color as the forewings; in the dark form, *P. interrogationis* f. *umbrosa*, the outer two-thirds of the upper surface of the hindwings are blackish and much darker than the forewings. Both forms occur in Georgia.

The dimorphism is seasonal, but not strictly so. Nearly all of the adults of the fall brood, which appears in September and October, are of the light form. These adults overwinter and reappear in early spring. The late spring and the summer broods, however, are nearly all of the dark form.

The presence of an individual of one form among those of the other form is of more than usual interest. A first-hand observation of this rare event has been given by Mrs. Ellen Robertson-Miller (1931, pp. 183–184). She became acquainted with *P. interrogationis* when she found two caterpillars feeding on a Hop vine. On July 2, both larvae became crysalids. Ten days later, when the butterflies emerged, they proved to be Violet-tips, but to her surprise, they were quite dissimilar.

The mystery of this variation was not made clear to her until she read that *P. interrogationis* appears in two forms, and that, although these forms are seasonal, they are not strictly so. It had chanced that one larva from the Hop vine had assumed the colors and markings of the light form while the other had retained those characteristics that distinguished it as the dark form.

The larva attains a length of about one and one-half inches. When fully grown, it is reddish brown with lighter markings of irregular dots and patches. There are many branched spines, including one pair on top of the head.

The larval food plants are Hop (*Humulus*), Elm (*Ulmus*), Nettle (*Urtica*), Hackberry (*Celtis*), and Basswood (*Tilia*). John Abbot (in Smith, 1797) states:

This feeds upon the plant called Warhew, which is very like the European lime-tree, except in being always a low bush or shrub; it eats also the sugarberry and the elm. It suspended itself by the tail May 29th, changed 30th, appeared on the wing June 7th. This species frequents swamps and oak woods, but is not very common.

The butterfly lives all the winter in places of shelter, coming forth very early in the spring. It occurs likewise in Virginia.

Abbot's reference to "Warhew" seems likely to have been to one of the several small trees in the genus *Tilia* (Basswood) that are found on the Georgia Coastal Plain. According to Harrar and Harrar (1962, p. 252), Sugarberry is a common name for certain species of hackberry in the southeast, particularly *Celtis laevigata*.

Comma Butterfly; Hop Merchant. *Polygonia comma*
T. W. Harris (Page 121)

Distribution and Records: *P. comma* is a woodland species that is found over most of the state.

Mountain Region—*Murray Co.*: Old Fort Mountain, 28 Mar 1963 LHJ (TTRS). *Fannin Co.*: Blue Ridge Wildlife Area, 16 Apr 1967 BMR. *Lumpkin Co.*: Blood Mountain, 6 July 1951 PWF (TTRS).

Piedmont Region—*Cobb Co.*: Marietta, Blackjack Mountain, 30 Mar 1952 LHT (TTRS). *Fulton Co.*: Atlanta, Indian Trail Road, 28 Mar 1956 LHJ; Atlanta, Indian Trail Road, 7 Apr 1961 LHJ. *Clarke Co.*: Athens, University of Georgia, Apr 1967 LRT. *Monroe Co.*: Forsyth, taken in light trap 22 May 1966 FTN. *Bibb Co.*: Macon, 8 July 1958 FTN. *Monroe Co.*: Forsyth, 1 Nov 1956 FTN.

Coastal Region—*Houston Co.*: Warner Robins, May 1958 JCBS. J. C. Brooks has also found *P. comma* in Laurens, Twiggs, and Ware counties.

There are three broods, the first appearing in March, the second in the last half of July, and the third in September. Individuals of the fall brood, which hibernate during the winter months, may be seen flying on warm winter days in sheltered sunny areas. There is some evidence that *P. comma* may also overwinter in the pupal state as fresh specimens are sometimes taken in the early spring. Adults of the summer brood are darker, and are known as *P. comma* f. *dryas*.

On June 6, 1951, the late Prof. P. W. Fattig collected one of

257

the first Georgia specimens of *P. comma* on Blood Mountain, near Vogel State Park, in the Mountain Region. On March 30, 1952, a colony was found by Abner Towers on Blackjack Mountain, near Marietta, in Cobb County, approximately twenty miles north of Atlanta, in the Piedmont Region.

J. P. Knudsen (1954) reported that a few specimens were taken in March in the vicinity of Oglethorpe College, on the edge of Atlanta. He commented that they were wary and hard to net. This area is also in the Piedmont Region. Two years later, on November 1, 1956, Fred T. Naumann collected a specimen in Forsyth, Monroe County, which is also in the Piedmont Region but farther south and less than fifty miles from the edge of the Upper Coastal Plain. Since that time, he has continued to find specimens of *P. comma* in the Forsyth area.

In May, 1958, J. C. Brooks found *P. comma* to be the commonest member of its genus in a river swamp near Warner Robins in Houston County. During several years of very active collecting, he found *P. comma* throughout the area in suitable habitats. He also found it farther south in the Coastal Region near Danville in Twiggs County, near Dublin in Laurens County, and near Waycross in Ware County, which is in the extreme southeastern part of Georgia, less than forty miles from the Florida state line.

The larva is one inch long. Its color has been described as varying from brown to greenish to nearly white. It is marked with blotches and transverse lines, and is variable both in color and markings. It is spiny, and bears one pair of spines on its head. The larval food plants are Elm (*Ulmus*), Hops (*Humulus*), and Nettles (*Urtica*).

Smyth's Angle-wing. *Polygonia faunus smythi*
A. H. Clark (Page 121)

Distribution and Records: *P. faunus smythi* occurs locally in the mountains of north Georgia, where it frequents woodland roads, clearings, and borders of wooded areas.

Mountain Region—*Fannin Co.*: near Margret, 16 Apr 1967 BMR (TTRS); Cooper Creek State Park, 28 June 1958 LNH (TTRS); Cooper Creek State Park, 29 June 1960 LHJ (TTRS). *Union Co.*: Cooper Creek State Park, Duncan Ridge Road, 29 June 1960 JCS. *Fannin Co.*: Cooper Creek State Park, 2 July 1958 LHJ (TTRS). *White Co.*: Unicoi Gap, 13 July 1953 JPK. *Union Co.*: Cooper Creek State Park, Duncan Ridge Road, 20 July 1960 JCS.
Piedmont Region—None.
Coastal Region—None.

There is one brood. Some adults may hibernate and re-appear on warm days in early spring. Bryant Mather collected a specimen on April 16, 1967, in Fannin County, which is the earliest Georgia record. The butterfly was in good condition, and whether it was a specimen that overwintered or had recently emerged cannot be stated with certainty. Adults emerge in June and July, and the population reaches its peak in the latter half of July; the butterfly may become locally common during this period. It flies through August and into September, with worn specimens being found in late summer and early fall.

P. f. smythi is a wary butterfly; it is easily frightened, and difficult to capture because of its erratic, fast flight. It is attracted to carrion at times. On one occasion, John C. Symmes collected a number of specimens on the remains of a skunk that he found on a mountain road.

In his description of *P. f. smythi*, Clark (1937) states that, among the watercolor drawings of the insects of Georgia by John Abbot dated 1792–1804 in the British Museum (Natural History), there is a figure, identified by Samuel H. Scudder as *Polygonia faunus*, that bears the manuscript note in Abbot's handwriting: "Met with by Mr. Elliot in his tour to the mountains." It was Mr. Elliot who also found *Speyeria idalia* in Georgia.

The larva of the subspecies *P. f. smythi* has not been described, but it may be assumed that it is similar to that of *P. faunus*, which has been described as follows: The mature larva is one and one-fifth inches long. Its head is black and bears a pair of spines. Its body is reddish or yellowish brown, with a large patch of white on the back and rows of light colored branching spines. The larva does not make a nest; it hides beneath the leaf of its food plant for protection.

According to Prof. Ellison A. Smyth, Jr. (in Clark, 1937), Gooseberry (*Ribes*) is an important food plant. Smyth wrote Clark that, in 1896, he had raised five individuals from larvae that he had found on Gooseberry in his garden at Blacksburg, Virginia.

Subfamily MELITAEINAE

The nomenclature of the subfamily Melitaeinae follows the new revision by Mr. Cyril F. dos Passos (1969).

Genus *Chlosyne*

Silvery Checkerspot. *Chlosyne nycteis* Doubleday
(Page 123)

Distribution and Records: *C. nycteis* is found in local colonies that are widely distributed over the state, except in the extreme southern and eastern portions of the Coastal Plain. Some colonies are very strong, and *C. nycteis* may be common to abundant in a favorable habitat, typically near a small stream in a grassy area in or near open woods.

Mountain Region—*Murray Co.*: Old Fort Mountain, 16 May 1950 LHT (TTRS); Old Fort Mountain, 22 May 1951 PWF (TTRS). *Fannin Co.*: Cooper Creek State Park, 28 June 1958 LHJ (TTRS); near Margret, 28 July 1959 LHJ (TTRS).

Piedmont Region—*Monroe Co.*: Forsyth, 5 May 1966 FTN. *Baldwin Co.*: Milledgeville, May 1958 JCBS. *Fulton Co.*: Atlanta area, 22 May 1955 LHJ (TTRS); Atlanta area, 26 May

1957 LHJ (TTRS); Atlanta area, 28 June 1957 JCS; Atlanta area, 6 July 1958 JCS; Atlanta area, 30 June 1957 LHJ (TTRS); Atlanta area, 12 July 1955 LHJ (TTRS); Atlanta area, 19 July 1958 LHJ (TTRS). *Bibb Co.*: Macon, 25 Aug 1960 FTN.
Coastal Region—*Houston Co.*: Warner Robins, May 1958 JCBS. *Laurens Co.*: Dublin, May 1958 JCBS.

Small colonies of *C. nycteis* are found in the mountains. Specimens were collected on Old Fort Mountain in Murray County on May 16, 1950, by Lucien Harris, III, and on May 22, 1951, by P. W. Fattig. I found a small colony in the mountain area of Fannin County near Cooper Creek State Park on June 28, 1958, and one near Margret on July 28, 1958.

John Symmes found a strong local colony in the Piedmont Region, not far from his home in Fulton County. The colony was flourishing in an area near a small stream. Some of the adults were unusually large in size.

Fred Naumann found *C. nycteis* around Forsyth in Monroe County and near Macon in Bibb County. J. C. Brooks found it abundant locally in the Macon area of Bibb County during May, and again in August, of 1958. He found it less common in 1959 and 1960, and none were seen in 1961. The colonies were very local and were found near water, especially rivers and large streams. Brooks also found *C. nycteis* very common in the upper Coastal Region, at Dublin in Laurens County and at Warner Robins in Houston County, in May, 1958.

The body of the larva is velvety black, with blackish barbed spines; a dull orange stripe extends along each side. The larval food plants are Asters (*Aster*) and Sunflowers (*Helianthus*).

Gorgone Checkerspot. *Chlosyne gorgone gorgone* Hübner (Page 123)

Distribution and Records: *C. g. gorgone* is apparently very rare and local in the Coastal Region. In the Piedmont and Mountain regions it is usually rare and local; at times, however, it may occur rather commonly in a limited area. It is most often found in open hardwood forests.

Mountain Region—*Murray Co.*: Old Fort Mountain, 2 May 1950 LHJ (TTRS); Old Fort Mountain, 5 May 1951 LHJ (TTRS); Old Fort Mountain, 6 May 1964 JCS; Old Fort Mountain, 10 May 1950 LHT (TTRS); Old Fort Mountain, 16 May 1950 LHT (TTRS); Old Fort Mountain, 17 May 1958 LHJ (TTRS). *Rabun Co.*: Coleman River, 26 May 1958 LHJ (TTRS). *Union Co.*: Cooper Creek State Park, Duncan Ridge Road, 29 June 1958 JCS. *Rabun Co.*: Coleman River, 16 July 1961 SSN.

Piedmont Region—*Fulton Co.*: Atlanta area, Indian Trail Road, 17 Apr 1955 LHJ (TTRS). *DeKalb Co.*: Stone Mountain, 20 Apr 1951 PWF (UGM). *Madison Co.*: Lake Beaver Dam Creek, 25 Apr 1942 HOL (UGM). *Hall Co.*: Lula, near Gainesville, 26 Apr 1953 PWF (TTRS). *Cobb Co.*: Kennesaw Mountain, 27 Apr 1957 LHJ (TTRS); Kennesaw Mountain, 28 Apr 1957 JCS. *DeKalb Co.*: Stone Mountain, 28 Apr 1953 LHJ. *Coweta Co.*: Madras, 29 Apr 1951 MES; Madras, 30 Apr 1950 MES. *DeKalb Co.*: Stone Mountain, 3 May 1954 LHJ (TTRS). *Harris Co.*: Pine Mountain, Chipley, 3 May 1958 HOL (UGM). *Monroe Co.*: Forsyth, near golf course, 7 May 1962 FTN. *Bibb Co.*: Macon, Arkwright Road, 11 May 1963 FTN. *Fulton Co.*: Buckhead area, 13 May 1950 LHT (TTRS); Atlanta area, Davis Drive, 18 May 1958 LHJ (TTRS); Atlanta area, Indian Trail Road, 6 June 1957 LHJ (TTRS); Atlanta area, 15 June 1944 GH (TTRS). *DeKalb Co.*: Stone Mountain, 17 June 1950 LHT (TTRS); Stone Mountain, 15 July 1950 LHT (TTRS); Stone Mountain, 1 Sept 1955 LHJ (TTRS).

Coastal Region—*Houston Co.*: Warner Robins, 3 June 1957 FTN. *Grady Co.*: Beachton, Birdsong Plantation, 18 Aug 1949 EVK.

I first became acquainted with this butterfly in the field on May 2, 1950, when collecting with Mrs. Harris and our two sons, Robin and Lucien, on Old Fort Mountain. We stopped to collect near the entrance marker to Fort Mountain State Park on US 76, several miles east of Chatsworth in Murray County. We saw some butterflies flying along the edge of a gravel road that has since been paved. They were flying close to the ground with a rapid zig-zag flight that was noticeably different from that of our commonest Checkerspot, *Phyclodes tharos*. We captured some specimens and identified them as the Gorgone Checkerspot. They were fairly common in a small area. The specimens, all males, were fresh. When we returned to the area two weeks later, females were present and fairly common.

Now that we were acquainted with the flight habits of *C. g. gorgone*, and found that we could distinguish it in flight from *P. tharos*, we began to look for it in other localities. An examination of the various Georgia localities listed under Distribution and Records will show how widely this butterfly has been collected in the state.

The first record known to me for the Piedmont Region of Georgia is a specimen in the collection of the University of Georgia Museum at Athens. The specimen was collected by Dr. Horace O. Lund on April 25, 1942, on Lake Beaver Dam Creek in Madison County. The second record is a specimen taken by Graham Heid on June 15, 1944, in the Atlanta area of Fulton County. The specimen is now in the collection at Tall Timbers Research Station.

A very important record for the Coastal Region is a specimen collected by E. V. Komarek on August 18, 1949, on Birdsong Plantation, near Beachton, in Grady County. This is only a few miles from the Georgia–Florida state line, and represents the southernmost point where *C. g. gorgone* has been found.

In September, 1950, through the courtesy of N. D. Riley of the Department of Entomology of the British Museum (Natural History), I learned that the museum had an original drawing of *C. gorgone* by Abbot.* On the drawing, Abbot wrote:

It frequents the oak woods of Burke County but is not common.

---

* Abbot's drawing is labeled "*Melitaea ismeria*," but the name *ismeria* has been placed in the synonymy of *C. gorgone* by dos Passos (1969). See the discussion of *M. ismeria* on pages 264–66.

Caterpillar feeds on crosswort and sunflower. It tied itself up by the tail 16 May, changed into chrysalis 17, bred 26th.

Riley noted that someone had written on the plate in pencil "*Helianthus trachelifolius*," presumably the name of the illustrated food plant.

The records indicate that there are two broods of *C. g. gorgone*, the first in April, May, and June, and the second in July, August, and early September.

The body of the larva is yellowish with three longitudinal black stripes and several rows of barbed, black spines. The larval food plants are Sunflower (*Helianthus*) and Crosswort (*Lysimachia*), according to Abbot. Klots (1951, p. 98) lists *Aster*, Sunflower (*H. scaberrimus*).

In his revision of the Melitaeinae, Cyril F. dos Passos (1969) included *Melitaea ismeria* Boisduval and LeConte in the synonomy of *C. gorgone*. Mr. dos Passos generously supplied me with an advance copy of his revision with permission for its use.

C. gorgone, type locality Georgia, was named by Hübner (1810) from an Abbot drawing of two males, showing the upper side only. *Melitaea ismeria* was a name provided by Boisduval and LeConte (1829–1833) on the basis of an Abbot drawing of a female only, showing the upper and lower sides of the butterfly. This drawing also figures the caterpillar and pupa. The only other illustration of *M. ismeria* is another Abbot drawing now in the British Museum, which illustrates the butterfly, the caterpillar and one of its food plants, and a pupa.

I do not know of any specimens attributed to *M. ismeria* that are still extant. It is possible that Abbot may have had an extreme female of *C. gorgone* as his model. This theory is strengthened by our having collected a few *C. gorgone* females that closely resemble Abbot's figure of *M. ismeria*. The specimens of *C. gorgone* (both male and female) that we have collected in Georgia differ consistently from specimens of the western subspecies *C. g. carlota* Reakirt that I have examined. The dark submarginal border on the lower side of the hindwing extends through the apex on *C. g. gorgone*, whereas on *C. g. carlota*, the apical area of the lower side of the hindwing is light.

The specimens Abbot depicted in his drawings, and from which *C. gorgone* and *M. ismeria* received their names, were found by him in the Coastal Region of Georgia. Hübner made no statement about the distribution of *C. gorgone*. Boisduval, with reference to *M. ismeria* (Boisduval and LeConte, 1829–1833, p. 169) states: "This *Melitaea* is found in Carolina and Georgia. It is rare in collections."

One may ask why these butterflies were present in Abbot's time but have been absent or overlooked since then. One explanation may be given on the basis of butterfly population cycles (Brown, 1964, p. 154). Some butterflies may, at times, expand into new territories when their population increases. They may also disappear from known territories when the population decreases. A tendency for increased variation sometimes seems to occur during the transitional stage when the population is increasing. The population may have been expanding when Abbot made the drawings of his specimens, which could have represented the male and female of only one species. We know that a population of *Melitaea* (in the broad sense) existed in Abbot's day, but whether both *C. gorgone* and *M. ismeria* were present or not we cannot know with certainty. We need specimens from the area where Abbot lived and collected before the problem can be fully resolved to the satisfaction of everyone.

Based on the information available to me, and on the absence of any supporting evidence for the existence of a "true" *M. ismeria*, my own conclusion is that the name *ismeria* was named for a variant specimen of *C. gorgone*. For the time being, *ismeria* can rest as a synonym, until such time as future captures might draw it from synonymy into established usage as a form name applicable to one or both sexes or as a valid name for a long-lost but rediscovered subspecies. When and if such specimens are found in the general area of the type locality in the Coastal Region, it is hoped that a full and early report of such discovery will be made by the captor in a periodical.

Genus *Phyciodes*

Seminole Crescent. *Phyciodes* (*Tritanassa*) *texana seminole* Skinner (Page 123)

Distribution and Records: *P. t. seminole* inhabits the Coastal Region. It is rare and very local.

Mountain Region—None.
Piedmont Region—None.
Coastal Region—*Chatham Co.*: Savannah, 22 May 1962 HLK; Savannah, 25 May 1960 JCS; Savannah, 27 May 1961 LHJ; Savannah, 28 May 1960 LHJ (TTRS); Savannah, 3 June 1963 HLK; Savannah, 15 and 16 Aug 1958 GBS. *Baker Co.* and *Mitchell Co.*: 15 and 16 Sept 1968 LN. *Decatur Co.*: Bainbridge, 19 Oct 1910 JCBY (CU). *Thomas Co.*: Boston area, Bar-M Ranch, 24 Sept 1967 ESS (TTRS).

P. t. seminole was described by Henry Skinner (1911, p. 412) from specimens taken by Dr. J. C. Bradley near Bainbridge, Georgia. The type specimens were placed in the Academy of Natural Science of Philadelphia. Some years ago, I was able to examine two of Bradleys specimens of this butterfly in the W. J. Mills collection, which was then located in the State Capitol in Atlanta. They were taken by Bradley on October 19, 1910, along Spring Creek, which forms part of the boundary between Seminole and Decatur counties in extreme southwest Georgia.

It was many years before *P. t. seminole* was rediscovered in Georgia. This was on the opposite side of the state at Savannah.

A thriving colony was found by Gordon B. Small, Jr. He collected his first specimens on August 15th, 1958. At that time, he was living in Providence, Rhode Island, and my first knowledge of his find came when he wrote to me on January 7, 1960:

While conversing with Dr. A. B. Klots recently, he mentioned that you are revising your work on the butterflies of Georgia. I mentioned that I had taken a series of *Phyciodes texana seminole* near the Savannah city limits and he suggested that you might be interested in this record. If you are interested in this and/or other Savannah records, drop me a line and I shall send you full details.

In addition to sending details, he extended an invitation to meet him in Savannah. John Symmes and I met him there on April 6, 1960. It was too early for *P. t. seminole*. We returned on May 28, when, for the first time, I saw live specimens of this butterfly that had eluded me for many years. Savannah is growing rapidly: in the spring of 1967, when H. L. King visited the locality where *P. t. seminole* once thrived, he found the area undergoing some changes that may, in time, eliminate the colony.

Gordon B. Small was the first to find *P. t. seminole* in eastern Georgia. This may also be the record for the eastern-most point of capture in the southeast, although Grossbeck (1917, p. 15) records a Florida record from La Grange (near Titusville) in Brevard County for September 9 and 10 (year not given).

Ellery Sedgwick, Jr., found *P. t. seminole* in south Georgia on September 24, 1967. It was collected near Linton Lake in Thomas County. This was an important discovery, because Thomas County is only two counties east of Decatur County, where the type specimens were collected.

The most recent discovery in a new area was made by Leon Neel on September 15, 1968. He found a thriving colony along the banks of the Flint River, which marks the boundary of Baker and Mitchell counties. He returned on September 16 and collected a few specimens in each county. These two counties are adjacent to Decatur County, where the type specimens were collected by Dr. J. C. Bradley in 1910.

The larva and its food plants are unknown.

Pearl Crescent. *Phyciodes tharos tharos* Drury
(Page 123)

Distribution and Records: *P. t. tharos* is abundant throughout the state.

Mountain Region—*Lumpkin Co.*: Auraria, 15 Apr 1967 LHJ (TTRS). *Fannin Co.*: near Margret, 16 Apr 1967 LHJ (TTRS). Cooper Creek State Park, 26 Apr 1959 LHJ (TTRS). *Murray Co.*: Old Fort Mountain, 5 May 1951 LHT (TTRS). *Banks Co.* and *Habersham Co.*: 26 May–1 Sept 1930 RWM (see Montgomery, 1931). *White Co.*: Helen, 15 June 1952 LHJ (TTRS). *Towns Co.*: Brasstown Bald (alt. 4700 ft), 12 Aug 1951 LHJ (TTRS).

Piedmont Region—*Monroe Co.*: Forsyth, 13 Mar 1955 FTN; Forsyth, 30 Mar 1957 FTN. *Fulton Co.*: Atlanta, Indian Trail Road, 17 Apr 1955 LHJ (TTRS); Atlanta, 13 May 1950 LHT (TTRS). *Forsyth Co.*: Lake Lanier, near Cummings, 2 June 1962 JRH (TTRS). *Fulton Co.*: Atlanta area, 9 July 1965 LHJ (TTRS); Atlanta, Buckhead area, 5 Sept 1949 LHT (TTRS). *Bibb Co.*: Macon, melanic aberration 23 Sept 1931 HFS (TTRS).

Coastal Region—*Grady Co.*: Beachton, Susina Plantation, 2 Jan 1965 LHJ (TTRS). *Charlton Co.*: Folkston, 9 Feb 1952 LHJ (TTRS). *Grady Co.*: Beachton, Susina Plantation, 28 Mar 1964 LHJ (TTRS). *Screven Co.*: near Sylvania, 7 Apr 1960 LHJ (TTRS). *Grady Co.*: Beachton, Sherwood Plantation, 9 May 1965 LN; Beachton, Susina Plantation, 19 July 1965 LNH (TTRS). *Charlton Co.*: Folkston, 11 Aug 1949 LHJ (TTRS). *Dougherty Co.*: ten miles west of Albany, 7 Sept 1964 LN. *Baker Co.*: Newton, 29 Nov 1964 LN. *Sumter Co.*: Americus, 29 Nov 1964 LN.

This familiar butterfly generally flies rather close to the ground. It may be found in a variety of habitats, including fields, pastures, orchards, roadsides, and open woods. It is one of the few butterflies that appears to be almost as abundant now as it was some years ago. There are three broods, with perhaps a fourth brood in the southern part of the state.

P. t. tharos is dimorphic. The two forms are seasonal; the cold-weather form, *P. t. tharos* f. *marcia* Edwards, is the typical form; it is darker than the warm-weather form, *P. t. tharos* f. *morpheus* Fabricius: The lower sides of the wings of the warm-weather form are noticeably lighter in color.

In addition to the seasonal forms, an occasional aberration may be found. An extremely dark (melanic) aberration was collected by Dr. H. F. Strohecker in Macon. It is now in the collection at Tall Timbers Research Station.

The body of the larva is black with yellow dots; there is also a yellow band along each side, and eight rows of yellowish-brown spines. The larval food plants are Asters (*Aster*) and other members of the family Compositae.

Tawny Crescent. *Phyciodes batesii* Reakirt
(Page 123)

Distribution and Records: *P. batesii* has been found in Georgia only in the Mountain Region. Three specimens which represent a new state record for Georgia, were collected by Jane and John Symmes on May 26, 1957, near the head of the Coleman River in Rabun County. The collectors generously presented one of their specimens to me. It is now in the collection of the Tall Timbers Research Station.

The location where the Symmeses found their specimens was the site of an abandoned saw mill about five miles north of an old cabin that may once have been Coleman's. This location marks the southern limit of the known range of this butterfly. There is a possibility—a remote one, perhaps—that it may be found in other favorable localities in the mountains of north Georgia.

The life history of *P. batesii* is not fully known. It is likely that it is similar to the life history of *P. tharos*, except in the number of broods: *P. batesii* is single-brooded, and *P. tharos* is multiple-brooded.

In Georgia, the adults should be sought in May and June in the northern tier of counties. North of Georgia, it occurs in late May and June.

Clark (1941, p. 49) states that W. T. M. Forbes has found that, in any given locality, *P. batesii* flies between the first two broods of *P. tharos*. This could be a good collecting tip, because *P. batesii* may be easily overlooked owing to its close resemblance to *P. tharos*, which is so numerous that collecting them in a search for the rare *P. batesii* can be discouraging. John Symmes, however, reports that both species were on the wing when he and his wife collected their specimens.

The larval food plant is *Aster*.

Phaon Crescent. *Phyciodes phaon* Edwards
(Page 123)

Distribution and Records: *P. phaon* inhabits the Coastal Region, where it is widely distributed but very local. It is usually uncommon, but it may be locally common at times. It has been recorded as a rare stray in the Piedmont Region.

Mountain Region—None.
Piedmont Region—*Bibb Co.*: Macon area, no dates JCBS. *Monroe Co.*: Forsyth, worn stray 8 Nov 1956 FTN.
Coastal Region—*Baker Co.*: Newton, 2 Mar 1965 LN. *Chatham Co.*: Savannah, 6 Apr 1960 LHJ (TTRS); Tybee Island, 7 Apr 1960 JCS. *Grady Co.*: Beachton, Sherwood Plantation, 10 Apr. 1965 LN; Beachton, Birdsong Plantation, 16 May 1953 EVK (TTRS); Beachton, Susina Plantation, 17 May 1967 LHJ. *Chatham Co.*: Tybee Island, 11 May 1958 JCS. *Glynn Co.*: St. Simons Island (type locality), 19 May 1965 LNH and LHJ (TTRS). *Screven Co.*: Sylvania, May and July 1946 OB (AMNH). *Twiggs Co.*: Danville, Sept 1957 JCBS. *Grady Co.*: Beachton, Susina Plantation, 7 Sept 1963 LNH (TTRS). *Baker Co.*: Newton, Blue Springs Plantation, 10 Nov 1964 LN. *Grady Co.*: Beachton, Birdsong Plantation, 3 Dec 1952 EVK (TTRS).

Fred T. Naumann collected a worn specimen in the Piedmont Region (at Forsyth, Monroe County) on November 8, 1956, and J. C. Brooks has collected a few rare specimens of *P. phaon* in the Piedmont Region near Macon. A few miles farther south, in the dry pine flats of Bibb and Houston counties, Brooks has found it flying in fair numbers in June and from August through September. He also found it very common at Danville (Twiggs County) in September, 1957.

Otto Buchholz found *P. phaon* rather common in May and July, 1946, in Screven County. I have found it locally common along the coast, as well as in south and southwest Georgia.

The larva, according to Klots (1951, p. 99), is olivaceous with longitudinal dark brown lines and mottled bands. There are many branching spines in rows. The head is creamy white with large brown spots on the sides and dorsum.

Charles P. Kimball (1965) reports *Lippia nodiflora* as a foodplant recorded in California. This plant, which is a member of the family Verbenaceae, is also found in Georgia (Greene and Blomquist, 1953, p. 108).

A nomenclatural problem related to *P. phaon* has been studied carefully and reported in detail by F. Martin Brown (1966). The problem arose from a mixed series of four figures on a plate published by Hübner (1806–1841, vol. 1, pl. 41). Two of the four figures (figs. 1 and 2) are males of *Chlosyne gorgone*, while the other two (figs. 3 and 4), supposedly females of the same species, are actually females of the species later recognized as *P. phaon*, a butterfly described from Georgia material by W. H. Edwards in 1864. The taxonomic complexities ensuing from this have just lately been resolved; it is hoped that *P. phaon* will enjoy nomenclatural stability henceforth.

Brown's research and discussion of the taxonomy related to this species have been most helpful to me. One of the specimens in a series that Mrs. Harris and I collected for Brown at St. Simons Island on May 19, 1965, was selected by him as the neotype that best fitted Edwards' original description: the specimen has been labelled as such and deposited with the Edwards Collection at the Carnegie Museum, Pittsburgh. A photograph of the specimen is reproduced on page 434 of Brown's (1966) article.

Genus *Euphydryas*

The Baltimore. *Euphydryas phaeton phaeton* Drury
(Page 127)

Distribution and Records: *E. p. phaeton* occurs in the Mountain and Piedmont regions, but is rare and local.

Mountain Region—*Murray Co.*: Old Fort Mountain, 17 May 1951 AT. *Fannin Co.*: near Margret, 28 June 1958 LHJ (TTRS).
Piedmont Region—*Fulton Co.*: Atlanta, Riverside Drive, 18 May 1957 JCS; Oglethorpe College, near Lake Phoebe, 19 May 1953 JPK. *DeKalb Co.*: Stone Mountain, 26 May 1953 JPK; Stone Mountain, 17 June 1950 LHT (TTRS). *Cobb Co.*: Kennesaw Mountain, 15 June 1959 JCS. *Bibb Co.*: near Macon June 1931 HFS.
Coastal Region—None.

The Baltimore is well named, as it wears the orange and black colors of Lord Baltimore. Of the few specimens collected in Georgia since 1950, nearly all are females. Instead of being collected in boggy areas where the usual food plant, Turtle-Head (*Chelone glabra*), might occur, the females were found mostly in open stands of mixed hardwoods on hillsides.

When my son Lucien and I were collecting on Stone Mountain on June 17, 1950, he collected a fresh female. It was flying up a hillside in open woods some distance above a small stream that flows through a wet area at the foot of the mountain. We searched the area for other specimens without success. We also looked for Turtle-Head in the wet area, but we did not find it. Later trips to the area failed to turn up either adults or larvae.

When John Symmes and I were collecting in some woods, predominantly pine, along Riverside Drive in Fulton County on May 18, 1959, we had a similar experience. We captured a female in the woods near the edge of the road, but our subsequent wide search of the area from which it came was met with no further success. We had collected in that area a number of times previously, and we did so many times afterwards, without seeing other Baltimores.

On May 17, 1951, Abner Towers collected a single specimen on Old Fort Mountain in Murray County. On May 19, 1953, J. P. Knudsen collected a fresh female flying near Lake Phoebe on the Oglethorpe College Campus, and on May 26, 1953, he collected one on Stone Mountain. In Cobb County, on June 15, 1959, John Symmes collected a worn female that was flying up the southeast slope of Kennesaw Mountain, about one-third of the way up the mountain.

On June 28, 1958, I picked up a specimen lying beside a forest road in Fannin County. It appeared to have been hit by a car. H. F. Strohecker positively identified a worn specimen he saw near Macon, in Bibb County, in June, 1931: the locality is near the center of the state, and this specimen is our southernmost Georgia record. A similar worn specimen was taken by M. Eugene Smith at Madras, in Coweta County.

The only reference to more than one specimen being found in a single area is contained in an old unidentified manuscript that was brought to my attention by A. Glenn Richards when he attended Cornell University. It may have been written by W. J. Mills, who formed a collection of Georgia butterflies around the turn of the century; the collection was on display in the State Capitol for many years. In the manuscript, *E. phaeton* was reported as rather common at Adairsville, which is located in the northwest corner of Bartow County in northwest

Georgia. A small, swampy area still exists on the western edge of Adairsville; a colony of *E. phaeton* may have existed there many years ago, but there are none there now.

Why have females of *E. phaeton* been captured on hillsides and mountain slopes in Georgia when they are found in boggy areas in the north? One explanation might be that the females were, perhaps, in search of another area having a fresh supply of a food plant on which to lay their eggs. But which food plant? Were they seeking the familiar Turtle-Head (*Chelone*) of the north, or a different plant, such as *Gerardia*, which grows mostly in open mixed hardwoods?

As long ago as 1930, Auburn E. Brower (1930, p. 287) wrote: "*E. phaeton*, scarce. All of the colonies of larvae which have been found were upon tall growing gerardias high up on dry, thinly wooded ridges." The colonies of larvae described by Brower were found in the Ozark Region of Greene County, Missouri, roughly 225 miles southwest of St. Louis.

The larva is about one inch long when fully grown. The head and first two segments are black, the middle segments are orange with narrow lines of black, and the last three segments are black with two orange bands around each. There are three rows of black spines along each side, and one row along the middle of the back.

The caterpillars are gregarious. They construct a silken web, usually over the tender leaves at the top of the food plant, and utilize it in a way that is reminiscent of the American tent caterpillars, which make their familiar webs in the forks of Wild Cherry and certain other trees.

The larval food plants are Turtle-Head (*Chelone glabra*) and, according to Klots (1951, p. 93) rarely *Wisteria*, Ash (*Fraxinus*), Japanese Honeysuckle (*Lonicera japonica*), and *Viburnum. Gerardia* has been reported by A. E. Brower (1930). Further study is needed to determine the food plants on which *E. phaeton* larvae feed in Georgia.

Subfamily ARGYNNINAE

Genus *Speyeria*

Regal Fritillary. *Speyeria idalia* Drury (Page 125)

Distribution and Records: *S. idalia* is included on the basis of a reference to it made by S. H. Scudder (1889, vol. 1, p. 541): "It occurs in the far south in the elevated parts of Georgia." The Georgia location shown by Scudder on his distribution map is between Clayton and Blairsville in the Mountain Region.

Scudder also quoted Abbot to the effect that a certain Mr. Elliot collected *S. idalia* in his journey to the mountains of Georgia. Abbot also made a similar comment about *Polygonia faunus smythi* being taken by Mr. Elliot in his journey to the mountains; undoubtedly, both species occurred there at the time of Mr. Elliot's journey. *P. f. smythi* is still found in the mountains, and is sometimes locally common in a few areas.

Once, when Professor P. W. Fattig and I were collecting along the Appalachian Trail above Neels Gap in Union County, he said that on two occasions he had seen a large fritillary, with white spots on the upper and lower sides of its wings, flying across the trail. He recalled seeing one in 1951 and the other in 1952. They could have been *S. idalia* strays from the Great Smoky Mountains of North Carolina and Tennessee.

An excellent account of the geographical distribution of *S. idalia*, together with other pertinent information, has been given by William Hovanitz (1963). The general range is reported as extending from New England southward to North Carolina and westward to Colorado and North Dakota.

Clark and Clark (1951, p. 55) have described the types of habitats where *S. idalia* occurs in Virginia. They are found in pastures with boggy or marshy areas; in damp, open grasslands; in extensive grassy bogs; and at high altitudes in dry pastures. South of Spotsylvania, Orange, and Albemarle counties, this species is found only in the mountains, and its distribution there is more localized. Should *S. idalia* occur regularly in the mountains of north Georgia, which seems doubtful, it would most likely be found in similar habitats.

There is one brood. The males appear about the middle of June and continue to emerge until about the middle of July. The females appear about two weeks later than the males, and continue to emerge until after the middle of August (Clark and Clark, 1951, p. 55).

The larva is about one and three-fourths inches long. The body is velvety black with dull yellow or reddish stripes. There are six rows of thorny spines, which are fleshy at the base. The spines along the back are silvery or yellowish white and tipped with black. Sometimes, the base of each spine along the sides of the body is orange. The larval food plants are Violets (*Viola* spp.).

Diana. *Speyeria diana* Cramer (Page 125)

Distribution and Records: *S. diana* is found sparingly in the Piedmont Region. Its chief habitat, however, is the Mountain Region.

Mountain Region—*White Co.*: Robertstown, 13 June 1957 LHT (TTRS). *Union Co.*: Blairsville, 27 June 1957 JCS (TTRS). *Fannin Co.*: near Margret, 28 June 1958 LNH (TTRS); near Margret, 29 June 1958 LHJ (TTRS). *Union Co.*: Cooper Creek State Park, 29 June 1960 LHJ (TTRS). *Fannin Co.*: Margret, 2 July 1958 LNH (TTRS). *Habersham Co.*: Cornelia, 10 July 1930 RWM (see Montgomery, 1931). *Rabun Co.*: near State Fish Hatchery, Dick's Creek Road, 18 Aug 1965 LHJ (TTRS). *Fannin Co.*: Margret, 30 Aug 1958 LHJ (TTRS). *Rabun Co.*: LaPrades Camp, Lake Burton, 21 Sept 1967 LNH (TTRS).
Piedmont Region—*DeKalb Co.*: Stone Mountain, 6 June 1952 HS. *Fulton Co.*: Atlanta, West Wesley Road, 4 July 1927 LHJ (TTRS). *Cherokee Co.*: Cox Road, 20 Aug 1960 JCS.
Coastal Region—None.

This beautiful butterfly has been decreasing in numbers for

several years. It has always been a prize for collectors and it is hoped that collectors will use restraint in the numbers they take when they happen to be so fortunate as to find a good local colony. It gladdens the eye of the lepidopterist who comes to a secluded mountain valley in July and August to find them eagerly feeding on the purple flower heads of Joe-Pye Weed (*Eupatorium maculatum*) and Ironweed (*Vernonia*). The males are also frequently found on the Orange Butterfly-Weed (*Asclepias tuberosa*).

S. diana is essentially a woodland species. It was in an open hardwood forest, with a small, clear stream flowing through, John Symmes called my attention to a female Diana walking about on the forest floor in what seemed, at first glance, to be an erratic course. Her wings were raised slightly as she went intently about her business, paying no attention to us as we watched her place her eggs singly in a seemingly haphazard manner, first on a dead twig and then on a dead leaf a few feet away. She deposited several eggs in this manner before flying a short distance to another area, where she repeated the performance with John and I following quietly along, fascinated by seeing this for the first time. We had learned that Diana does not search out the individual Violet plants, which provide food for the larvae, nor does she scatter her eggs by dropping them as she flies through the forest, as some have thought. Instead, she places her eggs in an area where they can hatch, and the caterpillars, in the first instar, remain protected under the leaves until spring. In this area, Violets are abundant in the spring when the caterpillars come forth from their hibernation in search of food.

An excellent account of the geographical distribution and variation of *S. diana* by William Hovanitz (1963), with two photographs in color, gives a great deal of information not found in more general articles about this butterfly. Through the courtesy of F. Martin Brown, my attention was directed to the life history of *S. diana* described in detail by W. H. Edwards

(1884). Strangely, the larva, egg, pupa, and adult of *S. diana* are figured on the plate devoted to *S. rupestris*. In this account, there is a comparison of the life histories of *S. diana*, *S. cybele*, and *S. aphrodite*.

When fully grown, the larva is rather large and its body is glossy black. There are a number of fleshy, barbed spines on the body. Each spine is bright red or orange on the lower one-third of its length, and black on the outer two-thirds. The head is black with dark orange along the upper part, which sometimes gives the head a brownish appearance. A complete description of the caterpillar through each instar has been given by W. H. Evans (1959, pp. 93–95).

Great Spangled Fritillary. *Speyeria cybele cybele* Fabricius
(Page 125)

Distribution and Records: *S. c. cybele* is common in the mountains; in the Piedmont Region, it decreases in numbers and becomes rare and local; in the Coastal Region, it occurs only as rare strays.

Mountain Region—*Murray Co.*: Old Fort Mountain, 3 June 1950 LHJ (TTRS). *Rabun Co.*: LaPrades, Lake Burton, 8 June 1967 LHJ; LaPrades, Lake Burton, 20 June 1950 LHT (TTRS). *Fannin Co.*: near Margret, 29 June 1958 LHJ (TTRS). *Union Co.*: Cooper Creek State Park, 29 June 1960 LHJ (TTRS); Cooper Creek State Park, Wolf Pen Gap, 2 July 1958 LHJ (TTRS). *Banks Co.* and *Habersham Co.*: 23 July and 10 Aug 1930 RWM (see Montgomery, 1931). *Towns Co.*: Brasstown Bald (alt. 4700 ft), 12 Aug 1951 LHJ (TTRS). *Rabun Co.*: LaPrades, Lake Burton, 12 Sept 1953 LHJ (TTRS); LaPrades, Lake Burton, 21 Sept 1967 LNH (TTRS).
Piedmont Region—*Fulton Co.*: Atlanta area, 18 June 1940 LHJ (TTRS). *Coweta Co.*: Madras, 2 July 1950 MES. *Baldwin Co.*: Sinclair Dam, Milledgeville, Aug 1958 JCBS. *Fulton Co.*: Oglethorpe College, frequent JPK (see Knudsen, 1954a).
Coastal Region—None.

The Great Spangled Fritillary visits flowers freely. The large purple flower heads of Ironweed (*Vernonia*) and Joe-Pye Weed (*Eupatorium maculatum*) are special favorites of this butterfly and the other large fritillaries.

S. c. *cybele* may be confused with S. a. *aphrodite*, but the two can be distinguished by the width of the buff submarginal band on the lower side of the hindwing: it is wide on S. c. *cybele* and very narrow and restricted on S. a. *aphrodite*.

S. c. *cybele* appears in early June and adults may be found through September.

The larva is similar to those of the other large fritillaries (see the descriptions of the larvae of S. *diana* and S. *idalia*). Fully grown larva are about one and three-fourths inches long, and are dark in color, with six rows of spines. The larval food plants are Violets (*Viola* spp.).

Aphrodite. *Speyeria aphrodite aphrodite* Fabricius
(Page 125)

Distribution and Records: S. a. *aphrodite* is rare in the mountains of north Georgia, which may be the southeastern limit of its range. It is not rare further northward. Clark and Clark (1951, p. 61) reported it common to abundant in the mountains of Virginia, especially at the higher altitudes.

Mountain Region—*Union Co.*: Cooper Creek State Park, Wolf Pen Gap, 29 June 1958 LHJ (TTRS). *Rabun Co.*: near La-Prades, Lake Burton, 25 Aug 1949 LHJ (TTRS).
Piedmont Region—None.
Coastal Region—None.

There is one brood, with adults appearing on the wing in June and remaining until September.

S. a. *aphrodite* resembles S. c. *cybele*, from which it may be distinguished by the width of the band of buff between the two outer rows of silver spots on the lower side of the hindwings: the band is narrow on S. a. *aphrodite* and wide on S. c. *cybele*; on S. c. *cybele*, the band of buff extends the full width of the

279

space between the rows of silver spots, but it does not extend the full width of this space on *S. a. aphrodite*.

The larva, which is dark brown or blackish with spines along the back, is similar to the larva of *S. cybele*. The larval food plants are Violets (*Viola* spp.).

Genus *Euptoieta*

Variegated Fritillary. *Euptoieta claudia* Cramer
(Page 127)

Distribution and Records: *E. claudia* is common throughout the state from early spring until late autumn.

Mountain Region—*Banks Co.* and *Habersham Co.*: 12 July–7 Sept 1930 RWM (see Montgomery, 1931). *Rabun Co.*: Lakemont, 3 Oct 1954 LHJ (TTRS).

Piedmont Region—*Cobb Co.*: near Marietta, 18 Mar 1950 LHT (TTRS). *DeKalb Co.*: Stone Mountain, 3 May 1952 LHJ (TTRS). *Clarke Co.*: Athens area, common May 1967 LRT. *Monroe Co.*: Forsyth, 5 June 1959 FTN. *DeKalb Co.*: Avondale Estates, 24 June 1944 LHJ (TTRS). *Clarke Co.*: Athens area, common July–Aug AGR (see Richards, 1931); Athens area, common July 1966 LRT. *Bibb Co.*: Macon, 11 Sept 1952 LHJ (TTRS). *Cobb Co.*: near Marietta, 24 Nov 1951 LHT (TTRS).

Coastal Region—*Screven Co.*: Sylvania, Mar–Sept 1946 OB (AMNH). *Chatham Co.*: Savannah, no dates MHM (CU). *Thomas Co.*: Boston, Bar-M Ranch, 11, 18, and 27 July 1967 ESS (TTRS). *Lee Co.*: Leesburg, Hickory Grove Plantation, 30 July 1965 LN. *Sumter Co.*: Americus, 1 Aug 1965 LN. *Thomas Co.*: Boston, Bar-M Ranch, 10 Aug 1967 ESS. *Grady Co.*: Beachton, Sherwood Plantation, 16 Sept 1964 LN.

The individuals of *E. claudia* vary in size, and an interesting series may be obtained. Very small specimens may be found at times, especially in early spring, and unusually large ones may be found in the summer.

The Variegated Fritillary seems to prefer open areas. It

frequents fields, orchards, roadsides, and uncultivated waste areas.

The larva is about one and one-fourth inches long. Its body is orange-red, and there are two dark stripes along each side containing whitish areas or blotches that give the appearance of an interrupted whitish band. There are six rows of spines on the body; the pair of horns on the first segment point forward over the head.

The larval food plants are Passion Flower (*Passiflora*), Violets and Pansies (*Viola*), and Moonseed (*Menispermum*).

Family HELICONIIDAE—Heliconians

Genus *Heliconius*

Zebra. *Heliconius charitonius tuckeri* Comstock and Brown
(Page 125)

Distribution and Records: *H. c. tuckeri* occurs in south Georgia as a casual to fairly common visitor from Florida, where, as Kimball (1965, p. 39) states, it is "general and common though perhaps not so abundant in the northern counties, but present at all times except during the coldest weather."

Mountain Region—None.
Piedmont Region—*Fulton Co.*: Atlanta, fresh female 13 Oct 1948 JPK. *Bibb Co.*: near Dry Branch, colony observed JCBS.
Coastal Region—*Chatham Co.*: Savannah, no date MHM (CU). *Richmond Co.*: Augusta, no date HWE. *Twiggs Co.*: near Danville, (no date) colony observed JCBS. *Camden Co.*: Coleraine Plantation, 17 Aug 1949 LHJ. *Grady Co.*: Beachton, Sherwood Plantation, 4 Sept 1965 LN; Beachton, Sherwood Plantation, 19 Sept 1965 LN; Beachton, Susina Plantation, 25 Sept 1965 LHJ (TTRS); Beachton, Sherwood Plantation, 12 and 13 Oct 1965 LN. *Thomas Co.*: Thomasville, Pebble Hill Plantation, 16 Oct 1965 LN. *Charlton Co.*: Billy's Island, Okefenokee Swamp, 21 Oct 1937 LHJ. *Grady Co.*: Beachton, Sherwood Plantation, 3 Dec 1965 JN and LN.

Individual strays have been taken in Georgia as far northward as Atlanta, Macon, Augusta, and Savannah. On August 17, 1949, I was shown an active colony by Johnny Burch, a woodsman working on the Coleraine Plantation in Camden County, eight miles east of Folkston. The butterflies were in a Live Oak and Magnolia hammock on a low hill overlooking the St. Marys River. The females were ovipositing on a type of vine unknown to me. Subsequent visits in November, 1949, and February, 1950, revealed that the colony was still thriving during the unusually mild winter. Flame Azaleas and other flowers were in bloom in December of 1949, and January, February, and March of 1950. However, a rather severe freeze early in April must have ended their existence, as I saw no butterflies when I visited the area on May 28, 1950, nor did I find any larvae on the food plants growing in the area.

J. C. Brooks found two colonies, one in Twiggs County and the other near Dry Branch in Bibb County.

The larva is greenish white in the earlier stages and white in the last stage, with transverse markings of brown or black spots and six longitudinal rows of long, black bristly spines. The food plant is Passion Flower (*Passiflora*).

Genus *Agraulis*

Gulf Fritillary. *Agraulis vanillae nigrior* Michener
(Page 125)

Distribution and Records: *A. v. nigrior* is common in the Coastal and Piedmont regions; it is of casual occurrence in the Mountain Region, except in the valleys, where it is common in areas where the food plant, Passion Flower (*Passiflora incarnata*), occurs.

Mountain Region—*Banks Co.* and *Habersham Co.*: 12 Aug–18 Sept 1930 RWM (see Montgomery, 1931).
Piedmont Region—*Bibb Co.*: Macon, partial albino 2 Sept 1923 HFS (TTRS). *Monroe Co.*: Forsyth, 15 Sept 1956 FTN. *Fulton Co.*: Atlanta, Indian Trail Road, 25 Sept 1960 JCS (TTRS).

Bibb Co.: Macon, melanic specimen 25 Sept 1930 HFS (TTRS). *Monroe Co.*: Forsyth, 30 and 31 Oct 1956 FTN. *Clarke Co.*: Athens, four specimens *A.v. nigrior* ab. *comstocki* Oct–Nov 1925–1931 AGR (see Richards, 1931). *Monroe Co.*: Forsyth, 1 Nov 1956 FTN.

Coastal Region—*Grady Co.*: Beachton, Sherwood Plantation, 2 Jan 1965 LHJ (TTRS); Beachton, 6 Jan 1965 LN; Beachton, Sherwood Plantation, 10 Jan 1965 LN. *Colquitt Co.*: Moultrie, 18 Apr 1945 HVAV (UWO). *Thomas Co.*: Boston, Bar-M Ranch, 7 July 1967 ESS (TTRS). *Screven Co.*: Sylvania, Mar–Sept 1946 OB (AMNH). *Grady Co.*: Beachton, Susina Plantation, 20 July 1963 LHJ (TTRS); Beachton, Sherwood Plantation, 10 Aug 1964 LN; Beachton, Susina Plantation, 7 Sept 1963 LHJ (TTRS).

The Gulf Fritillary, with its orange-red, black-bordered wings, adorned beneath with silver spots and bars, may often be seen in flower gardens eagerly sampling the nectar of the blossoms it visits briefly before flying away to seek others of its species. The adult population is most numerous from mid-July to early October.

Melanic specimens, their wings with areas suffused to varying degrees with black, are taken from time to time. Four specimens, two males and two females, of the aberration *A. v. nigrior* ab. *comstocki* Gunder were taken in Athens by Richards (1931, p. 244) in October and November. Over a period of six years, he took numerous specimens of the aberration *A. v. nigrior* ab. *fumosus* Gunder.

In the Macon area, Strohecker captured a partial albino on September 2, 1923. This specimen has a light area in the middle of each forewing. On September 25, 1930, he collected a melanic specimen with extensive black areas on the upper sides of both the forewings and the hindwings; on the lower side, the silver spots were fused into long silver bars.

The body of the larva is yellowish or pale brown, with two dark stripes along each side and (usually) a stripe along the back. There are six rows of spines on the body, and one pair on the head curving backward. The larval food plants, in addition to the Passion Flower, *Passiflora incarnata*, are various other members of the genus *Passiflora*.

Family DANAIDAE—Monarchs

Genus *Danaus*

Monarch; Milkweed Butterfly. *Danaus plexippus plexippus* Linnaeus (Page 125)

Distribution and Records: *D. p. plexippus* is found throughout the state. It is common in the spring and abundant in the fall when migrating. It is rare and sometimes apparently absent in many parts of the state in midsummer and in winter. Listed below are a few representative spring and summer records.

Mountain Region—*Banks Co.* and *Habersham Co.*: 24 Aug–7 Sept 1930 RWM (see Montgomery, 1931).
Piedmont Region—*Coweta Co.*: Madras, 29 Mar 1950 MES. *Monroe Co.*: Forsyth, 1 Apr 1956 FTN. *Troup Co.*: LaGrange, seven seen flying north 7 and 8 Apr 1956 LHJ. *Coweta Co.*: Madras, 13 Apr 1957 MES. *Monroe Co.*: Forsyth, 1 May 1956 FTN. *Morgan Co.*: Madison, 26 May 1967 JCS. *Bibb Co.*: Macon, uncommon (except in Sept migration—a few found each month, especially June), JCBS. *Morgan Co.*: Madison, 18 July 1967 JCS. *Monroe Co.*: Forsyth, common 19 Oct 1956 FTN.
Coastal Region—*Baker Co.*: Melton Place, 6 Jan 1965 LN. *Grady Co.*: Beachton, Susina Plantation, 6 and 7 Mar 1964 LHJ. *Glynn Co.*: Jekyll Island, three seen flying northward on beach 17 Mar 1956 LHJ; Jekyll Island, twenty-two seen feeding and flying casually 17 Mar 1956 LHJ; Jekyll Island, six seen (morning temp. 45° F) 18 Mar 1956 LHJ. *Coffee Co.*: Douglas, seen flying northward 30 Mar 1956 LHJ. *Colquitt Co.*: Moultrie, 8 Apr 1945 HVAV (UWO). *Camden Co.*: Kingsland area, Coleraine Plantation, 28 May 1950 LHJ (USNM). *Chatham Co.*: Blichton, 29 May 1964 LHJ.

The Monarch is well named: in late summer and fall, it makes its way southward in majestic flights from Canada to places as far away as Florida, Mexico, and California. In the spring, the survivors begin their return journey northward. Many of the females begin to lay eggs on the northward migration. John Abbot (in Smith, 1797) recorded that a caterpillar he observed feeding on Butterfly-Weed changed to a pupa on April 25, and that the butterfly emerged on May 11. Paul Kight found a freshly emerged adult near Stone Mountain in DeKalb County on May 13, 1957.

Georgia lepidopterists have observed that the Monarch becomes very rare in June and July after the migrants have passed through. Then, in late August, the population begins to increase noticeably—slowly, at first, and then rapidly, as the first migrants arrive from their northern breeding grounds. Studies have indicated that the Monarchs flying southward and southeastward through Georgia will, for the most part, spend the winter in Florida. The peak of the fall migration is reached in October. The numbers decline steadily in November.

An interesting event occurred on October 4, 1957: We had been away on a short trip, and upon reaching our home in Avondale Estates, near Atlanta, the telephone was ringing. It was our friends John and Jane Symmes, who excitedly reported that a spectacular migration of butterflies had been passing through Atlanta all day. They invited us to meet them near the State Capitol to see if any were settling in the trees for the night. Thousands of Monarchs had massed north of Atlanta at the edge of a low-pressure area, which had brought rain and poor visibility to the city for several days. The clouds lifted, the rain stopped, and the sun came out before noon. Monarchs appeared by the thousands flying down city streets, dodging people, automobiles, and office buildings. They were seen by hundreds of people who had never witnessed a butterfly migration. Newspaper offices and radio and television stations were deluged with telephone calls inquiring about the phenomenon.

On October 6, 1957, G. E. DuPree of Atlanta went into his

yard to take a picture of a Monarch and found a banded specimen. It had been tagged by Dr. F. A. Urquhart on September
18, 1957, and liberated at his home in West Hill, Ontario. This
butterfly had travelled more than 740 miles in eighteen days.
Many studies have been made on the migratory habits of the
Monarch. An outstanding contribution was made by Dr.
Urquhart, whose book (Urquhart, 1960) is a comprehensive
report based on the research he directed under the auspices of
the Royal Ontario Museum. Several hundred people cooper-
ated in the project, which included banding many thousands of
Monarchs to trace their routes and locate their wintering territories. A few records selected from Urquhart's book and included in the accompanying table will suffice to show the rate
of travel and distance covered by tagged Monarchs. The long-
distance record for a tagged Monarch is approximately 1,870
air miles (see the last line in accompanying table); the calcu-
lated rate of travel for the record holder, however, was a
leisurely 14.5 miles per day.

Rate of travel of tagged Monarchs (*Danaus plexippus plexippus*)

Monarchs tagged and released		Monarchs recovered		Distance traveled (miles)	Time elapsed (days)	Rate of travel (miles/day)
Date	Place	Date	Place			
22 Sept 1955	Liberty, Pa.	25 Oct 1955	Port St. Joe, Fla.	788	33	23.9
25 Oct 1955	Clarkston, Ga.	25 Nov 1955	Orlando, Fla.	404	31	13.0
19 Sept 1956	Highland Creek, Ont.	22 Oct 1956	Boston, Ga.	842	33	40.1
18 Sept 1957	Highland Creek, Ont.	6 Oct 1957	Atlanta, Ga.	740	18	41.1
18 Sept 1957	Highland Creek, Ont.	11 Oct 1957	Niceville, Fla.	985	23	42.8
18 Sept 1957	Highland Creek, Ont.	25 Jan 1958	San Luis Potosí, Mex.	1870	129	14.5

Source: Urquhart (1960).

For many years, Monarchs have been known to congregate
in clusters on trees during fall migration. On the Monterey
Peninsula of California, a certain group of Monterey Pines
(*Pinus radiata*) standing near the town of Pacific Grove have
been the home for overwintering Monarchs for many years.
They have become a valuable tourist attraction, and Pacific
Grove has passed a law protecting the Monarchs from
molestation.

Dr. Urquhart hoped to learn of such overwintering colonies in other states. Herbert L. Stoddard, Sr., a nationally known ornithologist, discovered a large gathering of Monarchs on groups of young pine trees at Alligator Point and Bald Point, on the Gulf coast of Florida, on November 4, 1954. He entered the event in his fieldbook as follows:

Saw several thousands of Monarch butterflies densely clustered out of wind on young pine saplings—thicker than the leaves on the trees. Such gatherings in several places over about 10 acre area. . . . Stiff SE wind up to 25 MPH. Just after a severe cold front—got down to 24 degrees at Sherwood yesterday but was 34 degrees this morning. Broken cloudy.

On December 20, 1955, more than a year later, Stoddard again took note of a large assemblage of Monarchs at Alligator Point and Bald Point. Florida maps usually refer to these locations on the Gulf of Mexico as Lighthouse Point. The area is about forty-five miles south of Tallahassee and seventy miles south of Stoddard's home in Grady County, Georgia. This was an important discovery, and some interesting data was obtained over a period of several years. Reference is made to this because of its importance and its proximity to Georgia.

During the first two weeks of January, 1956, Dr. Urquhart banded a thousand Monarch butterflies at Lighthouse Point. During the tagging operations, he saw birds (unidentified) picking up banded specimens and flying away with them.

On January 20, 1956, Herbert L. Stoddard, Sr., accompanied by E. V. Komarek, Sr., who is well known as a mammalogist, visited Lighthouse Point. Komarek took many fine photographs of the colony. They examined the butterflies and made a note of the tag numbers of the tagged individuals. They returned the next day and examined the area thoroughly, picking up 242 tagged and approximately 400 untagged right wings in two hours. The wings were lying on the ground in arborlike spots, each with a low perch, located beneath the trees in the underbrush within a radius of 100 yards of the pine trees used as a roost by the Monarchs. It seemed likely, in the expert opinion of these two men, that the killing was done by birds and not by mammals. The weather had been unusually cold for a number of days, and some birds that normally do not eat Monarchs may have done so when their usual food became scarce and hunger overcame their distaste for the Monarch.

At a later date, John and Jane Symmes and I visited the area and picked up many wings, including banded and unbanded right forewings. The wings were found in arborlike areas under Myrtle bushes, directly beneath low horizontal limbs that served as perches. Bird droppings were in evidence under the limbs. The number of perches in use in the area indicated that several birds, perhaps all of the same species, had caught and fed on the Monarchs after removing their wings. It was Herbert Stoddard's guess that the bird or birds that were feeding on the butterflies were distributed widely over the area and caught the flying Monarchs in their own territory, but that they took them to their favored insect-eating spots under the bushes, where they ate the butterflies after picking off their wings. A strong suspect is the Catbird (*Dumetella carolinensis*), which is common in the area and feeds in such spots.

This may be a rare occurrence. Urquhart (1960, p. 210) suggests that it is brought about only when there is a combination of the following unusual conditions: (1) the birds' normal food supply is absent or reduced in their regular feeding area; (2) Monarch butterflies are abundant in the feeding area; and (3) the weather conditions that have brought about the reduction of the birds' normal food supply have also caused the Monarchs to congregate in roosting trees in the general feeding area of the birds.

An important contribution can be made by someone identifying the birds that eat Monarchs under special circumstances in the wild. Bruce Petersen (1964) made some experimental tests in Iowa in which he observed that five common species of birds would eat Monarchs that he had de-winged and placed in a lively condition near the birds' usual feeding station. In an experiment he made during the winter in Colorado, he found that Scrub Oak Jays and Pinion Jays will eat Monarchs even with wings intact, provided the butterflies are lively but cannot fly, and are placed near the station where the birds usually feed.

I reported (Harris, 1950) seeing a very noticeable spring migration of Monarchs in March and April of 1950. Soon after publication, a letter arrived from Dr. C. B. Williams, the eminent authority on insect migration, asking for additional information. He mentioned that observations and accounts of northward migrations of Monarchs were rare.

Dr. Urquhart's (1960) research has shown that the spring migration varies from the fall migration in several important respects, including the following:

(1) overnight roosts are not established during spring migration; (2) spring migrants rarely stop to feed upon the nectar of spring flowers and further that they reach certain areas early in the spring before flowering plants are abundant; (3) the flight is direct, north or northeast, rather than meandering; (4) gravid females may retain fully developed eggs for a considerable length of time before ovipositing; (5) males take part in the flight as well as females, although in the more northern parts of the breeding range the males are rare; and (6) the fatty tissue is a fuel reserve for the spring migration because at this time there is a paucity of nectar-producing plants and the females take little, if any, time for feeding.

J. R. Heitzman (1962) reported a large spring migration in northern Mexico in 1962. The Monarchs were flying lazily to the northeast. At one point, he noted that between sixty to eighty butterflies were passing for every mile he travelled. When he stopped the car and got out to look about, the Monarchs were everywhere, some flying a few feet above the ground and others flying far up into the sky until hardly visible.

When he returned to Brownsville, Texas, on March 26, *D. plexippus* was common where not a one had been observed before.

Some studies were made in Mississippi by Bryant Mather (1955) on the flight period of the Monarch in the Gulf states. In the same report, he also discussed the length of the forewing, giving interesting examples of geographic variations in that character.

Geoffrey Beall (1952) published a report on the migration movements of the Monarch on the east coast of Florida during the winter (December 10 through May 5) based on data supplied by Mr. and Mrs. Karl Hodges. This report provides a good example of the valuable information that can be collected by local naturalists.

During the summers of 1964 and 1965, there was a marked drop in the numbers of Monarchs in Georgia. One of the several causative factors of the sharp reduction in the Monarch population was found to be a polyhedrosis virus. Both Brewer and Thomas (1966) and Urquhart (1966) reported on the virus and its effect on the eggs, larvae, and pupae. It seems likely that survivors of the virus epizootic will build up a resistance, and over a period of time, the population will gradually increase in numbers.

The larva is nearly two inches long when fully grown. Its body is white with narrow black and yellow bands around each segment, and the head is yellow with black stripes. The fully grown larva has four long, black, flexible horns, two of which project forward from behind the head at the second thoracic segment; the other two project backward from the rear or caudal extremity.

John Abbot (in Smith, 1797) wrote:

This caterpillar eats the butterfly weed. On the 24th of April it suspended itself by the tail; changed to a chrysalis the next day, and on the 11th of May the butterfly came out. It is not a very common species.

The Milkweed figured by Abbot is *Asclepias tuberosa*, the Orange Butterfly-Weed. Urquhart (1960) lists twenty species of Milkweed as occurring in Georgia.

Queen. *Danaus gilippus berenice* Cramer (Page 125)

Distribution and Records: *D. g. berenice* is found along the Georgia coast and in the counties of the Lower Coastal Plain where its chief foodplant, Blunt-leaved Milkweed (*Asclepias amplexicaulis*), occurs.

Mountain Region—None.
Piedmont Region—*Richmond Co.*: Augusta, no date HWE.
Coastal Region—*Colquitt Co.*: Moultrie, 8–27 Apr 1945 HVAV (UWO). *Charlton Co.*: Folkston, Coleraine Plantation, 28 May 1950 LHJ and BMR (see Mather, 1955a). *Thomas Co.*: Boston, Bar-M Ranch, Linton Lake, 9 July 1967 ESS (TTRS). *Grady Co.*: Beachton, Birdsong Plantation, 11 July 1944 LHJ (TTRS). *Screven Co.*: Sylvania, mid-May and late July 1946 OB (AMNH). *Glynn Co.*: Jekyll Island, 18 Aug 1960 JCS.

Otto Buchholz found *D. g. berenice* to be common in mid-May and again in late July in Screven County, where he collected extensively from March to September in 1946.

In an earlier publication (Harris, 1950), I incorrectly stated that the western subspecies *D. g. strigosa* was sometimes found in Georgia. The confusion arose from some specimens having grayish-bordered veins that are occasionally taken in Georgia and Florida. However, it has been noted by King (in Kimball, 1965) that the ground color in these specimens never tends to the pale brown of typical *D. g. strigosa* of the Southwest.

D. g. berenice is not much of a wanderer, although an occasional stray may be taken. H. W. Eustis collected a specimen in Augusta (Richmond County), and I have taken it on St. Simons Island (Glynn County). A few specimens have been taken in southwest Georgia, possibly strays from the Gulf Coast region of Florida. Mather (1955a) lists a number of records of this butterfly for the Gulf coast of Mississippi, along with records for other Gulf states.

John Abbot (in Smith, 1797) states: "After feeding on the plant here represented [*Asclepias amplexicaulis*], the caterpillar changed to a chrysalis June 18th, and the butterfly came forth the 26th."

The larva is similar to that of *D. plexippus*, but with six "horns" instead of four. One pair of horns is on the second thoracic segment, and the remaining two pairs are on the second and eighth abdominal segments.

Family SATYRIDAE—Satyrs and Wood Nymphs

Genus *Lethe*

Pearly-Eye. *Lethe portlandia* Fabricius (Page 152)

Distribution and Records: *L. portlandia* is widely distributed over the state. It is a woodland species usually found in local colonies not far from small streams where stands of maiden cane (*Arundinaria*) are growing in moist, shady areas. We do not have any Georgia records of the closely related *Lethe anthedon* Clark at the present time.

Mountain Region—None [but specimens have been collected by Richards (1931, p. 242) in June and August near Monteagle, Tennessee (alt. 1500 ft), roughly twenty miles northwest of the northwestern corner of Georgia].

Piedmont Region—*Monroe Co.*: Juliette, 19 Apr 1963 FTN; Juliette, 5 May 1966 FTN; Forsyth, two in light trap 18 May 1962 FTN. *Clarke Co.*: Athens, mid-Apr–late Aug AGR (see Richards, 1931). *Fulton Co.*: Buckhead area, 16 Sept 1949 LHT (TTRS).

Coastal Region—*Twiggs Co.*: Danville, 24 Apr 1961 JCBS. *Grady Co.*: Beachton, Sherwood Plantation, 4 May 1934 LHJ (TTRS); Beachton, Sherwood Plantation, 9 May 1965 LN. *Screven Co.*: Sylvania, 25 May 1968 BMR; Sylvania, several specimens May–Aug 1946 OB (AMNH). *Thomas Co.*: Boston, Bar-M Ranch, 2 July 1967 ESS (TTRS). *Grady Co.*: Beachton,

Susina Plantation, 28 July 1965 LHJ (TTRS). *Chatham Co.*: Savannah, 6 Aug 1962 JCS. *Grady Co.*: Beachton, Sherwood Plantation, 10 and 24 Sept 1964 LN; Beachton, Susina Plantation, 18 Oct 1963 LHJ (TTRS).

Austin H. Clark (1936) found recognizable differences between *L. anthedon* and *L. portlandia*. An important difference was noted in the row of spots on the lower side of the forewings, which is straight on *L. anthedon* and curved on *L. portlandia*.

Another important difference was noted by William D. Field. He found that the antennal clubs of specimens of *L. portlandia* were orange above and below, but that those of *L. anthedon* were completely ringed with black behind the tip (Mather and Mather, 1958, p. 73).

J. C. Brooks observed that the courtship ritual of *L. portlandia* takes place at nightfall, whereas the closely related species *L. creola* mates in the daytime, thus possibly explaining the lack of hybridization between these butterflies when they are found in the same local area.

The larva is about one and one-fourth inches long and yellowish green. There are two sets of horns, one pair on the head and the other on the last segment of the body; the horns are tipped with red. The larval food plant is Cane (*Arundinaria gigantea*). It is likely that Maiden Cane (*Arundinaria tecta*) is also a food plant, because this butterfly and *L. creola* both appear to be associated with it.

Creole Pearly-Eye. *Lethe creola* Skinner (Page 154)

Distribution and Records: *L. creola*, although rare and local, is widely distributed over the state.

Mountain Region—*White Co.*: Cleveland, Yonah Mountain, 27 July 1934 PWF and DE.
Piedmont Region—*Fulton Co.*: Atlanta, Indian Trail Road, 14 May 1965 HAF; Atlanta, Riverside Drive, 21 May 1957 LHJ (TTRS). *Monroe Co.*: Forsyth, taken at light trap 22 May

1966 FTN. *Fulton Co.*: Atlanta, Harris Trail, 2 June 1956 LHJ (TTRS). Atlanta, Indian Trail Road, 6 June 1957 LHJ (TTRS). *Monroe Co.*: Forsyth, taken in light trap 9 June 1966 FTN. *DeKalb Co.*: Stone Mountain, 17 June 1950 LHJ. *Fulton Co.*: Atlanta, 10 July 1937 LHJ (TTRS); Atlanta, Harris Trail, 25 July 1965 JCS. *Monroe Co.*: Forsyth, three males in bait trap 7 Aug 1960 FTN. *Clarke Co.*: Athens, early June and early Aug AGR (see Richards, 1931).
Coastal Region—*Chatham Co.*: Savannah, 14 May 1951 HLK.

This is a woodland butterfly, preferring moist, shady areas where Maiden Cane (*Arundinaria tecta*) is growing, especially near small streams. This is also the type of habitat frequented by *L. portlandia*, and the two are sometimes, but not always, found in the same area.

J. C. Brooks has observed that, in local colonies containing both *L. creola* and *L. portlandia*, the former species constitutes about 5 percent of the total population. He also observed that *L. creola* does not participate in a courtship ritual at nightfall as does *L. portlandia*, thus possibly explaining the lack of hybridization of these closely related species.

Clark and Clark (1951, p. 30) state that *L. creola* is easily overlooked because it is crepuscular, seldom flying during the day but becoming very active just before dark. The collector may most readily obtain specimens by beating them out of the Cane, in which they rest during daylight hours.

The males of *L. creola* are easily distinguishable from those of *L. portlandia* by the olive sex-scaling and their narrower, more triangular wings. The females, however, are difficult to distinguish, because their wings are almost the same shape; but they do differ in the number of eyespots on the lower sides of the forewings—*L. creola* has five well-developed eyespots, whereas *L. portlandia* has only four. Some females of *L. portlandia* have a fifth spot, which appears as a dot or as a very small eyespot.

The larva is lighter in color than that of *L. portlandia*, ac-

294

cording to Brooks. The larval food plant is *Arundinaria tecta* (Clark, 1951, p. 30; Kimball, 1965, p. 38).

Eyed Brown; Grass Nymph. *Lethe eurydice appalachia*
Chermock (Page 152)

Distribution and Records: *L. e. appalachia* is found throughout the state. It is rare and local in the Mountain and Piedmont regions, and very rare in the Coastal Region.

Mountain Region—*Union Co.*: Cooper Creek State Park, Duncan Ridge Road, 6 June 1958 JCS. *White Co.*: Cleveland, 13 June 1957 LHT (TTRS). *Fannin Co.*: near Cooper Creek, 18 June 1962 JCS. *Union Co.*: Cooper Creek State Park, 16 July 1961 JCS (TTRS); Cooper Creek State Park, 18 July 1962 JCS. *Rabun Co.*: Dicks Creek Road, near State Fish Hatchery, 19 Aug 1965 LHT. *Union Co.*: Duncan Ridge Road, 22 Aug 1959 JCS.
Piedmont Region—*DeKalb Co.*: Avondale Estates, 16 June 1944 LHJ (TTRS). *Fulton Co.*: Atlanta, near Westview Cemetery, 4 July 1937 LHJ; Atlanta, Harris Trail, 29 July 1960 JCS; Atlanta, Harris Trail, 20 Aug 1961 JCS; Atlanta, Harris Trail, 26 Aug 1961 LHJ (TTRS).
Coastal Region—*Thomas Co.*: Boston, Merrily Plantation, Linton Lake, 9 Aug 1967 ESS (TTRS); Boston, Merrily Plantation, 29 Aug 1967 LN and WB.

This subspecies, the type locality of which is Brevard, North Carolina, is darker than typical *L. eurydice*. It seems to prefer grassy areas in open woods, but it has also been found in grassy areas near streams and along roads near wooded areas. The dull colors of this butterfly blend well with grasses, thus causing it to be easily overlooked by collectors. This may explain the paucity of Georgia records.

Kimball (1965, p. 38) reported that J. R. Watson collected specimens from Monticello, Florida, only eleven miles from the Georgia state line. Leon Neel collected specimens there on September 12, 1966.

On August 9, 1967, Ellery Sedgwick, Jr., collected *L. e. appalachia* at Linton Lake on Merrily Plantation in Thomas County, very near the Florida state line. On August 29, 1967, Leon Neel and Wilson Baker visited the colony at Linton Lake and collected one specimen. The habitat was a Black Gum "pond" with a coarse green grass and Button-Bush understory.

In Virginia, Clark and Clark (1951, p. 32) found *L. e. appalachia* in the Mountain and Piedmont regions in permanently wet sedgy areas, almost invariably with Alders, in and near woods. On the Coastal Plain, they found that it lives in wet woods and swamps with abundant *Arundinaria* and always in association with *L. p. portlandia*. Throughout the state of Virginia, they found it to be very local and rare.

The larva is about one and one-fourth inches when fully grown. The body is downy and is striped lengthwise with shades of green; the head and last abdominal segment each have a pair of red-tipped horns. The larva overwinters when partially grown. The larval food plants are various grasses and sedges.

Genus *Euptychia*

Gemmed Satyr; Gemmed Brown. *Euptychia gemma* Hübner
(Page 152)

Distribution and Records: *E. gemma* is found throughout the state. It is local and usually rare.

Mountain Region—*Murray Co.*: Old Fort Mountain, 23 Apr 1961 JCS. *Banks Co.* and *Habersham Co.*: five specimens 16 June and one specimen 28 Aug 1930 RWM (see Montgomery, 1931). *Rabun Co.*: specimens taken above 3000 ft AGR (see Richards, 1931).

Piedmont Region—*Clarke Co.*: Athens, Mar–Sept AGR (see Richards, 1931). *Coweta Co.*: Madras, Mar–Apr 1950 MES. *Monroe Co.*: Forsyth, 10 Apr 1966 HAF. *DeKalb Co.*: Stone Mountain, 11 Apr 1951 LHJ and DE. *Bibb Co.*: Stone Creek,

11 Apr 1960 FTN. *Fulton Co.*: Atlanta, 8 June 1955 JCS. *Bibb Co.*: Macon, 20 Oct 1928 HFS and DE.
Coastal Region—*Camden Co.*: Kingsland, Coleraine Plantation, 9 Feb 1952 LHJ and DE. *Screven Co.*: Sylvania, Mar–Sept 1946 OB (AMNH). *Thomas Co.*: Thomasville, Mill Pond Plantation, 19 Apr 1967 ESS; Boston, Bar-M Ranch, 12 July 1967 ESS (TTRS). *Grady Co.*: Beachton, Susina Plantation, 26 Aug 1966 LHJ; Beachton, Sherwood Plantation, 25 Sept 1964 LN; Beachton, Sherwood Plantation, 13 Oct 1965 LN; Beachton, Sherwood Plantation, 26 Nov 1964 LN.

There are two broods, the first usually appearing in March and April (but sometimes earlier in south Georgia) and the second in July and August (some individuals of the second brood have been found as late as September and October).

On the Coastal Plain, it is found in grassy areas in open woods where there are moist or wet areas, and also near streams and ponds. In the Piedmont Region, it is found in grassy woodland areas near streams. It strays, however, to grassy areas in open woods on hillsides and hilltops, where individuals may sometimes be collected.

In the area around Macon, J. C. Brooks found *E. gemma* to be common in March, April, and early May, with a second brood in August. He found *E. gemma* along woodland trails and observed that it seldom enters heavily populated areas.

A. Glenn Richards, Jr. (1931, p. 244) states:

Clarke County in all shady environs, even in the center of town but like all Satyrs commonest on the Bridle Path, late March—Sept., odd specimens taken at several points in pure Transition parts of the mountains, and taken at over 3000 feet in Rabun County.

Richards' reference to "the center of town" refers to Athens, where the University of Georgia is located. The campus is almost in the center of town, and has lawns shaded by old trees, which may have given a restful haven to some of the wandering Gemmed Satyrs.

The larvae are dimorphic: those of the first brood are green

297

with darker lengthwise stripes, and those of the second brood are brown with darker lengthwise stripes. The larvae of both broods have long tubercles on the head and last segment. Comstock and Comstock (1920, p. 196) report that the larval dimorphism is an adaptation for protection during the respective seasons in which the larvae appear. Then, with delightful humor, they ask, "How does this caterpillar know when to be green and when to be brown?"

The larval food plants are various grasses.

Georgia Satyr. *Euptychia areolata areolata* J. E. Smith
(Page 152)

Distribution and Records: *E. a. areolata*, the type locality of which is Georgia—John Abbot's notes and drawing (in Smith, 1797) were very likely made from specimens he found in Screven County—occurs locally in the Coastal Region.

Mountain Region—None.
Piedmont Region—None.
Coastal Region—*Colquitt Co.*: Moultrie, 21–27 Apr 1945 HVAV (UWO). *Chatham Co.*: near Savannah, 27 May 1961 LHJ (TTRS). *Camden Co.*: Kingsland, Coleraine Plantation, 28 May 1950 LHJ (USNM). *Bryan Co.*: near Blichton, 30 May 1960 LHJ (TTRS). *Thomas Co.*: Thomasville, Greenwood Plantation, 21 June 1954 EVK (TTRS). *Screven Co.*: several collected Mar–Sept 1946 OB (AMNH).

In keeping with other species in the same genus, *E. a. areolata* prefers grassy areas. It occurs in moist grassy areas, and it seems to prefer grasses of the coarse, sedgy type.

John Symmes and I found a good collecting spot for *E. a. areolata* on US 80, about three miles west of Blichton, which is located between Statesboro and Savannah. We found a small pond in open pine woods surrounded by a wet, almost marshy area with coarse grasses. The butterflies in the tall grass are easily overlooked until they are disturbed and take flight.

Klots (1951, pl. 7) figures the upper and lower sides of a

specimen of *E. a. areolata* from Deenwood, near Waycross (Ware County), Georgia.

Mather (1965) reported the results of a study of the distribution and variation of *Euptychia areolata*, with special reference to Mississippi. He noted that the spots on the hindwing of the Georgia specimen figured by Klots had an average ratio of length to width of below 2.8. This value, taken with others, was used by him in constructing a map that suggested that, in Georgia, this ratio would be expected, on the average, to diminish from about 2.9 in the extreme southeast to 2.2 in the northwest part of the state. Mather found that the ratio for subspecies *E. a. septentrionalis* would be about 1.5, which indicates that it does not occur in Georgia.

The body of the larva is yellow-green with darker stripes. The head is green, and bears tubercles that are brownish; the tubercles on the last segment are tipped with red.

The larval food plants are various grasses. Abbot (in Smith, 1797) states:

Feeds on the drooping andropogon grass [*A. nutans*]. . . . The caterpillar changed May 22nd, the fly appeared June 1st. It frequents the sides of rivulets, or branches, as they are called in America.

Carolina Satyr. *Euptychia hermes sosybia* Fabricius
(Page 152)

Distribution and Records: *E. h. sosybia* is found throughout the state. It is common over most of the state, but uncommon in the mountains.

Mountain Region—*Rabun Co.*: Lake Rabun and surrounding ridges to alt. 3000 ft, June 1927 AGR (see Richards, 1931).
Piedmont Region—*Monroe Co.*: Forsyth, 7 Apr 1959 FTN. *Coweta Co.*: Madras, 9 Apr 1950 MES. *Monroe Co.*: Forsyth, 27 Apr 1955 FTN. *Coweta Co.*: Madras, 29 Apr 1951 MES.
Coastal Region—*Grady Co.*: Sherwood Plantation, 10 Jan 1965 LN. *Charlton Co.*: Folkston, 9 Feb 1952 LHJ (TTRS). *Grady*

Co.: Beachton, Sherwood Plantation, 19 Mar 1966 LN. *Colquitt Co.*: Moultrie, 11, 17, and 18 Mar 1945 HVAV (UWO). *Thomas Co.*: Boston, Bar-M Ranch, 10 Aug 1967 ESS (TTRS). *Screven Co.*: Sylvania, several specimens Mar–Sept 1946 OB (AMNH). *Grady Co.*: Beachton, Sherwood Plantation, 18 Sept 1964 LN. *Baker Co.*: Newton, 30 Oct 1964 LN.

Richards (1931, p. 244) reported taking specimens at Lake Rabun (Rabun County) and higher on the surrounding ridges up to 3000 feet.

The Carolina Satyr flies close to the ground and may be found in grassy areas (shady spots are preferred) and in open woods. It is smaller and darker than our other Wood Satyrs. There are two broods in the northern portion of the state and three in the southern.

The larva has a light green body with dark green stripes running lengthwise. It has many small, hairy, yellow tubercles. The larval food plants are various grasses.

Little Wood Satyr. *Euptychia cymela cymela* Cramer
(Page 152)

Distribution and Records: *E. c. cymela* is a common woodland species found throughout the state.

Mountain Region—*Murray Co.*: Old Fort Mountain, 3 June 1950 LHT (TTRS). *Rabun Co.*: common, June–July AGR (see Richards, 1931).
Piedmont Region—*Clarke Co.*: Athens, uncommon May 1967 LRT. *Bibb Co.*: Macon, 11 May 1963 FTN. *DeKalb Co.*: Stone Mountain, 24 May 1952 LHJ (TTRS). *Fulton Co.*: Atlanta, Mt. Vernon Road, 31 May 1958 LHJ (TTRS). *DeKalb Co.*: Avondale Estates, 24 June 1944 LHJ (TTRS). *Bibb Co.*: Macon, 24 June 1961 FTN. *Clarke Co.*: Athens, July 1966 LRT.
Coastal Region—*Charlton Co.*: Folkston, 1 Apr 1955 LHJ (TTRS). *Screven Co.*: Sylvania, Mar–Sept 1946 OB (AMNH). *Grady Co.*: Beachton, Sherwood Plantation, 9 May 1965 LN.

This is the largest of our small Wood Satyrs. It is easy to

identify by the presence of prominent eyespots on the upper and lower sides of its wings. It flies close to the ground with a rapid skipping and dancing flight.

Knudsen (1954) wrote: "It comes out later than its congeners, but is usually to be found in moist woods throughout the summer." It is said to have one brood in the northern portion of its range, and two broods in the southern.

The larva is a downy, pale, greenish brown, with dark stripes running lengthwise on its body. The tubercles on its head and last segment are whitish. The larval food plants are various grasses.

Genus *Cercyonis*

Wood Nymph. *Cercyonis pegala* Fabricius (Page 154)

Distribution and Records: *C. pegala* is found throughout the state.

Mountain Region—*Union Co.*: Cooper Creek State Park, Shope Gap (alt. 2500 ft), 2 July 1958 LHJ (TTRS); Cooper Creek State Park, Shope Gap (alt. 2500 ft), 9 July 1960 LHJ (TTRS). *White Co.*: Cleveland, Yonah Mountain, 15 July 1934 PWF. *Towns Co.*: Brasstown Bald (alt. 4700 ft), 12 Aug 1951 LHJ (TTRS). *Habersham Co.*: Cornelia area, 25 Aug 1930 RWM (see Montgomery, 1931). *Union Co.*: Cooper Creek State Park, Shope Gap (alt. 2500 ft), 30 Aug 1958 LHJ (TTRS).
Piedmont Region—*Monroe Co.*: Forsyth, 18 June 1962 FTN. *DeKalb Co.*: Mount Arabia, near Lithonia, 19 July 1961 LHJ (TTRS). *Coweta Co.*: Madras, 23 July 1950 MES. *DeKalb Co.*: Stone Mountain, 27 July 1953 LHJ (TTRS); Avondale Estates, 29 July 1941 LHJ (TTRS). *Washington Co.*: "common in certain woods," 9–12 Aug 1926 AGR (see Richards, 1931). *Cobb Co.*: Kennesaw Mountain, 22 Aug 1967 JCS. *Fulton Co.*: Cox near Roswell, 26 Aug 1961 LHJ (TTRS).
Coastal Region—*Thomas Co.*: Boston, Bar-M Ranch, 15 July 1967 ESS (TTRS). *Camden Co.*: Kingsland, Coleraine Plantation, 16 July 1944 LHJ (TTRS). *Grady Co.*: Midway, 17 July 1965 LN. *Thomas Co.*: Metcalf, 20 July 1965 LN. *Screven Co.*: "large specimens collected in July and August, 1946" OB

(AMNH). *Baker Co.*: Newton, 14 Aug 1964 LN. *Camden Co.*: Kingsland, Coleraine Plantation, 17 Aug 1947 LHJ (USNM). *Dougherty Co.*: ten miles west of Albany, 20 Aug 1964 LN.

C. p. abbotti, the typical subspecies, was described from Charleston, South Carolina (Brown, 1965).* It is known as "Pegala" or "The Large Southern Wood Nymph," and is found in coastal woodlands of the Lower Coastal Plain. It is the largest in size. The orange patches or bands on the forewings range from rusty yellow to orange yellow.

The subspecies *C. p. alope*, described from Burke, Screven, and Bulloch counties, Georgia (Brown, 1965), is found in the upper Coastal Plain and in the Piedmont Region. It is known as "Wood Nymph" or "Grayling." The patches or bands on the forewings of *C. p. alope* are yellow. A form of this subspecies, *C. p. alope* f. *carolina* Chermock, was described from Conestee Falls, North Carolina, and is known as the "Carolina Wood Nymph." It is found in the Mountain Region of Georgia. The patches or bands on the forewings range from light yellow to a creamy white.

All three butterflies are found in woodlands in their respective geographic areas. They are usually found in local colonies; whether they are common or not depends upon the size of the colony, which, in turn, depends upon the extent of favorable habitat. Individuals may wander quite some distance from the area of the colony.

With reference to the original description of *C. p. pegala* (now known as *C. p. abbotti*), F. M. Brown (1965, p. 133) wrote: "The key phrase in the original description is 'anticus fascia rufa ocelloque unico.'" This subspecies is recognized by the rust-tinted yellow field on the upper side of the forewing in which there is a single (anterior) ocellus. It is found in the coastal woodlands of southern Georgia and from there north-

* This butterfly was originally described as *C. p. pegala*. In 1969, F. M. Brown restudied the nomenclature and changed the subspecies name to *C. p. abbotti*.

ward. It is distinctly maritime. Inland, its place is taken by *C. p. alope*. There is a tendency for *C. p. abbotti* to be somewhat larger than *C. p. alope*, especially among the females. Also, on the lower side of the hindwings of *C. p. abbotti*, the ocelli that compose the anterior triad are all clearly oval, or at least the second and third are. In *C. p. alope*, the third ocellus in the group is almost entirely circular.

With reference to the original description of *C. p. alope*, Brown (1965, p. 136) wrote:

The key phrases in this description are 'fascia flava; ocellis duobus.' True *alope* bears a yellow field on the forewing in which there are two ocelli. This is the characteristic form from the North Atlantic states. . . . There is no question but Fabricius had before him the North American butterfly known as *alope*.

Brown (1965, pp. 136–137) wrote:

It seems most probable that Abbot was the collector of the type of *alope* . . . Abbot first settled in Burke County, Georgia, and spent most of his sixty years in America in that county, Screven County and Bulloch County, although he lived for short periods around Savannah. I believe that the most likely source of the type of *alope* is the Burke-Screven-Bulloch Counties region of Georgia and here restrict it to that region. When a neotype is selected for the name *alope* it should come from that area and then the locality from which the neotype came will further restrict the type locality.

Ehrlich and Ehrlich (1961, p. 95) figure a female *C. pegala alope* (labeled *C. pegala*) from Screven County, Georgia. Klots (1951, p. 64, pl. 7) figures a male *C. p. abbotti* (labeled *C. p. pegala*) from Currituck County, North Carolina. Boisduval and LeConte (1829–1833, pl. 59) figured Abbot's drawing of the upper and lower sides of *C. p. alope*, the larva, pupa, and a food plant, which is one of the coarse grasses.

Mather (1966) found that males and females of *C. p. abbotti* collected in Mississippi could not be separated on the basis of males having one eyespot and females two eyespots in the yellow patch on the upper side of the forewing. He noted that about one-third of the individuals in the population of *C. p. abbotti* in southern Mississippi, judging from his sample, have two eyespots, and that the presence or absence of a second spot is not related to the sex of the individual.

In a sampling of fourteen specimens (eight males and six females) of *C. pegala* from middle and southern Georgia (which, it now seems likely, included a predominance of *C. p. alope*), it was found that five males had one spot; three males had two spots, with the lower (posterior) spot much reduced in size; five females had two spots of equal size; and one female had two spots, with the lower (posterior) one somewhat reduced.

From all of the data he gathered, which included some from additional states and sources, Mather (1966) concluded that the use of the number of eyespots on the upper sides of the forewings as a basis for determining the sex of individuals of *C. p. abbotti* is unreliable. He suggested that the variation of number of these eyespots merits further study.

The larva of this species has been described as downy and yellowish green, with four lighter, lengthwise stripes; the anal fork is reddish (Klots, 1951, p. 72). The larval food plants are various grasses.

GENERAL BIBLIOGRAPHY

Abbot, Charles H., 1950. Twenty-five years of migration of the Painted Lady Butterfly, *Vanessa cardui*, in southern California. *Pan-Pac. Entomol.* 26:161–172.

————, 1951. A quantitative study of the migrations of the Painted Lady Butterfly, *Vanessa cardui. Ecology* 32:155–171.

————, 1962. A migration problem—*Vanessa cardui*, The Painted Lady Butterfly. *J. Lepidopterists' Soc.* 16(4):229–233.

Ae, S. Albert, 1957. Effects of photoperiod on *Colias cyrytheme. Lepidopterists' News* 11(6): 207–214.

Barnes, William, and James H. McDunnough, 1912. Revision of the *Megathymidae. Contr. Nat. Hist. Lepidoptera N. Amer.* 1(3).

Beall, Geoffrey, 1952. Migration of the Monarch Butterfly during the winter. *Lepidopterists' News* 6(4–5).

————, 1953. Congregation of butterflies at hilltops. *Lepidopterists' News* 7(2):41–43.

Boisduval, Jean Alphouse, and John E. LeConte, 1829–1833. *Histoire Generale et Iconographie des Lepidopteres et des Chenilles de L'Amerique Septentrionale.* Paris.

Bonniwell, J. G., 1916. Location of pupae of *Meg. cofaqui. Entomol. News* 27:372.

————, 1917. Article dealing with *Meg. yuccae* gives reference to *Meg. cofaqui* larvae and pupae. *Lepidoptera* 2:108–109.

Bouton, D. W., 1964. Venation aberration in *Papilio glaucus. J. Lepidopterists' Soc.* 18(3):157–158.

Brewer, Jo, and Gerard M. Thomas, 1966. Causes of death encountered during rearing *Danaus plexippus* (Danaidae). *J. Lepidopterists' Soc.* 20(4):235–238.

Brooks, James C., 1962. Foodplants of *Papilio palamedes* in Georgia. *J. Lepidopterists' Soc.* 16(3):198.

Brower, Auburn E., 1930. A list of the butterflies of the Ozark Region of Missouri. *Entomol. News* 41:286–289.

Brower, L. P., 1958. Larval foodplants of the *Papilio glaucus* group. *Lepidopterists' News* 12(3–4):103–114.

Brown, F. M., 1960. Description of *Papilio glaucus* yellow and black female received by W. H. Edwards. *J. New York Entomol. Soc.* 68:157–175.

———, 1964. Butterflies, natural history of the Boulder area. *Univ. Colorado Mus. Leaflet* 13.

———, 1965. Comments on the genus *Cercyonis* Scudder, with figures of types (Satyridae). *J. Res. Lepidoptera* 4(2):131–148.

———, 1966. The types of nympholid butterflies described by William H. Edwards, Part II. Melitaeinae. *Trans. Amer. Entomol. Soc.* 92:357–468.

———, Donald Eff, and Bernard Rotger, 1957. *Colorado Butterflies*, Denver, Colo.: Denver Museum of Natural History.

———, 1969. *Cercyonis pegala abbotti*, new subspecies. *Entomol. News* 80(7):193–196.

Buchholz, Otto, 1950. Additions to Butterflies of Georgia. *Lepidopterists' News* 4(6–7):62.

Burns, John M., 1964. *Evolution in the Skipper Butterflies of the Genus Erynnis*. Berkeley and Los Angeles: University of California Press.

Butler, Robert B., and Charles V. Covell, Jr., 1957. *Megathymus yuccae* in North Carolina. *Lepidopterists' News* 11(4–5):137–141.

Cantwell, Robert, 1961. *Alexander Wilson, Naturalist and Pioneer*. Philadelphia and New York: Lippincott. (Abbot on pp. 181–185.)

Catesby, Mark, 1731–1743. *The Natural History of Carolina, Florida, and the Bahama Islands*, vols. 1 and 2. London.

Chermock, Ralph L., 1942. Notes on collecting *Argynnis diana*. *Proc. Penn. Acad. Sci.* 16:59–61.

Clark, Austin H., 1932. The butterflies of the District of Columbia and vicinity. *Bull. U.S. Natl. Mus.* 157.

———, 1936a. Notes on the butterflies of the genus *Enodia*, etc. *Proc. U. S. Natl. Mus.* 83 (2983):251–259.

———, 1936b. The Golden Banded Skipper (*Rhabdoides cellus*). *Smithsonian Misc. Collect.* 95(7).

———, 1936c. A portion of the above with 1 color plate appeared in "Who's Who Among the Butterflies," in *Natl. Geogr.* 69(5):679–792.

————, 1937. A new species of the nymphalid butterfly *Polygonia faunus. Proc. U. S. Natl. Mus.* 84(3013):219–222.

————, 1941. Notes on some North American danaid butterflies. *Proc. U. S. Natl. Mus.* 90(3118):531–542.

————, 1948. A new subspecies of *Glaucopsyche lygdamus. Proc. Entomol. Soc.* 50(7):176–178.

————, and Leila F. Clark, 1951. The butterflies of Virginia. *Smithsonian Misc. Collect.* 116(7).

Clench, H. K., 1955. Some observations on the habits of *Strymon falacer. Lepidopterists' News* 9(4–5):105–117.

————, 1961. *Panthiades m-album* (Lycaenidae): remarks on its early stages and on its occurrence in Pennsylvania. *J. Lepidopterists' Soc.* 15(4).

Comstock, J. H., and Anna B. Comstock, 1920. *How to Know the Butterflies.* Ithaca, N. Y.: Comstock Publishing Co., Inc.

Covell, C. V., Jr., 1962. The occurrence of *Satyrium kingi* (Lycaenidae) in Virginia. *J. Lepidopterists' Soc.* 16(3):197–198.

dos Passos, C. F., 1958. Names proposed in *The Rarer Lepidopterous Insects of Georgia* by Sir James E. Smith. *Lepidopterists' News* 12(5–6):191–192.

————, 1958. Names proposed by Boisduval and LeConte. *Lepidopterists' News* 12(3–4):121–122.

————, 1959. Further notes on the dates of publication of some generic and specific names proposed by Boisduval and LeConte. *J. Lepidopterists' Soc.* 13(4):212.

————, 1964. A synonymic list of the nearctic Rhopalocera. *Mem. Lepidopterists' Soc.* 1.

————, 1969. A revised synonymic list of the nearctic Melitaeinae with taxonomic notes (Nymphalidae). *J. Lepidopterists' Soc.* 23(2):115–125.

————, and A. B. Klots, 1969. The systematics of *Anthocharis midea* Hübner. *Entomol. Amer.* 45:1–34.

Doubleday, Edward, 1840–1842. Description of a new North American *Polyommatus* (*P. lygdamus*). *The Entomologist* Vol. I: 209–211.

Duncan, W. H., 1941. *Guide to Georgia Trees.* Athens, Ga.: University of Georgia Press.

Ebner, J. A., 1960. A striking male of *Papilo glaucus. J. Lepidopterists' Soc.* 14(2):157–158.

Edwards, W. H., 1884. Revised catalogue of the diurnal Lepidoptera of America north of Mexico. *Trans. Amer. Entomol. Soc.* 11:235–237.

———, 1868. Notes on a remarkable variety of *Papilio turnus* and descriptions of two species of diurnal Lepidoptera. *Amer. Entomol. Soc.* 2:207–210. (1st series, Philadelphia; 2nd series, Boston & New York; 3rd series, Boston & New York)

———, 1868–1872. *The Butterflies of North America*, first series.

———, 1884. *The Butterflies of North America*, second series.

———, 1887–1897. *The Butterflies of North America*, third series.

———, 1894. Description of the preparatory stages of *Phyciodes carlota* Reakirt (*Charidryas ismeria* Scudder). *Can. Entomol.* 26(1):3–8.

Ehrlich, P. R., and Anne H. Ehrlich, 1961. *How to Know the Butterflies.* Dubuque, Iowa: W. C. Brown.

Emmel, T. C., and R. A. Wobus, 1966. A southward migration of *Vanessa cardui* in late summer and fall, 1965. *J. Lepidopterists' Soc.* 20(2):123–124.

Evans, W. H., 1951–1955. *A catalogue of the American Hesperiidae in the British Museum*, vols. 1–4. London: British Museum (Natural History).

———, 1959. The saga of an orphan *Speyeria diana* larva. *J. Lepidopterists' Soc.* 13(2):93–94.

Forbes, W. T. M., 1960. Lepidoptera of New York and Neighboring States, part IV. *Cornell Univ. Mem.* 371.

Freeman, H. A., 1951. Ecological and systematic study of the Hesperioidea of Texas. *S. Methodist Univ. Studies* 6(1):61–67.

———, 1952. Notes on *Megathymus yuccae*, with a description of a new subspecies. *Field Lab.* 20(1):29–33.

———, 1955. Four new species of *Megathymus*. *Amer. Mus. Novitates* (1711):1–20.

———, 1958. A revision of the genera of the *Megathymidae* with a description of three new genera. *Lepidopterists' News* 12(3–4):81–92.

———, 1963. Type localities of the Megathymidae. *J. Res. Lepidoptera* 2(2):137–141.

French, G. H., 1886. *The Butterflies of the Eastern United States.* Philadelphia.

Greene, W. J., and H. L. Blomquist, 1953. *Flowers of the South.* Chapel Hill, N. C.: University of North Carolina Press.

Grossbeck, J. A. 1917. Insects of Florida, IV. Lepidoptera. *Bull. Amer. Mus. Nat. Hist.* 37.

Grote, A. R., and C. T. Robinson, 1867–1868. Description of American lepidoptera. *Trans. Amer. Entomol. Soc.* Vol. 1, pp. 1–30 (June, 1867); Vol. 2, pp. 171–192 (August, 1867); Vol. 3, pp. 323–360 (January, 1868).

Harrar, E. S., and J. G. Harrar, 1946–1962. *Guide to Southern Trees.* New York: Dover.

Harris, L., Jr. 1931. *A List of the Butterflies of Georgia.* Avondale Estates, Ga.: Georgia Naturalists' Club.

————, 1950. *The Butterflies of Georgia, Revised.* Avondale Estates, Ga.: Georgia Society of Naturalists.

————, 1950. Notes and range extensions of butterflies in Georgia. *Lepidopterists' News* 4(4–5):43–44.

————, 1955. Life History of a rare Yucca Skipper (Megathymidae). *Lepidopterists' News* 8(6):153–162.

Haskin, J. R., 1933. Life history of *Eurema demoditas, Lycaena theonus,* and *Lycaena hanno. Entomol. News* 44:153–156.

Hebard, Morgan, 1903. Notes on the collecting about Thomasville, Ga. *Entomol. News* 14(8):260–261.

Heitzman, J. R., 1962. Butterfly migrations in March in northern Mexico. *J. Lepidopterists' Soc.* 16(4):249–250.

————, 1963. The Complete Life History of Staphylus Hayhursti. *J. Res. Lepidoptera* 2(2):170–172.

————, 1964. Early stages of *Euphyes vestris. J. Res. Lepidoptera* 3(3):151–153.

————, 1965. The life history of *Amblyscirtes belli* in Missouri. *J. Res. Lepidoptera* 4(1):75–78.

————, 1965. The life history of *Problema byssus* (Hesperiidae). *J. Lepidopterists' Soc.* 19(2):77–81.

————, 1966. The life history of *Atrytone arogos* (Hesperiidae). *J. Lepidopterists' Soc.* 20(3):177–181.

Hessel, S. A., 1952. A new altitudinal high for *Erora laeta. Lepidopterists' News* 6(1–3):34.

————, 1963. I gave up collecting Lepidoptera (for 45 minutes). *J. Lepidopterists' Soc.* 17(1):43–44.

Holland, W. J., 1931. *The Butterfly Book* (revised ed.). New York: Doubleday, Doran.

Hopf, Alice L., 1954. Sex differences observed in larvae of *Danaus gilippus berenice. Lepidopterists' News* 8(5):123–124.

Hovanitz, W., 1963a. Geographical distribution and variation of the genus *Argynnis*, Part II. *A. idalia. J. Res. Lepidoptera* 1(2):119–123.

——, 1963b. Geographical distribution and variation of the genus *Argynnis*, Part 3. *A. diana. J. Res. Lepidoptera* 1(3): 201–208.

Howe, W. H., 1966. A melanic female of *Colias eurytheme* (Pieridae). *J. Lepidopterists' Soc.* 20(4):215–216.

——, 1967. A migration of *Vanessa cardui* in Montana and Wyoming. *J. Lepidopterists' Soc.* 21(1):39–40.

Hübner, Jacob, 1806–1841. *Sammlung Exotischer Schmetterlinge*, vols. 1–3. Augsburg.

——, 1818–1837. *Zutrage zur Sammlung exotischer Schmetterlinge bestehend in Bekindigung einzelner Fleigmuster neuer oder rarer nichteuropaischer Gattungen*, vols. 1–5. Augsburg.

Hume, I. N., 1966. *1775, Another Part of the Field*. New York: Alfred A. Knopf.

Jones, F. M., 1926. The rediscovery of *Hesperia bulenta* Bdv. and LeC., with notes on other species (Lepidoptera; Hesperiidae). *Entomol. News* 37(7):193–198.

Karalus, K. E., Jr., 1957. An unusual method of collecting a rare yucca skipper (*Megathymus harrisi*). *Lepidopterists' News*. 11(1–3).

Kendall, R. O., 1960. New larval foodplant for *Erynnis zarucco* (Hesperiidae) from Louisiana. *J. Lepidopterists' Soc.* 14(3): 176.

Kimball, C. P., 1957. On describing distributions. *Lepidopterists' News* 11(1–3):21.

——, 1965. *The Lepidoptera of Florida*. Gainesville, Fla.: Division of Plant Industry, Florida Department of Agriculture.

Klots, A. B., 1951. *A Field Guide to the Butterflies*. Boston: Houghton Mifflin.

——, and H. K. Clench, 1952. A new species of *Strymon* Hübner from Georgia (Lepid. Lycaenidae). *Amer. Museum Novitates* (1600):2–21.

——, 1960. Notes on *Strymon carysevorus* McDunnough. *J. New York Entomol. Soc.* 68:190–198.

Knudsen, J. P., 1954a Butterflies and conspicuous moths of the Oglethorpe College campus.

——, 1954b Butterflies and hilltops. *Lepidopterists' News* 8(5):141–142.

——, 1955. A new host plant for *Strymon liparops*. *Lepidopterists' News* 9(1):11–12.

Kolyer, J. M., 1966. The effect of certain environmental factors and chemicals on the markings of *Pieris rapae* (Pieridae). *J. Lepidopterists' Soc.* 20(1):13–27.

Lambremont, E. N., 1954. The butterflies and skippers of Louisiana. *Tulane Studies Zool.* 10:125–164.

Lawrence, D. A., and John C. Downey, 1966. Morphology of the immature stages of *Everes comyntas* Godart. *J. Res. Lepidoptera* 5(2):61–96.

Lindsey, A. W., E. L. Bell, and R. C. Williams, Jr., 1931. The Hesperioidea of North America. *J. Sci. Lab. Denison Univ.* 26:1–142.

Martin, L. M., and F. S. Truxal, 1955. A list of the North American lepidoptera in the Los Angeles County Museum. Los Angeles, Cal. Part I, Sci. Series, No. 18; Zool., No. 8:1–35.

Masters, J. H., 1967. Observations on Arkansas Rhopalocera. *J. Lepidopterists' Soc.* 21(3):206–209.

Mather, Bryant. 1953. A migration of *Ascia monuste* in Mississippi. *Lepidopterists' News* 7(1):13–14.

———, 1954. Size of *Papilio glaucus* in Mississippi. *Lepidopterists' News*. 8(5):131–134.

———, 1955a. *Danaus gilippus* in Mississippi. *Lepidopterists' News* 9(2–3):67–68.

———, 1955b. Forewing length and flight period of *Danaus plexippus* in the Gulf states. *Lepidopterists' News* 9(4–5):119–124.

———, 1956. *Eurema daira daira* in Mississippi. *Lepidopterists' News*, 10(6):204–206.

———, 1963. *Euphyes dukesi*, a review of knowledge of its distribution in time and space, and its habitat. *J. Res. Lepidoptera* 2(2):161–169.

———, 1964. The southern limits of the range of *Pieris napi* and *Pieris virginiensis*. *J. Res. Lepidoptera* 3(1):45–48.

———, 1965. *Euptychia areolata*, distribution and variation, with special reference to Mississippi. *J. Lepidopterists' Soc.* 19(3):139–160.

———, 1966. *Cercyonis pegala pegala* (Satyr.): occurrence in Mississippi and variation in forewing maculation. *J. Lepidopterists' Soc.* 20(3):186–188.

———, 1967. Variation in *Junonia coenia* in Mississippi (Nymphalidae). *J. Lepidopterists' Soc.* 21(1):59–67.

———, and Katharine Mather, 1958. The butterflies of Mississippi. *Tulane Studies Zool.* 6(2):64–109.

————, and ————, 1959. The butterflies of Mississippi, Supplement 1. *J. Lepidopterists' Soc.* 13(2):71–72.

Maynard, C. J., 1891. *A Manual of North American Butterflies.* Boston.

Megerle, J. K., 1801–1805. *Catalog Insectorum Quae Viennae Austriae Distrahunter.*

Merritt, J. R., 1952. Butterflies and hilltops. *Lepidopterists' News* 6(6–8):101–102.

————, 1953. Southeastern season summary for North Carolina. *Lepidopterists' News* 7(3–4):103–104.

Montgomery, R. W., 1931. Notes on some butterflies of northeastern Georgia. *Entomol. News* 42(4):109–111.

Morris, J. G., 1860. Catalogue of the described lepidoptera of North America. *Smithsonian Misc. Collect.* 3(2):1–68.

Muspratt, Vera M., 1954. Butterflies on hilltops. *Lepidopterists' News* 8(5):143–145.

Nielsen, E. T., and Astrid Nielsen, 1950. Contribution toward the knowledge of the migration of butterflies. *Amer. Mus. Novitates* (1471):1–29.

Pease, R. W., 1962. Factors causing seasonal forms in *Ascia monuste* (Lepid.). *Science* 137:987–988.

————, 1963. Extension of known range of Mitoura hesselis. *J. Lepidopterists' Soc.* 17(1):27.

Peterson, B., 1964. Monarch butterflies are eaten by birds. *J. Lepidopterists' Soc.* 18(3):165–169.

Pliske, T. E., 1957. Notes on *Atrytone dukesi*, a rare species new to southern Michigan. *Lepidopterists' News* 11(1–3):42.

Rawson, G. W., 1955. More on hilltop butterflies. *Lepidopterists' News* 9(4–5):133–134.

————, 1961. The early stages of *Brephidium pseudofea* (Morrison). *J. New York Entomol. Soc.* 69:88–91.

————, and Sidney A. Hessel, 1951. The life history of *Strymon cecrops* Fabricius. *Bull. Brooklyn Entomol. Soc.* 46(3):79–84.

————, and J. B. Ziegler, 1950. A new species of *Mitoura* Scudder from the pine barrens if New Jersey. *J. New York Entomol. Soc.* 58:69–82.

————, ————, and S. A. Hessel, 1951. The immature stages of *Mitoura hesseli. Bull. Brooklyn Entomol. Soc.* 46(5):123–130.

Reinthal, W. J., 1956. A search for *Pieris virginiensis* in Massachusetts. *Lepidopterists' News* 10(1–2):25–28.

Remington, C. L., 1950. A review of the butterflies of Georgia, Revised. *Lepidopterists' News* 4(4–5):42.

————, 1953. Two new genes, "whitish" and "blond," giving pale males and females of *Colias philodice*. *Lepidopterists' News* 7(5–6): 139–145.

Remington, C. L., 1954. A new pale male of *Colias philodice*. *Lepidopterists' News* 8(3–4):76.

————, 1959. Review of the butterflies of Mississippi. *J. Lepidopterists' Soc.* 13(1):33–34.

————, and R. W. Pease, 1955. Studies in foodplant specificity, 1. The suitability of Swamp White Cedar for *Mitoura gryneus*. *Lepidopterists' News* 9(1):4–6.

Richards, A. G., Jr., 1931. Distributional studies on southeastern Rhopalocera. *Bull. Brooklyn Entomol. Soc.* 26(5):234–255.

Rindge, F. H., 1958. Buchholz collection obtained by The American Museum of Natural History. *Lepidoptorists' News* 12(5–6): 208.

Robertson-Miller, Ellen, 1931. *Butterfly and Moth Book*. New York: Scribner's.

Roever, K., 1962. Notes on *Erora* (Lycaenidae). *J. Lepidopterists' Soc.* 16(1):1–4.

Rothschild, W., and K. Jordon, 1906. A revision of the American Papilios. *Novitates Zool.* 13(3):411–744.

Scudder, S. H., 1889. *The butterflies of the Eastern United States and Canada, with Special Reference to New England*, vols. 1–3. Cambridge, Mass.

Seitz, A., et al. 1924. *The Macrolepidoptera of the World*, vol. 5 (*The American Rhopalocera*). Stuttgart.

Shapiro, A. M., 1965. Ecological and behavioral notes on *Hesperia metea* and *Atrytomopsis hianna* (Hes.). *J. Lepidopterists' Soc.* 19(4):215–221.

————, 1966. *Butterflies of the Delaware Valley*. Philadelphia: American Entomological Society.

Shepard, P. M., 1965. The Monarch Butterfly and mimicry. *J. Lepidopterists' Soc.* 19(4):227–230.

Sicher, H., 1962. A mosaic melanic male of *Papilio glaucus*. *J. Lepidopterists' Soc.* 16(2):98.

Skinner, H., 1897. *Debis creola*. *Entomol. News* 8(10):236.

————, 1911. New species or subspecies of North American butterflies. *Entomol. News* 22(8):412–414.

————, 1917a. *Lycaena lygdamus* Doubleday and its races, with a description of a new one. *Entomol. News* 28(5):212–214.

————, 1917b. *Anthocharis genutia* and a new variety. *Entomol. News* 28(10):438.

————, and R. C. Williams, Jr., 1922. On the male genitalia of the larger Hesperiidae of North America. *Trans. Amer. Entomol. Soc.* 48(2):109–127.

Small, G. B., Jr., 1962. Notes on *Euristrymon ontario ontario* and *Satyrium caryaevorus* (Lycaenidae). *J. Lepidopterists' Soc.* 16(3):195–196.

Smith, J. E., 1797. *The Natural History of the Rarer Lepidopterous Insects of Georgia*, vols. 1 and 2. London.

Syme, P. D., 1961. Observations on *Strymon liparops. J. Lepidopterists' Soc.* 15(2):108.

Tilden, J. W., 1962. General characteristics of the movements of *V. cardui. J. Res. Lepidoptera* 1(1):43–49.

Urquhart, F. A., 1960. *The Monarch Butterfly.* Toronto: University of Toronto Press.

————, 1966. Virus-caused epizootic as a factor in population fluctuations of the monarch butterfly. *J. Invert. Pathol.* 8:492–495.

Van Someren, V. G. L., 1955. Butterflies and hilltops in East Africa. *Lepidopterists' News* 9(4–5):127–132.

Voss, E. G., and W. H. Wagner. 1956. Notes on *Pieris virginiensis* and *Erora laeta*, two butterflies hitherto unreported from Michigan. *Lepidopterists' News* 10(1–2):18–24.

Wagner, W. H. Jr., 1955. Biographical obituary of Austin H. Clark. *Lepidopterists' News* 9(4–5):153–159.

Williams, C. B., 1937. Butterfly travelers. *Natl. Geogr.* 81(5):568–585.

————, 1949. Presidential address to the Fellows of the Royal Entomological Society of London. *Proc. Roy. Entomol. Soc. London* 13(12):70–84.

————, 1958. *Insect Migration.* London: Collins.

Ziegler, J. B., 1953. Notes on the life history of *Incisalia augustinus* and a new host plant record. *Lepidopterists' News* 7(2):33.

BIBLIOGRAPHY ON JOHN ABBOT

Allen, Elsa G., 1942. A third set of John Abbot bird drawings. *Auk* 59:536.

————, A resume of John Abbot's "Notes on My life." *Oriole* 13(4):31–32.

————, 1951. The history of American ornithology before Audubon, John Abbot of Georgia. *Trans. Amer. Phil. Soc.* (NS)41 (3):593.

————, 1953. A report on John Abbot, ornithologist of Georgia. *Yearb. Amer. Phil. Soc.* 1952:300–305.

————, 1957. John Abbot, pioneer naturalist. *Georgia Hist. Quart.* 41(2):143–157.

Baker, Woolford B., 1959. John Abbot's "Insects of Georgia." *Emory Univ. Quart.* 15(3):146.

Bassett, Anna Stovall, 1938. Some Georgia records of John Abbot, naturalist. *Auk* 55(2):244–254.

Beirne, Bryan P., 1950. Some original paintings by John Abbot. *Lepidopterists' News* 4(3):25–26.

Cantwell, Robert, 1961. Alexander Wilson–Naturalist and Pioneer. Philadelphia and New York: Lippincott. (Abbot on pp. 181–185.)

Faxon, Walter, 1896. John Abbot's drawings of the birds of Georgia. *Auk* 11(3):28.

Remington, L., 1948. Brief biographies, No. 10, John Abbot. *Lepidopterists' News* 2(3):28.

Rhodes, S. H., 1918. Georgia rarities further discovered, a second American portfolio of John Abbot's bird plates. *Auk* 35:27.

Scudder, Samuel H., 1889. *Butterflies of the Eastern United States and Canada, with Special Reference to New England.* Cambridge, Mass. (A portrait and a brief biography of Abbot in vol. 1, pp. 651–654.)

Smith, J. E., 1797. *The Rarer Lepidopterous Insects of Georgia*, vols. 1 and 2. London. (Contains Abbot's observations on each species.)

Stone, Witmer, 1906. Letter from John Abbot to George Ord. *Auk* 23.

INDEX

317